TRAUMA-INFORMED PRACTICES FOR EARLY CHILDHOOD EDUCATORS

Trauma-Informed Practices for Early Childhood Educators guides child care providers and early educators working with infants, toddlers, preschoolers, and early elementary aged children to understand trauma as well as its impact on young children's brains, behavior, learning, and development. The book introduces a range of trauma-informed teaching and family engagement strategies that readers can use in their early childhood programs to create strength-based environments that support children's health, healing, and resiliency. Supervisors and coaches will learn a range of powerful trauma-informed practices that they can use to support workforce development and enhance their quality improvement initiatives.

Julie Nicholson, PhD, is Deputy Director for WestEd's Center for Child and Family Studies.

Linda Perez, PhD, Licensed Clinical Psychologist and Professor of Education at Mills College, is Co-Director of the Mills Infant Mental Health Program and Clinical Director of the Epiphany Center Family Treatment Program.

Julie Kurtz, MS, LMFT, is Co-Director for the Trauma-Informed Practices in Early Childhood Education Project and a Regional Director for California's Center on the Social and Emotional Foundations for Early Learning/Teaching Pyramid at WestEd's Center for Child and Family Studies. She also operates a private therapy practice in the California Bay Area Region.

OTHER EYE ON EDUCATION BOOKS
AVAILABLE FROM ROUTLEDGE
(www.routledge.com/eyeoneducation)

Coding as a Playground
Programming and Computational Thinking in the Early Childhood Classroom
Marina Umaschi Bers

Eco-Education for Young Children
Revolutionary Ways to Teach and Learn Environmental Sciences
Ann Lewin-Benham

The Bridge to School
Aligning Teaching with Development for Ages Four to Six
Claire Bainer, Liisa Hale, and Gail Myers

Teaching Children with Challenging Behaviors
Practical Strategies for Early Childhood Educators
Edited by Gayle Mindes

Anti-Bias Education in the Early Childhood Classroom
Hand in Hand, Step by Step
Katie Kissinger

Developing Natural Curiosity through Project-Based Learning
Five Strategies for the PreK–3 Classroom
Dayna Laur and Jill Ackers

Five Teaching and Learning Myths—Debunked
A Guide for Teachers
Adam Brown and Althea Need Kaminske

Nurturing Young Thinkers Across the Standards
K–2
Wynne A. Shilling and Sydney L. Schwartz

TRAUMA-INFORMED PRACTICES FOR EARLY CHILDHOOD EDUCATORS

Relationship-Based Approaches that Support Healing and Build Resilience in Young Children

Julie Nicholson, Linda Perez, and Julie Kurtz

Routledge
Taylor & Francis Group

NEW YORK AND LONDON

First published 2019
by Routledge
711 Third Avenue, New York, NY 10017

and by Routledge
2 Park Square, Milton Park, Abingdon, Oxon, OX14 4RN

Routledge is an imprint of the Taylor & Francis Group, an informa business

Library of Congress Cataloging-in-Publication Data
Names: Nicholson, Julie, 1965- author. | Perez, Linda, author. |
Kurtz, Julie, author.
Title: Trauma informed practices for early childhood educators:
relationship-based approaches that support healing and build resilience
in young children / Julie Nicholson, Ph.D., Linda Perez, Ph.D., and
Julie Kurtz, M.S.
Description: New York, NY: Routledge, 2019. | Includes bibliographical
references.
Identifiers: LCCN 2018025057 (print) | LCCN 2018029411 (ebook) |
ISBN 9781315141756 (e-book) | ISBN 9781138306387 (hbk.) |
ISBN 9781138306394 (pbk.) | ISBN 9781315141756 (ebk.)
Subjects: LCSH: Early childhood education–Psychological aspects. |
Psychic trauma in children. | Child mental health. | Early childhood
education–Case studies. | Psychic trauma in children–Case studies. |
Child mental health–Case studies.
Classification: LCC LB1775.6 (ebook) | LCC LB1775.6 .N55 2019 (print) |
DDC 372.2101/9–dc23
LC record available at https://lccn.loc.gov/2018025057

ISBN: 978-1-138-30638-7 (hbk)
ISBN: 978-1-138-30639-4 (pbk)
ISBN: 978-1-315-14175-6 (ebk)

Typeset in Minion Pro
by Deanta Global Publishing Services, Chennai, India

CONTENTS

INTRODUCTION

Anthony is riding a tricycle at his preschool when a loud airplane flies overhead. He starts to cover his ears and screams repeatedly "no, no, no, no" over and over. His preschool teacher, Lawanda, walks over to Anthony, bends down to his eye level and using a calm and reassuring voice tells him, "Anthony, you are safe, you are here in preschool where the teachers will take care of you. That loud sound was an airplane way up high in the sky. You are safe down here on the ground with me. Let's take some deep breaths together."

Anthony's teacher, Lawanda, is using trauma-sensitive strategies to guide Anthony back to a self-regulated state after his stress response system was triggered by the loud sound of the airplane. Loud sounds like that remind Anthony of a serious and very scary car accident he recently witnessed on the highway that involved multiple cars and several fatalities. Whenever Anthony hears a loud sound that frightens him at his preschool, he now runs over to his teachers and says, "Hold me and tell me I will be safe," a coping strategy he has learned by having the consistent and predictable trauma-informed approach at his preschool. Recently, Lawanda observed Anthony practicing these strategies in the dramatic play area where he was pretending to be driving a car with two dogs in the back seat. When the dogs started to bark, Anthony turned around and said to them, "You are safe, you are going to be okay." He then gestured as if he was turning on the radio in his pretend car and said, "I am putting on a song for you so you can take a nap and feel better." Through his imaginary play, Anthony was communicating how children—with the support of adults who understand traumatic stress and its impact on young children's behavior—can learn strategies to heal from traumatic experiences they have early in life.

Why is it Important to be Trauma-Informed?

Childhood trauma has been named our nation's single most important public health challenge.

(van der Kolk, 2014)

Research and decades of clinical practice provide ample evidence that **trauma** experienced in the first five years of life can have a significant negative impact on children's developmental processes with lifelong consequences.

> *Trauma is an actual or perceived danger that undermines a child's sense of physical or emotional safety or poses a threat to the safety of the child's parents or caregivers, overwhelms their coping ability, and impacts their functioning and development.*

Trauma disrupts healthy development by interfering with a child's capacity to develop positive relationships with adults and peers, to learn and play, and to self-regulate their emotions, attention, and behavior. Exposure to trauma is unfortunately a very common experience for our youngest children (Ghosh Ippen, Harris, Van Horn, & Lieberman, 2011). Research demonstrates that a majority of children in the United States have been exposed to trauma and the prevalence of trauma is highest for children in their early childhood years (Briggs-Gowan, Ford, Fraleigh, McCarthy, & Carter, 2010; Shahinfar, Fox, & Leavitt, 2000). In fact, childhood trauma has been named our nation's single most important public health challenge (van der Kolk, 2014).

The Adverse Childhood Experiences Study

The Adverse Childhood Experiences (ACEs) study was a landmark research project that catapulted the discussion of trauma and trauma-informed practices into our national dialogue. The ACEs study was sponsored and conducted by Kaiser Permanente and the Center for Disease Control and Prevention from 1995 through 1997. The goal of the study was to investigate the impact trauma and stressful experiences during the childhood years have on adult health outcomes. Over 17,000 members of Kaiser participated in the original ACEs study. The study found that 63% of those who participated reported at least one experience of childhood trauma and that 20% of the participants reported trauma in three or more categories, defined as adverse childhood experiences or ACEs (www.cdc.gov/violenceprevention/acestudy/).

The original study measured the prevalence of seven adverse childhood experiences asking whether a child ever had exposure to:

1. Physical abuse
2. Sexual abuse

3. Emotional abuse
4. Household substance abuse
5. Household mental illness
6. Domestic violence (mother treated violently)
7. Incarcerated household member (criminal behavior in household)

Three additional items were added in subsequent research including:

8. Parental separation or divorce
9. Physical neglect
10. Emotional neglect

These ten ACEs survey questions have since been adapted for international use and also updated to include additional types of adversity that were not included on the original questionnaire including:

- Racism
- Witnessing violence outside the home
- Bullying
- Losing a parent to deportation
- Living in an unsafe neighborhood
- Involvement with the foster care system
- Experiencing homelessness
- Living in a war zone
- Being an immigrant
- Witnessing a sibling, father, other caregiver, or extended family member being abused
- Involvement with the criminal justice system
- Attending a school that enforces a zero-tolerance discipline policy (Figure 0.1).

The ACEs study found that the more ACEs an individual has in childhood, the more likely they are to experience disrupted brain development, which puts them at risk for social, emotional, and cognitive delays in childhood. Such delays increase the likelihood that youth will engage in risky behaviors in adolescence, which is correlated with increased mental, social, and physical health problems in adulthood, all conditions that can lead to premature death (Felliti & Anda, 2010; Felliti et al., 1998; Koplan & Chard, 2014). The ACEs study documented a relationship between early adverse childhood experiences and increased risk for a range of negative outcomes in adulthood including:

• Alcoholism and alcohol abuse	• Depression	• Smoking
	• Illicit drug use	• Obesity
• Chronic obstructive pulmonary disease	• Intimate partner violence	• Suicide attempts
		• Unintended pregnancies
• Ischemic heart disease	• Sexually transmitted diseases (STDs)	• Fetal death
• Liver disease		

The ACEs study was revolutionary as it provided evidence about the significant prevalence of adverse experiences in the lives of children and the youth across our nation *and* the critical need to invest in interventions to prevent and interrupt the long-term consequences of ACEs as early as possible. Since the ACEs study was first completed, a wide range of trauma-informed interventions have been developed primarily within the field of child welfare to improve screening and intervention for child maltreatment.

Adverse childhood experiences are especially problematic for young children who do not have strong attachments with caring adults. We now know from research that supportive, responsive relationships with caring adults significantly help to buffer the negative impact of ACEs and traumatic stress for young children. In fact, nurturing relationships can prevent or reverse the toxic impact of trauma for young children.

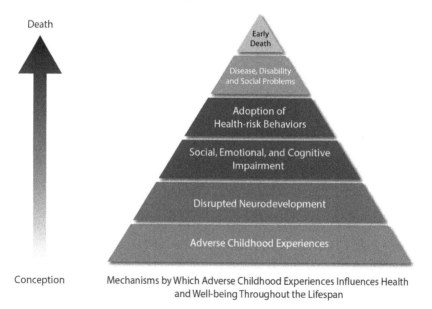

Figure 0.1 The Influence of Adverse Childhood Experiences Across the Lifespan

RECENT STATE AND NATIONAL DATA ON PREVALENCE OF ACES FOR CHILDREN BIRTH TO 17

A recent analysis of the *2016 National Survey of Children's Health* (NSCH) examined the prevalence of one or more ACEs among children from birth through age 17, as reported by a parent or guardian. The data are representative at national and state levels. Key findings include:

- **Economic hardship and divorce or separation of a parent or guardian** are the most common ACEs reported nationally, and in all states.
- **45% of children in the United States have experienced at least one ACE.**
- **One in ten children nationally has experienced three or more ACEs**, placing them in a category of especially high risk. In five states—Arizona, Arkansas, Montana, New Mexico, and Ohio—as many as one in seven children had experienced three or more ACEs.
- **Children of different races and ethnicities do not experience ACEs equally**. National percentages of children with at least one ACE: 61% of black non-Hispanic children, 51% of Hispanic, 40% of white non-Hispanic children, and 23% of Asian non-Hispanic children. In every region, the prevalence of ACEs is lowest among Asian non-Hispanic children and, in most regions, is highest among black non-Hispanic children.

Source: www.childtrends.org/publications/prevalence-adverse-childhood-experiences-nationally-state-race-ethnicity/

Intergenerational Transmission of Trauma

Research on ACEs provides preliminary evidence that their negative impacts can be transmitted across generations (Buss et al., 2017; Monk, Feng, Lee, Krupska, Champagne & Tycko, 2016). Toxic stress experienced by women during pregnancy can negatively affect genetic "programming" during fetal development, which can contribute to a host of bad outcomes, sometimes much later in life (Almond & Currie, 2011). Infants born to women who experienced four or more childhood adversities were two to five times more likely to have poor physical and emotional health outcomes by 18 months of age, according to one recently published study (www.childtrends.org/publications/prevalence-adverse-child hood-experiences-nationally-state-race-ethnicity/).

What Implications Does the ACES Study Have for Early Childhood Educators?

The ACES research identified the high prevalence of trauma impacting young children all across the country. Given this information, child care providers and early childhood teachers need to acknowledge trauma's existence in children's lives and to begin to discuss what its prevalence means for their own teaching and caregiving practice.

As the developing brain has the most plasticity in the early childhood years, early childhood teachers need to learn how to create trauma sensitive, trauma-informed early learning programs. They need to learn how to identify children's physiological reactions to stress, how to reduce traumatic triggers in their early learning environments, how to calm children's central nervous systems, and bring them back to a place of regulation. And importantly, teachers need to learn to engage in their own self-care so they can sustain the hard work of caring for children and families impacted by trauma.

Traditional wisdom and best practices discussed in child development and early childhood courses and training are often unsuccessful when applied to children with histories of trauma. This is especially the case when it comes to the strategies recommended for supporting children's "challenging behaviors." Learning about brain research on traumatic stress provides teachers with a whole new perspective on what children are communicating to them when they display these behaviors.

At its foundation, trauma-informed practice (TIP) recognizes that a child's history of trauma impacts their development, learning, emotions, and behavior. TIP is not a specific theory but instead, an integration of various strengths-based and relationship-based approaches and theories that all aim to do no further harm—i.e., not to re-traumatize a child—and to guide a child toward health and healing.

BEING A TRAUMA-INFORMED EARLY CHILDHOOD TEACHER MEANS THAT YOU:

- Have an understanding of the neurobiology of trauma and its impact on young children's development and ability to learn
- Acknowledge the existence and prevalence of many different types of trauma in young children's lives
- Recognize your responsibility to learn about trauma-sensitive strategies for supporting the young children and families you work with so you support their health and healing instead of further traumatizing them

- Engage in systematic self-care to replenish your energy and sustain your ability to work with the extra demands of children and families with trauma histories
- Commit to engaging in an ongoing reflection, inquiry, and continuous professional learning to improve your ability to develop sensitive, caring, responsive, and attuned relationships with children exposed to trauma and their families

Early childhood professionals are communicating that they are not prepared with the skills, knowledge, or tools they require to understand and work effectively with children who have experienced trauma. This is no surprise as the early childhood field has few resources on trauma-informed practices developed specifically for child care providers and early childhood teachers working with young children in early learning programs. The books, websites, and resources on trauma and young children that currently exist are primarily written from a clinical perspective by early childhood mental health practitioners, psychologists, therapists, social workers, and doctors. These resources are extremely valuable; however, many emphasize relationship-based therapeutic supports and focus on parent-child attachment relationships and interactions instead of teacher-child relationships. This makes it challenging to transfer the strategies directly to early childhood settings.

What Is Trauma-Informed Care and How Does It Relate to Trauma-Informed Practices?

Trauma-informed care (TIC) is an organizational structure and treatment framework that involves understanding, recognizing, and responding to the effects of all types of trauma. TIC includes a commitment to children, families, and staff that promotes:

1. Understanding trauma and the impact on children, families, and staff
2. Procedures for early identification of trauma
3. Responding to the effects of trauma with key evidence-based strategies
4. Supporting relationship practices and environments that promote safety, predictability, empowerment, and control
5. Identifying and recommending resources and referrals
   www.traumainformedcareproject.org/

In this book, TIP is the practical application of strategies with a TIC framework in an educational context.

Moving from Trauma-Inducing to Trauma-Reducing Early Childhood Programs, Organizations, and Systems

Teachers cannot support and heal children in silos on their own. Teachers' success in meeting the needs of children and families impacted by trauma is deeply influenced by the level of trauma-sensitivity of the programs, organizations, and systems they are working within. As a result, the North Star we all need to strive for is to integrate knowledge of trauma and TIPs across every level of the early childhood field. Our collective goal must be to create workplace cultures, policies, services, and daily practices that are trauma-sensitive, trauma-informed, and healing for young children, families, and the workforce serving them (www.traumatransformed.org) (Figure 0.2).

Trauma-organized programs, agencies, and systems have several characteristics. The people working within them or impacted by their services do not feel an inherent sense of safety. Relationships are lacking trust or frequently disrupted before trust can be built. Information, communication, and work feels fragmented, people and systems/processes are overwhelmed, leadership and the climate are fear driven, and rules are rigid—i.e., they leave no room for local variation or equity—and as a result, people do not feel a sense of agency to influence the conditions that impact them, leading to feelings of numb and hopelessness.

TRAUMA-ORGANIZED

- Reactive
- Reliving/Retelling
- Avoiding/Numbing
- Fragmented
- Us Vs. Them
- Inequity
- Authoritarian Leadership

TRAUMA-INFORMED

- Understanding of the Nature and Impact of Trauma and Recovery
- Shared Language
- Recognizing Socio-Cultural Trauma and Structural Oppression

HEALING ORGANIZATION

- Reflective
- Making Meaning Out of the Past
- Growth and Prevention-Oriented
- Collaborative
- Equity and Accountability
- Relational Leadership

TRAUMA INDUCING   TO   TRAUMA REDUCING

Figure 0.2 Moving from Trauma-Inducing to Trauma-Reducing Early Childhood Programs, Organizations and Systems.

Trauma-informed programs, agencies, and systems realize the widespread impact of trauma, are knowledgeable about the neurobiological impact of trauma and its effects on children, youth, families, communities, and systems and they share a common language to talk about trauma. They act on this knowledge by changing practices and policies to actively work to resist re-traumatization of people and to address the impacts of trauma.

Healing programs, agencies, and systems acknowledge that it is not enough to just be trauma-informed. Instead, we want to move toward becoming healing environments. A healing environment is integrated, collaborative, and promotes authenticity. There are intentional spaces included to create time to pause and to reflect, to make meaning of, and learn from difficult experiences. There is a value for human connection, for taking care of ourselves and each other, celebrating successes, and striving together to create a culture of wellness. There is an explicit focus on learning, growth, and optimism. Individuals work together to contribute toward a greater good. Joy, creativity, and innovation are valued and supported.

Teachers will be most effective in learning to support young children and their families impacted by trauma if they are not working alone. Everyone working directly with or on behalf of young children and their families has a responsibility to help create early learning environments that are not only trauma-sensitive and trauma-informed but genuine places of safety and healing.

Goals and Overview of the Book

The goal of this book is to provide early childhood professionals working with infants, toddlers, preschool, and early elementary-aged children with the knowledge and skills they need to understand trauma, its impact on young children's learning and development, and a range of TIPs they can use to create safe and predictable classroom environments that support children's health, healing, and well-being. Through many authentic vignettes and teacher-friendly strategies, everything in this book is written specifically for the early childhood field with a particular focus on the adults directly serving young children and their families. We offer a wide range of ideas teachers can use to support children in their programs who have experienced trauma.

Chapter Outline

Each chapter begins with an **inquiry question** to model the importance of reflective practice in TIP. In each chapter, we provide definitions of key terms, cite relevant research, introduce teacher-friendly strategies for applying TIP in early childhood programs, and provide authentic vignettes drawn from diverse early learning programs.

Throughout the book **we use the word "teacher"** to represent the diverse range of early childhood professionals who work with young children and their families. We understand that many adults who serve our youngest children use a range of other formal titles—e.g., *provider, caregiver, care teacher, care provider, child care provider, teacher aide, instructional aide, home care provider, substitute, volunteer, parent, caregiver, and others.* Our decision to refer to "teachers" throughout the book is only to provide a consistent term for readers. The content of the book applies to all adults who work directly with, or on behalf of, infants, toddlers, preschoolers, and early elementary-aged children.

Four chapters include **case studies and reflection questions**. The narratives of children's experiences of trauma and early learning environments included in these case studies were constructed as composites that draw from our authentic experiences working with young children and families. None of the stories represent a specific child, family, or teacher, however, they are entirely authentic and based in our collective experiences in our work as an educator, social worker, and clinical psychologist.

Chapter 1, "Understanding the Neurobiology of Trauma," begins with an introduction to the different parts of the brain and the impact of stress on the developing brain. Next, we define trauma, describe the different types of trauma, and discuss the impact of trauma on young children's development and capacity to learn. We also introduce the importance of attunement, adult-child co-regulation and the role of mirror neurons in supporting young children to calm when their stress response systems are triggered. This chapter ends by introducing readers to the concept of resiliency and the factors that strengthen it in young children.

Chapter 2, "Foundations of Trauma-Informed Practice for Early Childhood Education," introduces several principles for guiding a discussion of trauma and TIPs for early childhood. A thriving coastal redwood tree is introduced as a metaphor to represent the image of a child whose health, well-being, and ability to grow and thrive are dependent upon the adult caregivers and the environment around them.

Chapters 3, "Trauma-Sensitive Early Childhood Programs," begins with a description of the most important trauma-sensitive strategy in early childhood classrooms, building attuned and responsive relationships between teachers and young children. We then describe other important trauma-sensitive strategies including the use of self-reflection and inquiry to strengthen self-awareness and adult self-regulation, the importance of using a strengths-based approach, implementing culturally responsive practices, use of consistent routines and schedules, support for transitions, and direct teaching of social-emotional skills.

Chapter 4, "Case Study: Infant and Mother Living in a Homeless Shelter," illustrates a case study of a single mother and her 14-month-old infant experiencing homelessness. We describe several TIPs for supporting a hyper-aroused fight response in a young infant. We then introduce trauma-sensitive family engagement strategies for communicating with and supporting a mother in this situation. We end with reflection questions to guide teachers' discussion of the concepts in the case and how they can apply them to their practice.

Chapter 5, "Case Study: Toddler with a History of Neglect and Three Foster Home Placements," presents a case study of a 28-month old toddler with an experience of neglect placed in foster care. We describe several TIP practices for supporting a hypo-aroused freeze response in a toddler. We also introduce several family engagement strategies for communicating with and supporting a foster parent caring for a child with a history of trauma. The chapter closes with reflection questions to guide teachers' discussion of the concepts in the case and how they can apply them to their practice.

Chapter 6, "Case Study: Preschooler with an Undocumented Father Who Suddenly Disappears Due to Deportation," describes a case study of a 4-year-old boy experiencing the loss of his father due to a sudden deportation order. We describe several TIP practices for supporting a withdrawn freeze response in a preschooler. We also introduce trauma-sensitive family engagement strategies for working with a family with two generational traumatic stress. Reflection questions are included to inform teachers' discussion of the concepts in the case and how they can apply them to their practice.

Chapter 7, "Case Study: First Grader Who Recently Witnessed a Drive-by Shooting While Playing at School," presents a case study describing a first-grade boy impacted by community violence. The chapter begins with a description of several TIP practices appropriate for supporting a child with a withdrawn freeze response. We also describe how a TIP approach can be expanded beyond classrooms to create trauma-informed and trauma-sensitive school environments. The chapter ends with reflection questions to guide teachers' discussion of the concepts in the case and planning for how to apply them in their practice.

Chapter 8, "The Importance of Self-Care in TIP Work: Taking Care of Yourself in Order to Prevent Burnout, Compassion Fatigue, and Secondary Traumatic Stress," begins with a brief summary of the research on the impact of burnout, compassion fatigue, and secondary traumatic stress for adults working in caring professions. Next, we introduce the importance of self-care for teachers working with young children and their families experiencing traumatic stress. We describe several self-care strategies teachers can implement at home and work to support their health and well-being. We end with the introduction of a tool teachers can use to create a quality self-care plan.

The end of the book includes several **recommendations** for teachers and administrators interested in transforming their classrooms and programs to become trauma-informed and trauma-sensitive. We also describe important **resources** on trauma and TIP including books for adults and children, videos, websites, and a self-care app. The **appendices** include three case scenarios with accompanying teacher observation forms and trauma-sensitive support planning sheets to help teachers learn to identify factors that contribute to an individual child being triggered and the trauma-sensitive strategies they can use to support children in a dysregulated fight, flight, or freeze state.

1

UNDERSTANDING THE NEUROBIOLOGY OF TRAUMA

What Role Do Caregivers Play in Facilitating Early Brain Development?

Key Topics Covered

- Brainstem, limbic brain, neo-cortex
- Arousal states
- The impact of stress on the developing brain
- Defining trauma and the different types of trauma
- The impact of trauma on young children's development and capacity to learn
- Attunement, co-regulation, and mirror neurons
- Neuro-plasticity, resiliency, and healing

Neurobiology 101: Brain Development in the Earliest Years

Brain development begins when a baby is growing in the womb. Neurons are the foundational elements of a baby's brain growth. **Neurogenesis**, or the process of growing new neurons, is a process that occurs throughout an individual's lifetime, although neural growth is most active during the first two trimesters of pregnancy. An estimated 86 billion neurons form the basic structure of a baby's brain at birth (Azeveo et al., 2009; Herculano-Houzel, 2009). At birth, every neuron in a baby's cerebral cortex has approximately 2,500 **synapses** (the gaps between neurons), by 2 years of age the number closely approximates an average adult's brain, and by the time a child reaches their third birthday, every neuron has approximately 15,000 synapses, an amount that is about twice the number in a typical adult's brain (Conkbayier, 2017; Rogers, 2011). This is why the early childhood years are so critical. Synaptic growth—where neurons are connected to other neurons—is strongly influenced by environmental conditions and a direct result of the various experiences a child has whether developmentally supportive or traumatic and impairing.

WHEN DOES BRAIN DEVELOPMENT START?

Brain development begins when a baby is growing in the womb. Brain growth is significant and extremely fast while a baby is growing in utero, which is why the prenatal environment is so critical. Many factors can have a profound impact on a vulnerable and developing fetal brain, particularly maternal health. Such factors include diet/nutrition, exercise, substance abuse, mental health challenges (depression, anxiety, etc.), exposure to environmental toxins, and most significantly, experiences of prolonged traumatic stress. Young children's healthy brain development starts with the health and well-being of their mothers. This is why supporting maternal health before, during, and after pregnancy is a critical foundation for healthy child development.

Through healthy and caring relationships, play, exploration of their environment, and responsive communication where adults help children feel safe and belonging in their families and communities, children develop healthy synaptic connections that become a neurobiological foundation supporting their future academic learning and social-emotional health. Similarly, early traumatic experiences can interrupt normal synaptic growth from occurring, leading a young child's brain to develop differently with negative outcomes that can last a lifetime without proper intervention. This is why **neural plasticity**—or the brain's ability to alter its structure and function in response to internal bodily changes or external environmental changes—is most rapid during a child's first few years of life when their brains are most influenced by environmental factors. As Conkbayier (2017) explains:

> Neural connections grow and are strengthened in response to [environmental] experiences, be they positive or negative. Repetition of experiences leads to neurons creating pathways in different parts of the brain, based on experiences. Perry (2001) tells us that experience, good and bad, literally becomes the neuroarcheology of the individual's brain.
>
> (p. 14)

What Is Pruning?

A process called **pruning** is essential for young children's healthy brain growth. During the pruning process, synaptic connections that are used in a child's brain are strengthened and those that are not used are eliminated. As children develop relationships and have experiences, the neural connections that have the most "usage"—the neurons that fire most often in the child's brain—will be strengthened and maintained and those that are used least often will be "pruned away" making room for new neural growth to take place. This is often referred to as "Use It or Lose It" (Perry et al., 1995).

The process of pruning is most active during infancy (especially just after birth) and throughout the adolescent years. This is why the quality of early interactions and experiences can have such significant and long-term effects for children. If, for example, a child does not have caring attuned relationships with adults in their earliest years, the neural pathways that support emotions and emotional regulation can be significantly impaired. Additionally, if a child is not exposed to rich vocabulary or provided with many opportunities to actively explore their environment, the healthy neural networks they need for future academic learning may be lost instead of developed and strengthened through the pruning process.

Young children's caregivers have a tremendously important role in guiding their healthy brain development. It is important that early childhood teachers understand how neural structures are created and form the building blocks of children's development and their potential to learn. They have a tremendous responsibility to support young children's brain development. As Wolfe (2007) explains, they must understand that every child they care for, "represents a virtual explosion of dendritic growth. [Early childhood educators] are so fortunate to be in a profession where [they] can create learning opportunities to best support young children's development and their biological wiring" (cited in Rushton, 2011, p. 92).

The Hierarchical Nature of Children's Brain Development

The process of neural growth occurs sequentially from the "bottom up" (Perry et al., 1995). The first areas of the brain to fully develop are the brainstem and midbrain (the midbrain is part of the brainstem), as they are responsible for the bodily functions necessary for life, which are called the autonomic functions (e.g., breathing, sleeping, blood pressure). The last regions of the brain to fully develop are the limbic system, involved in regulating emotions, and then the cortex, involved in language, abstract thought, reasoning, and problem-solving. Because of the sequential nature of neural growth, if one "layer" of the brain's development is interrupted and/or impaired, the subsequent parts of the brain will also not develop properly. For example, if trauma damages the healthy development of a child's brainstem, the child's limbic system and cortex will not function optimally, which may show up as delays or impairments with language development or difficulty with social-emotional skills or cognitive processing (Figure 1.1).

The Brainstem (Primitive or "Reptilian" Brain). The first part of the human brain to develop in the womb is the brainstem, whose function is similar to the brain of reptiles. Thus, the nickname, reptilian brain. The primitive part of the brain is responsible for the FLIGHT, FIGHT, and FREEZE response humans have when they perceive danger. We all need this part of our brain to mobilize an emergency or survival response in situations of crisis. If a child puts their hand on a hot stove, their brainstem gives them the ability to react quickly and remove their hand so that they do not sustain burns. If an adult driver gets cut off on the freeway, it is their brainstem that quickly reacts and makes them swerve quickly away from a potentially fatal situation. This part of the brain is referred to as the "alarm center" or "smoke detector" (van der Kolk, 2014) and it continually scans the environment for red flags and sends messages that lead us to perceive whether we are safe or should mobilize to prepare for danger.

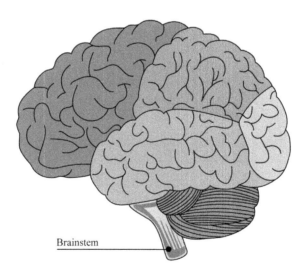

Brainstem

Figure 1.1 Brainstem.

Courtney Vickery

A WINDOW INTO YOUR BRAINSTEM AT WORK ...

Imagine you are driving on the freeway and out of nowhere, someone cuts you off. Your reptile brain kicks into high gear and serves a life-saving function of helping you immediately mobilize your energy to focus quickly to avoid the car swerving into your lane. Your brain sends signals to increase your heart rate and blood flow to your extremities shutting down all other bodily functions so that you can quickly save your life by escaping the potential danger.

Or, if your supervisor sends you a very direct and extensive email about your performance deficits, this could also immediately trigger a reaction that sends you into your reptile brain. With your heart racing, you quickly respond by pounding out an email solely authored by either the fight, flight, or freeze reptile brainstem.

FIGHT: You immediately email back to your supervisor a defensive, attacking, and reactive response to prove them wrong.

FLIGHT: Another response while in this part of your brain is the need to run away. You "decide" right then to state that you are sick and will send it in the evening so you will not have to deal with any confrontation.

FREEZE: When in freeze mode, you find ways to completely disconnect and avoid the situation. Unhealthy freeze strategies for an adult may be binge eating with food, abusing drugs, alcohol, or other similar strategies that help you numb out and disconnect from the world.

Perhaps you have been working with a child where you just set a firm limit. If the child yells "I hate you and I hope you die," the adult caregiver may be triggered emotionally and default directly to their reptile brain. If you have a reptilian brain reaction toward the child, you would use punishment or other punitive strategies such as criticism, threats, or shaming.

The reptile part of your brain is life saving and helps you in an emergency such as a fire, an unexpected car swerving in your lane, a tornado, or even day to day stressors. You need this part of your brain to mobilize your personal physical resources for survival. However, if you habitually default to your reptile brain during normal day to day stressors, then you will be more reactive and punitive, thus causing more harm to children impacted by trauma (Figure 1.2).

The Limbic Brain (Emotional or Mammalian Brain). We share this part of our brain with mammals. The functionality of the mammalian brain differentiates us from our more primitive reptilian brainstem. It generates our feelings, emotional intensity of feelings, and creates our desire for attachment, significance, and belonging. Attachments, emotions, and emotional regulation of our behavior are all generated and expressed through this part

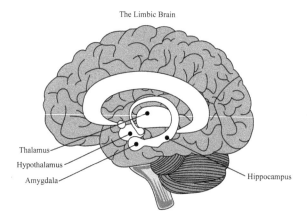

Figure 1.2 Limbic system.

Courtney Vickery

of the limbic brain. Young babies are born with what is called "an experience-dependent limbic system," which means they need lots of repeated positive emotional, social, and cognitive interactions to support the development of a healthy limbic system (Conkbayir, 2017, p. 43; Twardosz, 2012). The limbic brain includes several different elements:

- **Thalamus**. Among the roles of the thalamus is the process of receiving sensory information and through synaptic connections sharing it with the neo-cortex (discussed below).
- **Hypothalamus**. The hypothalamus is responsible for autonomic functions including our perception of thirst and hunger, maintenance of our body temperature, and sleep. It also controls the release of hormones from the pituitary gland including the secretion of adrenocorticotropic hormone (ACTH), which stimulates the production of cortisol and oxytocin. In this way, the hypothalamus creates a bridge between the endocrine system and the nervous system.
- **Amygdala**. The amygdala controls our survival responses and allows us to react within fractions of a second to the presence of anything we perceive to be threatening or dangerous. The amygdala supports our ability to feel emotions and to perceive them in others around us and the physical sensations in our bodies that result when we are fearful or threatened (e.g., racing heartbeat resulting from a sudden and very loud siren). The amygdala is the reason we are scared of things that are out of our control. It controls how we react to the events, experiences, and stimuli in our environments that are perceived as potentially threatening or dangerous. The amygdala is the emotional center of our brain and responsible for the development of fear.

Young children are less capable of regulating their emotions because the neural connections that communicate information from the cortex to the limbic system are not fully developed. Although the neo-cortex continues to develop until early adulthood, the amygdala is fully developed at birth, and for this reason, has a strong influence on young children's emotions and behavior.

- **Hippocampus.** This part of the brain is responsible for processing our long-term memories including our memories of the location of objects and people. The hippocampus is vulnerable to the negative biochemical effects of severe and prolonged early stress (Cozolino, 2006; Pally, 2000). The hippocampus plays an essential role in the formation of new memories about past experiences and in regulating our emotions and learning. It does not fully myelinate until at least three years of age (van der Kolk, 1994). Myelination is essential for the proper function of the nervous system and it helps messages to move more quickly and clearly from the brain to the correct body part (Figure 1.3).

The Pre-Frontal Cortex or Neo-Cortex (Executive or Thinking Brain). Mammals and reptiles do not have the neo-cortex that exists only in the human brain. Only humans have a neo-cortex allowing us to have more advanced processing capabilities. This part of the brain is responsible for making logical decisions, problem-solving, rational thought, perspective taking, and abstract thinking. The neo-cortex is considered the "Boss or Chief Executive Officer" of the brain, but it is not born that way. Just as a person does not become a CEO of a company overnight, it takes years of rich experiences and skill building to learn to manage a complex organization.

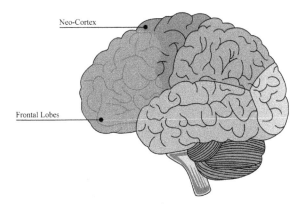

Figure 1.3 Neo-cortex.

Courtney Vickery

Similarly, it takes our entire childhood, and into early adulthood, to build a strong neo-cortex. Positive experiences, nurturing caregivers and supportive environments help build this part of the brain to full potential, helping us solve complex problems by:

- Identifying how we feel;
- Recognizing how intense our emotions are;
- Using healthy self-regulation strategies;
- (When calm and regulated), allowing us to think through all the possible choices and outcomes to solve a problem;
- Choosing a solution that is for the greater good that does not hurt ourselves, others, or the environment;
- Seeing the "big picture" of a dilemma and map the small steps to a solution.

The frontal lobes (part of the prefrontal cortex of the brain) are responsible for the development of our complex cognitive processes and executive functions that are central to emotional and behavior self-regulation (Center on the Developing Child, 2011; Pally, 2000). Neuroscientists have discovered that the development of the frontal lobes occurs over a long period of time. Development begins close to the eighth month of life, increases between 12 and 24 months when the brain is organizing (Hanson, 2009; Pally, 2000), continues to rapidly develop through the first six years, reduces by age 16 (Schore, 1994), but continues to develop throughout the mid-20s (Hanson, 2009)! The frontal lobe is the part of the brain that governs both self-regulation and executive functioning skills:

- **Self-regulation skills** include the ability of a child to express emotions and maintain an optimal level of arousal so they can pay attention, focus on something specific, and be in control of their behavior (Blair & Diamond, 2008; Bronson, 2000).
- **Executive function skills** include *working memory* (holding information in the short term), *behavior inhibition* (ability to pause before responding to a stimuli), and *cognitive and behavioral flexibility* (ability to change one's thinking and behavior in response to environmental stimuli) (Blair & Diamond, 2008; 18Center on the Developing Child, 2011; Greenland, 2010; Posner & Rothbart, 2007; Rothbart & Posner, 2006). Executive functions work together to facilitate complex levels of self-regulation needed for children to pursue goals. For example, children use their executive functions to manage their strong emotions, motivations, and arousal levels to assist their ability to self-regulate and engage in learning and positive interactions.

Self-regulation skills and executive function skills work together to promote young children's emotional resiliency (Center on the Developing Child, 2011).

Brainstem our "Reptilian Brain": Alarm Center of the Brain

- Fight, flight, freeze
- Breathing
- Heart rate
- Motor regulation
- Body temperature
- Blood pressure
- Reflex response
- Sensorial memory (anxiety or arousal states associated with a traumatic event)

Limbic "Mammal" Brain: The Emotion Center of the Brain

- Attachment
- Emotional memory (e.g., fear, pleasure, sadness)
- Emotional state/Affect
- Emotional reactions
- Appetite

Neo-Cortex "Executive" Brain: The CEO of the Brain

- Abstract thought
- Logic and reasoning
- Impulse control
- Self-regulation
- Problem-solving
- Critical thinking
- Cognitive memory (e.g., names, faces, and facts)

Supporting Children to be in their Optimal Zone of Arousal

Arousal is a state of physiological and mental alertness. Each child has an individual **zone of optimal arousal**, which is the arousal level where they are the most regulated and learn best (Figure 1.4). Too much or too little arousal

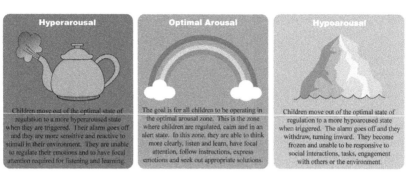

Figure 1.4 Zones of Arousal.

Courtney Vickery

can negatively influence children's behavior and their ability to learn. There is a strong relationship between environmental stimuli and the arousal system. In considering how to support children to be in their zone of optimal arousal, teachers need to identify the type and number of stimuli children are exposed to:

- **High Arousal State**: If children experience too much stimulation, their arousal level shifts above their optimal threshold and they become hyper-aroused, which leads to behavior that is dysregulated and hyper-reactive. This may look like a child yelling and running in the classroom and not listening to the teacher when asked to calm down.
- **Low/Under Arousal State**: If children experience too little stimulation, their arousal level shifts below their optimal threshold and they become hypo-aroused, which leads to behavior that is withdrawn and hypo-reactive. This may look like a child who is alone in the corner of the room and staring at the wall.
- **Optimal Arousal**: The state of physiological and mental alertness that is optimal for children's behavior and ability to learn.
- **Hyper-arousal**: Increased physiological and psychological activity that requires a need to release huge amounts of energy such as running away, throwing objects, throwing a tantrum, hurting others, yelling or screaming (*fight/flight response*).
- **Hypo-arousal**: Low physical energy, low emotion, and low cognitive activity such as being despondent, shut down, hiding, unresponsive or uninvolved (*freeze response*).

Environmental Stimuli that Affect Young Children's Arousal States

New child or adult	Quick movements	Disorganized materials
Stranger entering the space	Unexpected touch	Unpredictable schedule
Noise levels	Harsh touch	The absence of caregiver
A smell	Another child crying	A particular texture
Unexpected noise	Someone taking something away	Taking the child's shoes off while they are lying down
Change in lighting	New room arrangement	Someone approaching while a child is lying on a cot
Change in schedule	New piece of equipment	Tickling a child
Too many transitions	Nap time	An adult towering over a child
Harsh words or harsh tone of voice	Someone approaching the child too quickly	Angry or fearful facial expression

Source: Sorrels, 2015, p. 38.

Early childhood teachers want to strive to support each child to increase the amount of time they are in their optimal zone of arousal each day. Not over-stimulated and not under-stimulated, but in that "just right" zone for their brains and bodies. Unfortunately, many children with histories of trauma spend the majority of their day outside of their optimal zone either in a High Arousal State (hyper-arousal; fight/flight response) or in a Low Arousal State (hypo-arousal; freeze/withdrawn response). This happens because their brains have learned to perceive the world as a dangerous place and they automatically shift out of their optimal arousal states in order to do everything they can to keep themselves safe (this happens automatically in the child's body, they are not in control of this process).

Understanding how to support children with histories of trauma to increase the amount of time they are in their Optimal Zone of Arousal requires learning about the role of stress in children's brain development.

The Role of Stress in Children's Development

Developing a healthy stress response system is important for all children so they grow up with the ability to cope with stress and the challenges they will face throughout their lives. To understand how early childhood teachers can support children to develop healthy stress response systems, it is helpful to consider the impact of stress along a continuum. The Center for the Developing Child at Harvard University (https://developingchild.

harvard.edu/science/key-concepts/toxic-stress/) distinguishes among three types of stress responses: positive, tolerable, and toxic. As described below, these three terms refer to the stress response system's effects on the child's body, not necessarily the intensity of a stressful event or experience itself.

POSITIVE Stress Response. Learning how to manage stress is a normal and healthy part of young children's development. When children face developmentally appropriate levels of stress, they can develop coping skills that become an important foundation for their resiliency and ability to manage life's ongoing challenges as they mature. Positive stress responses result from developmentally responsive stressors in a young child's life (e.g., first day of school, learning to ride a bike, a new sibling, mastering a new skill) when their body has a brief increase in heart rate and a mild elevation in stress hormones.

Children are best able to learn how to manage their stress when they are in an environment with supportive adults who can buffer or decrease the impact of a stressful experience on the child. For example, if a young toddler is suddenly frightened by the sound of a very loud thunderstorm and her fear triggers a release of cortisol and other stress chemicals throughout her body, a supportive adult can help to buffer the stress she feels by communicating messages of safety, calm, predictability, and providing the child with some agency or sense of control in responding to the situation. *What does this buffering effect look like*:

- **The adult stays near the toddler until the storm is over and reassures her that she is safe and she will be taken care of by the adult.** She also reassures her that although the thunder is loud, she is safe inside her house and nothing bad will happen to her. The storm will stop in a little while (communicating safety).
- **The adult reminds the toddler about the daily routines they will continue to do even though the thunderstorm is happening outside**: washing hands, eating snack, nap time, playtime (creating a sense of predictability and reducing fear associated with uncertainty).
- **The adult invites the toddler to draw a picture of the thunderstorm, or to choose a storybook to read together or to push "play" to turn on some calming classical music they can listen to together** (providing an opportunity for the toddler to experience a sense of control in the situation).

All of these actions by the adult are strategies that help to buffer or decrease the child's feeling of fear, powerlessness, and lack of control; the key indicators of a traumatic stressor for a young child. In this way, the presence of a caring and responsive adult helped this toddler to learn to manage the stress created by the storm and to develop coping skills (e.g., drawing, reading, listening to music, sitting in an adult's lap) that reinforced the development of a healthy stress response system. Stress that is developmentally supportive is predictable and moderate. Resilience is developed from patterns of predictable moderate controlled stress as highlighted in the example above.

Children are best able to learn how to manage their stress when they are in an environment with supportive adults who can buffer or decrease the impact of the stressful experience on the child.

TOLERABLE Stress Response. *Tolerable stress* occurs when children are faced with a more severe, persistent, and longer-term threat. Examples include the loss of a loved one, experiencing a natural disaster (earthquake, flood, hurricane, tornado) or similarly frightening experience (car accident, medical procedure, fall that leads to injury). The brain activates a survival fight, flight, freeze stress response and the body releases stress hormones. The impact of this activation can be damaging on the brain and organs if the child does not have a strong support system and at least one attuned, caring relationship with an adult who can buffer their stress. However, if the activation of the stress response system is limited in time (versus ongoing) and a caring adult helps the child cope and manage her stress, the child will likely recover without any enduring neurobiological, psychological, or physical damage. We might see this with a young preschool child whose family had to evacuate their home in the middle of the night as a wildfire appeared suddenly and burned their home to the ground. *What does adult buffering look like in this context?*

- **Despite the adult's own stress, she keeps the child physically close to her during the evacuation and reassures the child that she (the adult) is taking care of her and taking her out of danger to a safe place.** The adult has coping skills to support the child to feel safe even though they are in a threatening situation. The adult is able to act quickly to remove the child from danger as quickly as possible (communicating safety).

- **Once the adult and child are out of harm's way, the adult communicates that helpers (firefighters and others) are rescuing the people and animals and bringing them to safety** and **working to put out the fire.** (Creating a sense of predictability and reducing fear associated with uncertainty for the child).

- **The adult provides opportunities for the preschooler to release the additional "discharge" of survival energy from the triggering of her stress response system.** The adult guides the child to run, jump up and down, shake her body, tap her hands or feet, or engage in any movement that releases the excess energy in her body, so the stress chemicals are not frozen into the child's nervous system, which can create lasting damage. When the child is ready, the adult might also help her verbalize her experience including how she felt and the actions she took to get to safety (providing an opportunity for the child to experience a sense of control in the situation).

TOXIC Stress Response. *Toxic or traumatic stress* occurs when a child endures frequent, severe, and/or prolonged exposure to adversity with no caring adult available to buffer the distress for the child. Physical or sexual abuse, physical or emotional neglect, extreme poverty, caregiver mental illness, and exposure to violence are examples of the types of stress that without the support of consistent caring adults, can lead to toxic stress. Toxic stress leads to prolonged activation of a child's stress response system and a significant release of stress chemicals throughout a child's developing brain and body. This can result in damage to the developing circuits in the child's brain (e.g., underdevelopment of their limbic brain and neo-cortex and over-activation of the right hemisphere of the brain) and impaired functioning for the child across all domains of their development (physical, social-emotional, and cognitive).

When children repeatedly experience stress, especially toxic or traumatic stress, and they do not have supportive relationships with adults who can buffer their stress, the result can be poorly developed and damaged stress response systems—alterations in the very neural tissue and architecture of their brains—that impair their ability to learn and pay attention, to cope with daily stressors, and to self-regulate their emotions and behavior, consequences that can endure throughout their lives. The fear associated with traumatic stress overwhelms young children's fragile and developing nervous systems and reduces their capacity to modulate their body's arousal levels (their ability to remain alert, attentive, and awake), important foundations for children's healthy development and early learning (Blair & Diamond, 2008). Additionally, the fear children experience as a result of traumatic stress negatively influences the development of their stress response system. When the development of children's stress response system is interrupted due to stress, a common result is that young children respond to everyday experiences with a heightened early stress reaction, that is, their brains overly perceive danger even when little to no danger exists in the environment (Schore, 2003a, Schuder & Lyons-Ruth, 2004).

As these descriptions highlight, it is important for early childhood professionals to fully absorb how young children react to traumatic or toxic stress. It is a whole mind and body experience as they react neurobiologically (e.g., their bodies release stress hormones), physiologically (e.g., rapid heart rate), and behaviorally (e.g., inability to pay attention) when traumatic events stir up the children's feelings of helplessness and fear and trigger a complex set of chemical and neurological events known as a body's **stress response** (Massachusetts Advocates for Children, 2005). We know from research that if children grow up with persistent traumatic stress and fear, they can easily find themselves on an unhealthy neurological trajectory with significant damage to the development of their vulnerable brains (Siegel, 2012). Traumatic stress is most harmful in children's earliest years because it undermines typical development of the right brain, which governs children's coping abilities and their emotional regulation (Schore, 2005, 2010).

Epigenetic Changes

Epigenetics is the study of variations in the expression of genes—how genes are switched on or off in tissues and cells during conception—that get passed from one generation to another without altering the genetic DNA. Epigenetic research has demonstrated that genes can be silenced (switched off) or expressed (switched on) as a result of many factors (maternal health, environment, lifestyle, etc.) including the *presence of stress and trauma* in a mother's life.

Animal research has demonstrated that mothers who are unresponsive in their care have babies with higher stress-reactivity and increased anxiety and fearfulness in comparison with the offspring of mothers who provide more responsive caregiving. Research in humans has confirmed and extended these findings demonstrating that pregnancy, infancy, and early childhood are sensitive periods during which exposure to stress and adverse experiences can lead to behavioral, psychological, and epigenetic changes that may persist into adulthood (Cunliffe, 2016).

Epigenetic research demonstrates that a range of adverse experiences in early childhood (e.g., intimate partner violence, maternal exposure to genocidal war, childhood abuse, neglect, and deprivation) can induce prenatal stress and lead to epigenetic changes in a child's gene expression. Said in another way, the presence of consistent activation of stress chemicals can change children's brains at a genetic level as new neural circuits are created in response to stress.

We need additional research to deepen our understanding of epigenetic effects in young children. Specifically, how experiences of prenatal stress, childhood maltreatment and unresponsive parental care become biologically embedded in a child's genes leading to long-term negative impacts that persist across their lifetime.

The Central Nervous System: The Command Center for the Stress Response System

Stress is a biological and psychological response that a person experiences when they are faced with social challenges and do not have the resources to cope. The hypothalamic-pituitary-adrenal (HPA) axis in the brain is in charge of the stress response. The HPA system works with the autonomic nervous system to release hormones that are vital to manage stress (Pally, 2000). The HPA system is not completely developed at birth but instead, forms in response to the quality of infant-caregiver attachment relationships in the first years of life. When infants have caregivers who help to buffer or regulate their stressors, the HPA system supports the development of a healthy stress response system. In contrast, when a young child does not have a consistent and supportive adult to help manage their stress, the child's brain develops in a manner that significantly compromises their ability to self-regulate their emotions and/or behavior.

The **autonomic nervous system** is responsible for our survival and regulates our body's central unconscious processes (breathing, sleeping, hunger). It is divided into two systems: the sympathetic nervous system (SNS) and the parasympathetic nervous system (PNS) and both are involved in our neurobiological reaction to stress.

The **SNS** activates the fight or flight response and also maintains homeostasis (balance of the body's functions including body temperature and balance of body fluids) in the body. Prolonged activation of the SNS can lead to the release of adrenaline in the body and is associated with increased arousal and increased activity. Moreover, the more often the SNS is activated, the more easily it is activated.

The **PNS** is responsible for the stimulation of several actions in the body including salivation, urination/defecation, digestion, and production of tears. Similar to the SNS, the more often the PNS is activated, the more easily it is activated. Too much activation of the PNS increases the risk of developing psychiatric symptoms including withdrawal, depression, helplessness, and anxiety (Perry et al., 1995).

Neurochemicals Released by the Body When the Stress Response System is Activated

Adrenaline. A neurochemical commonly referred to as the fight or flight hormone. It is produced by the body's adrenal glands after receiving a message from the amygdala that there is a potential threat or immediate danger. Adrenaline increases the body's heart rate, provides a surge of energy that helps us survive when we are in danger (e.g., helps us run away or move quickly), and helps to focus our attention (e.g., helps us scan our environment for signs of danger).

Norepinephrine (also called noradrenaline). A stress chemical similar to adrenaline released from the adrenal glands and from the brain that primarily increases arousal—responding to stress by increasing a person's ability to very quickly become more aware, awake, focused, and responsive. Norepinephrine also creates the signal that leads blood to shift in ways that support survival (away from skin toward muscles to allow for "fleeing" and away from limbs and toward organs to protect from injury).

Cortisol. Also a stress chemical released from the adrenal glands in a multistep process: (a) The alarm center of the brain—the amygdala—perceives a threat and (b) signals the hypothalamus to release a hormone (corticotro-pin-releasing hormone), which then (c) signals the pituitary gland to release another hormone (adrenocorticotropic hormone) that then (d) tells the adrenal glands to produce cortisol. Cortisol is a helpful life-saving hormone when it is released in the body in moderate amounts. However, chronic stress elevates the production of cortisol in the body. When cortisol is continuously released in the body and the level of cortisol in the body is elevated on a per-sistent basis—as is the case with children who experience toxic stress—it can cause tremendous damage to the brain and body suppressing the immune system, increasing blood pressure and blood sugars, breaking down muscle, bone and connective tissue, contributing to obesity, leading to hypothyroid, and interfering with sleep causing insomnia and night waking.

Polyvagal Theory and Neuroception

Stephen Porges is a trauma researcher who developed some foundational theories and concepts that are widely used by trauma scholars around the world. One is **polyvagal theory** that emphasizes the relationship between the brain, facial muscles, our hearts and gut, and our emotions. This theory suggests that children's nervous systems are genetically wired to scan the environment to determine whether they are safe or not. What they per-ceive from this process influences whether their autonomic nervous system (brainstem) responds with a survival response (i.e., fight/flight or freeze) to protect them and keep them out of harm's way.

Porges coined the word **neuroception** to describe how humans are geneti-cally wired to detect safety, danger, or threat, well below their level of conscious awareness. As humans, our nervous systems are continually scanning for signs of danger even though we are not consciously aware of this process. What information does the brain scan for during neuroception? A sense of physical or emotional safety. When a child feels safe and protected, they are able to use their **social engagement system** (face, eyes, mouth, and middle ear) and their heart to positively interact with others, to learn, and to function well.

Porges describes **prosody of voice** (intonation, tone, rhythm) and **facial expressions** as two of the most important sources of information our nerv-ous systems use during neuroception to assess our level of safety or danger. This means that a young child is more likely to sense danger and trigger a strong survival stress response when adults are using a harsh or angry tone of voice and when their facial expressions communicate frustration, lack of empathy, anger, or fear. Using the same logic, the process of calming a dis-tressed child is best achieved by adults who use a calm and nurturing tone of voice with facial expressions that communicate, "I'm here for you. I'm lis-tening to you. I care about you and want to support you and keep you safe." When a child has an experience of "feeling felt" by a caring adult (Levine &

Kline, 2007), the process of neuroception helps to change their autonomic state (calming their central nervous system). However, this outcome is compromised if children's neuroception is impaired due to a traumatic event that may undermine their sense of physical or emotional safety. In this case, the stress or trauma impairs a child's ability to use their social engagement system, leaving them in a survival state of fight/flight or freeze. The trauma becomes imprinted on the child's brain and body leaving them in a constant state of over-arousal and fear (Porges, 2011; van der Kolk, 2014).

Defining Trauma

Trauma affects children in every state, county, and city in America. Trauma impacts children and their families across all racial, ethnic, income and education levels, family constellations, geographic locations, and community groups. Trauma has been described as our nation's single most important public health challenge (van der Kolk, 2014) that is too often silenced and unacknowledged for its significant prevalence and devastating impact in our public dialogue (Craig, 2016). Trauma has been defined in a variety of ways by different scholars, clinicians, and agencies. Three important sources use the following definitions:

Child trauma refers to a child's witnessing or experiencing an event that poses a real or perceived threat to the life or well-being of the child or someone close to the child (such as a parent or sibling). The event overwhelms the child's ability to cope and causes feelings of fear, helplessness, or horror, which may be expressed by disorganized or agitated behavior.
(National Traumatic Stress Network)

Individual trauma results from an event, series of events, or set of circumstances that is experienced by an individual as physically or emotionally harmful, and that has lasting adverse effects on the individual's functioning and mental, physical, social, emotional, or spiritual well-being.
(Substance Abuse and Mental Health Services Administration;
SAMHSA, www.integration.samhsa.gov/clinical-practice/trauma)

Trauma is the result of an overwhelming amount of stress that exceeds one's ability to cope or integrate the emotions involved with that experience. Trauma differs among individuals by their subjective experiences, not the objective facts.
(Statman-Weil, 2018)

Although trauma crosses all demographic groups affecting children in every community in the United States, young children of color and children living in poverty are inequitably represented in the child welfare system, foster care placements, and the national statistics on child maltreatment.

Early childhood trauma is a broad term that describes a range of reactions young children have in response to a stressful experience in which their ability to cope is seriously weakened (Massachusetts Advocates for Children, 2005). An event becomes traumatic for a young child when it overwhelms their nervous system's ability to cope with stress leaving them feeling unsafe, vulnerable, and out of control (Macy et al., 2004). Traumatic experiences, whether real or perceived, lead children to feel significant levels of helplessness, powerlessness, and intense fear; experiences they perceive to be life threatening to themselves or others.

> Young children who experience trauma see the world as a dangerous place and their stress response systems are continually activated, communicating to them that they are not safe.

It is important to note that adults cannot determine whether a particular experience is traumatic for a child based on the intensity of a circumstance. This is because the experience of trauma is subjective and defined by its effect on a particular child's nervous system. While the intensity of a particular stressor is an important factor, this alone does not define trauma. As Peter Levine and Maggie Kline explain, *"trauma is not in the event itself; rather, trauma resides in the nervous system"* (Levine & Kline, 2007, p. 4, italics in original).

Types of Trauma

Experts studying and treating trauma in children and adults have categorized trauma into different categories. These individual types of trauma are not mutually exclusive as children and adults often have traumatic experiences that cross over these different categories:

Acute trauma. Acute trauma is a single traumatic event that is limited in time. Examples of acute trauma include loss of a loved one (divorce, death), accidents and falls (falling off a bike, a car accident), near drowning or suffocation, natural disaster (earthquake, flood, tornado), school shooting, sexual assault, painful/invasive medical or surgical procedures, fetal distress and birth complications, poisoning, life-threatening illness or high fevers, animal attack (dog bite).

Complex trauma. Complex trauma is defined as the experience of multiple traumatic events over a period of time. Complex trauma involves repetitive, persistent, and unpredictable significant stressors for a child. Children who have experienced complex trauma have endured multiple interpersonal traumatic events from a very young age (e.g., early loss and lack of consistent caregivers, placement in the foster care system, sexual abuse, significant neglect, and domestic violence). Complex trauma has profound effects on nearly every aspect of a child's development and functioning. For example, a child lives in a family with domestic violence, endures sexual abuse, resides in a neighborhood with a significant level of community violence, and experiences food insecurity on a daily basis. Complex trauma has a cumulative effect with each traumatic experience deepening the child's sense of fear, overwhelm, vulnerability, and lack of safety.

Childhood neglect, defined as the failure to provide for a child's basic physical, medical, educational, and emotional needs, is the most common type of maltreatment among young children. Neglect is defined as the omission of caretaking behavior that a child needs for healthy development and can lead to serious and lifelong consequences. Experiencing neglect can feel acutely threatening, particularly for very young children who are completely dependent on caregivers for their survival. Neglect often occurs in the context of other maltreatment, such as periods of abandonment and abuse, and is frequently associated with other psychosocial stressors and forms of adversity such as extreme poverty and parental substance abuse. Neglect is usually the most difficult type of trauma to identify.

Historical/cultural trauma. Historical trauma is a personal or historical event or prolonged experience that continues to have an impact over several generations. Cultural trauma is an attack on the fabric of a society, affecting the essence of the community and its members, leading some to feel a pervasive sense of hopelessness (e.g., racism, prejudice, discrimination, poverty, and health disparities that persist in many ethnic minority communities). Historical and cultural forms of trauma are multigenerational/intergenerational involving a collective and cumulative emotional wounding that persists unresolved and over time becomes internalized and passed from one generation to the next. Examples include slavery, racism, removal from one's homeland, massacres, genocides, or ethnocides, cultural, racial, and immigrant oppression, and forced placement.

PREVALENCE OF CHILDHOOD TRAUMA

Almost half the nation's children have experienced at least one or more types of serious childhood trauma (National Survey of Children's Health, www.childhealthdata.org/learn/NSCH) This translates into an estimated 34,825,978 children nationwide.

In 2016, an estimated 1,750 children died from abuse and neglect in the United States.

Nearly 700,000 children are abused in the US annually.

CPS protects more than 3 million children.

The youngest children are most vulnerable to maltreatment. Children in the first year of their life have the highest rate of victimization of 24.8 per 1,000 children in the national population of the same age.

Neglect is the most common form of maltreatment. Of the children who experienced maltreatment or abuse, three-quarters (74.8%) suffer neglect; 18.2% suffer physical abuse; and 8.5% suffer sexual abuse. (And tragically, some children are polyvictimized—they have suffered more than one form of maltreatment.)

About four out of five abusers are the victims' parents. A parent of the child victim was the perpetrator in 77.5% of substantiated cases of child maltreatment.

Source: US Administration for Children and Families, Child Maltreatment 2016. www.acf.hhs.gov/cb/resource/child-maltreatment-2016

How are Trauma Memories Stored in the Brain?

Memory is the way the brain anticipates and prepares for the future based on what has happened in the past. Memories shape our current perceptions by creating a filter through which we automatically anticipate what will happen next. There are two types of memory, implicit and explicit.

Implicit Memories (Unconscious Memories). Implicit memories are stored as images or sensations in the brain and they are unconscious (not in our awareness). For example, if a caregiver was nurturing and every time the baby cried, she hummed a lullaby and rocked the baby, then the baby would store that memory as a sound, sensation, or feeling (mother's voice tone, warm sensation in the body, feeling safe). Babies can perceive their environment and retain unconscious memories (e.g., recognizing caregiver's voice). In fact, memories during the first 18 months of life before a child has language are all implicit memories. Trauma is stored as implicit memories for children and adults.

Explicit Memories (Conscious Memories). Explicit memories begin to emerge by the second year of life. These memories are stored in the brain with words and when retrieved the child can share the memory in a logical, sequential order with a coherent story that has a beginning, middle, and end.

Explicit memories may also be called conscious memories and are tied to language development.

Trauma and Implicit and Explicit Memory. Explicit, or conscious, memories can be created for children around age two, when toddlers are able to use language to encode their experiences into a memory. Children with early trauma often retain implicit memories of abuse without an awareness of the abuse. Essentially, they carry memories of being distressed and dysregulated. Physical or emotional sensations (sights, sounds, textures, smells) can trigger these memories, causing flashbacks, nightmares, or other distressing reactions (Applegate & Shapiro, 2005).

Survival Stress Response in Young Children: Fight, Flight, Freeze

When children's fear activates their stress response system, their immature brains activate a **fight, flight, or freeze** survival response based on the type and intensity of the threat (Balberni, 2001; Perry et al., 1995; Schore, 2003a; Stein & Kendall, 2004). Infants and toddlers most often react to traumatic stress using a combination of crying or vocalizing to elicit the caregiver's protection. When these adaptive behaviors are not responded to, young children may throw a tantrum or act out (a fight response). If at this point the caregiver still does not respond, they may move from initially becoming compliant and immobile (freezing), followed by surrender and **dissociation**, a defense in which the children escape internally from the stress, when there is no external support and relief from a caregiver, through altering their bodies through such means as decreasing their heart rate (Porges, 2011).

Activating the stress response system is an automatic survival response from the child's brain. This triggering response is involuntary—it happens automatically and is not under the child's control. It is driven the by lower brainstem for the sole purpose of self-preservation and survival (Porges, 2011). In a threatening condition, children are unable to process information because their brainstem prevents the use of the pre-frontal cortex necessary for cognitive functioning. This means that children who are in a fight, flight, or freeze survival state, are less able to engage in problem-solving, rational thought, focused attention, self-regulation of their emotions or behavior or to verbalize their experience because the neural networks to their cortex are literally shut off in order to focus on survival. Only after the child no longer perceives they are in danger, has calmed their central nervous system, and returned to an optimal state of arousal, can they begin to engage their cortex again.

When children's stress response system is repeatedly triggered, their neural networks can become **sensitized** becoming more easily activated and result in long-term changes that weaken young children's ability to return to a calm state and cope. When this happens, minor stressors can easily activate children's fear response system and lead to severe traumatic reactions to environmental stimuli, for example, a child hears a dog bark and starts to scream at the top of her lungs and hyperventilate (Perry et al, 1995).

Behaviors Teachers May See When Young Children's Fight, Flight, Freeze Survival Response Has Been Activated

	Fight	Flight	Freeze
Infants	Startles Irritability Arching away from caregiver Does not want to be touched or held Separation distress Arousal	Resists food and sleep	Social withdrawal, tunes out More acute and increased episodes of clinging Decrease in the capacity for pleasure Disruptions in vocalization Limited interest in play Avoidance
Toddlers	Cries Screams Kicking Banging head	Runs from caregiver Hides under table or out of sight of caregiver Pulls jacket over head Sits in corner of room and just watches	Restricted play Restricted social interactions No response to name Becomes absorbs with something and seems unaware of people Falls asleep when things are noisy, chaotic, and stimulating
Preschool	Cursing Biting Kicking Screams and yells Talks back Destructive to property Throws objects Tantrums Hits or hurts others	Runs away from teachers Runs out of the room or building Hides from others Covers face, eyes, or ears Avoiding an activity Redirects attention elsewhere Refuses to listen to adult directions	Withdraws Shuts down Daydreams, appears sleepy Blank look on face Child engages in repetitive movements or perseverating on something like picking at skin over and over, head banging, rocking Reverting behaviors such as sucking thumb Falls asleep when not nap time Not able to vocalize Unresponsive to comments, requests, questions, or name being called
Early Elementary	Yelling or screaming Cursing Making threats Arguing Destroys property Hurts others physically Anger outbursts Irritable Difficulty staying calm Reactive emotionally Aggressive	Running away Refuses to participate Late for classes Wears glasses, hoodie, or hats to cover face	Isolated Withdrawn Daydreaming Restricted movement Apathy Difficulty focusing Memory problems Self-injurious behaviors Sleepiness

One of the most common questions asked in the field of early education from teachers new to learning about trauma is ... *How will I know the difference between a developmentally appropriate challenging behavior and a trauma trigger or trauma-related challenging behavior?* The answer is complex but following are some thoughts to inform teachers' thinking about this important question:

- **Challenging behavior such as biting, hitting, or tantrums does not mean a child has experienced trauma.** A challenging behavior may indicate that the child is displaying developmentally appropriate and responsive behaviors. A child is communicating a need with their challenging behavior. Since their brain is in the early stages of development, children have difficulty making sense of their emotions and communicating how they feel or what they need, and have not yet mastered the ability to self-regulate or problem solve. Thus, challenging behaviors are expected from all children as they learn to navigate the complex social and emotional skills needed in the world around them.

- **Promoting the development of social and emotional skills is good for all children.** Teaching emotional literacy, self-regulation, friendship skills, and problem-solving are social skills that every child needs to learn. Teachers do not need to know if there is a trauma history or if the child is typically developing to implement these strategies.

- **Observing a child over time that has persistent challenging behaviors is important to gather data about patterns of behavior to determine appropriate interventions.** Conducting an observation and tracking data at different times of the day over a period of weeks helps gather important information. Information that can be tracked over time may be what happens BEFORE the challenging behavior, what happens DURING the challenging behavior, and then what occurs AFTER the behavior of concern. Finding recurring patterns in these three areas can help teachers determine what type of interventions may be indicated as appropriate for an individual child. Other data to gather are where the challenges usually occur, when the behavior does *not* occur, and the strategies that have/have not worked historically to support the child. Teachers can also document whether there is a particular setting the challenge occurs in more often (e.g., during a transition, outdoor play, free play, block area, with other children)? Observing with intention can help teachers formulate a sensitive response for intervention and support.

- **Using trauma-sensitive strategies are critical and recommended for children impacted by trauma AND are also considered supportive to all children.** Using trauma-sensitive strategies will not cause any harm if a child does not have a history of trauma. However, if typical strategies are not working for a child then it might be assumed that a trauma-sensitive strategy and intervention may be important to try.
- **A developmentally appropriate challenging behavior is a response to a situation that happens in the present moment.** For example, a child's toy was taken away from a peer, a teacher told a child "no" to something she wanted, a child has to transition from something they love to something they did not want to do such as washing their hands. It is typical for a child to have challenges around these types of events every day. It is typical as the child begins to learn the life skills to manage these experiences with a healthy social and emotional response. However, a trauma trigger is about a nonthreatening event that occurs in the present that triggers a past trauma memory. For example, a young girl takes the last tortilla at lunch, which triggers her classmate to remember a past trauma of food scarcity and severe deprivation and neglect in his home. When this past trauma memory is triggered, he responds with an intense emotional reaction of FIGHT, FLIGHT, or FREEZE. Essentially, his sensory system communicated to him that he was in danger and activated the release of stress chemicals and for his body to go into survival mode. Challenging behaviors related to trauma are triggers usually to nonthreatening events that are perceived by the child as a threatening trigger, which brings them back to a memory they begin to relive from their past. The behaviors they express when triggered are adaptive behaviors that represent the child's best attempts to keep themselves safe in the moment. These are moments of terror for the child where it is critical that the adults they trust understand trauma-sensitive strategies to support the child in that moment to feel safe and protected.

Trauma-sensitive strategies will promote healing over time, create a sense of trust, build relationships, and create safe and predictable environments.

WHAT DOES "FIGHT, FLIGHT, AND FREEZE" LOOK LIKE FOR YOUNG CHILDREN?

Two-year-old Mateo and his family are experiencing homelessness. Over the last few months, Mateo has been moving from one relative's house to another. Because of the constant disruptions in his life and his mother's need to quickly pack their clothes and move at night to whatever house they can find to give them a place to sleep, Mateo no longer has any toys that he can play with when he leaves his child care center. He worries that just like he lost his home, he will lose other things that he cares about including the toys he plays with when he is at the center. One morning he arrived at the center, started playing with Legos™ and spent a long time trying to build a tower. Another child in the toddler class, John, walked up to Mateo and started taking some of the Legos™. Mateo immediately responded by hitting, kicking, and pulling John's hair until he got the Legos™ back (Fight response).

Suriya, a visitor who has permission to be in the kindergarten classroom at a public elementary school, but who the children have never seen before, starts observing the children as part of an assignment she is completing in her teaching training program at the local university. Suriya has hair just like Ella's mother (a child in the center) who used to abuse Ella before she was removed by Child Protective Services and placed in care with her aunt and uncle. Ella starts to cry the moment Suriya enters the classroom and she runs and hides under a table and starts to shake all over her body (Flight response).

Benji, a four-year-old child in Head Start classroom, was home when a water heater in his apartment building exploded, starting a fire and leading to the evacuation of his building and two of the residents being transported by ambulance to the local emergency room. Ever since this traumatic event, Benji has been very sensitive and frightened when he hears loud noises. One morning, the school fire alarm is accidentally triggered and all the children are told by their teacher to line up and walk outside to wait on the playground until the firefighters come and determine that the site is safe and they can return to their classroom. All the children walk outside as they are asked to do except Benji who is later found by the program director who sees him standing in the corner of the room, holding his ears, completely frozen and unable to move. He is unresponsive to the director's touch, verbal direction, or guidance. Benji is staring into space completely unresponsive to all the stimulation and sounds around him (Freeze response).

The Impact of Trauma on the Right Hemisphere of the Brain

If children grow up with repeated exposure to traumatic stress and fear, there is often a disruption of the development of the right brain, which governs coping and emotional regulation (Schore, 2005, 2010). When the right brain is not able to develop properly, children often perceive the people and stimuli in the environments around them to be dangerous. If this becomes a pattern during young children's earliest years, there is a risk that their stress response systems will remain activated in a perpetually fearful state (Siegel, 2003, 2012).

Living in fear distorts young children's sensory perceptions and it leads to over development of the parts of the right brain associated with decoding facial expressions and reading threatening social cues (Perez, 2009) and underdevelopment of the parts of the right brain governing self-control. When this happens, young children are often on high alert, scanning nonverbal behavior for signs of danger (Perry, 2002; Perry et al., 1995), constantly focusing on keeping themselves emotionally and physically safe. When this happens, there is less activation of their neo-cortex or thinking brain, which decreases their ability to learn and manage the complex social interactions they need to navigate in a busy early childhood environment.

BECAUSE THE AMYGDALA IS WELL DEVELOPED AT BIRTH, FEAR IS THE STRONGEST EARLY EMOTION

The amygdala, the emotional center of the brain, stores memories of frightening experiences (Cozolino, 2006, 2012). Because the amygdala is well developed at birth, fear is the strongest early emotion (Cozolino, 2006). This has important consequences for young children. One, it can lead them to a tendency to misperceive people, events, experiences, and/or stimuli in their environments as dangerous when they are not. And two, the combination of young children's immature perceptions and the fully developed amygdala means that they often interpret stimuli that even remotely resemble those associated with the trauma as dangerous (e.g., anything "red" frightens a child because the child remembers a man wearing a red shirt yelling and threatening his mom with a gun).

When children continue to perceive that everyday events in their life are frightening, this becomes their worldview (Siegel, 2003). When this happens, children impacted by trauma become focused on scanning the environment and reading nonverbal cues (e.g., facial expressions, body language, tone of voice) and they become hypervigilant to signs of negativity or criticism (Perry, 2002; Perry et al., 1995). This means, they frequently misinterpret body language and facial cues, incorrectly assuming that adults and peers are intentionally trying to criticize or harm them when this is not the case.

Trauma can interfere with every aspect of a young child's development including their ability to form relationships with others and their ability to learn. Although not a comprehensive description of the consequences of trauma, the following are some of the many ways trauma impacts young children's learning and development.

When Traumatic Stress Leads to a Misreading of the World as Dangerous and Critical

Young children whose neurochemistry has been altered by early trauma may continually perceive the world to be a dangerous and continually threatening place. Their amygdala continually activates, leaving them in a state of persistent hypervigilance. Similarly, they often perceive that others are judging or trying to harm them. Because of the under-development of their relational (limbic) and self-control (neo-cortex) systems, they judge situations as personally threatening when they are not. For example, a young little girl with a history of trauma might observe a classmate laughing across the playground and immediately react by perceiving that he is laughing *at* her. If a child has a "fight" stress response, this could lead her to go over and hit, kick, or yell at the little boy, a "flight" response could be the girl running away in tears to hide, and a "freeze" response would look like she is suddenly daydreaming as the children swirl in activity around her on the playground.

As children mature and their verbal abilities increase, teachers can provide support by helping them to learn to read social cues more accurately. Teachers can help children ask questions to create a "pause" in their reactivity. For example, a child can be encouraged to ask her classmate, "why are you laughing?" As children provide explanations ("I was laughing at Benjamin who is making funny faces at me"), a child who misperceives the intentions of her peers can be supported to begin to build trust and feel safe at school.

IMPACT ON COGNITIVE/LINGUISTIC DEVELOPMENT

- *Difficulty with symbolic or representational thinking*. Trauma impacts children's ability to use words or symbols to represent concepts. For example, to use a block in imaginary play to represent a pretend phone, or when a child's "lovey" brought from home represents their strong attachment to their primary caregiver/family. Being able to use representational thinking is a foundation for literacy and mathematical thinking.
- *Learning to see from another perspective*. As the development of object permanence—the understanding that something (person, object) exists even when it is no longer in view—is often interrupted for young children with histories of trauma, these children may struggle to learn that other people exist with their own thoughts and intentions

that are separate from their own. This leads to difficulty in learning how to see a situation from different points of view, which is the foundation for the development of empathy.

- *Language development*. Children learn language through their social interactions with caregivers. When babies and young children have caregivers who do not respond to their early vocalizations (coos, cries, babbling), they do not have adults modeling language use for them. These children often have delays in their language development. When children have responsive caregivers who use language throughout the day to label experiences and feelings, children learn that words are used to represent things in their world. For children who do not have consistent caregivers or experience maltreatment, they may have difficulty understanding how to connect their internal thoughts and feelings to words because of the nonverbal nature of their traumatic memories and the poor language modeling they experience in their home environments. When children are in a continual state of heightened arousal, it is difficult for them to access their ability to use language and verbalize their feelings and needs. As a result, many children with histories of trauma have language delays, limited vocabulary, challenges communicating effectively with their peers (they may have delays in the development of receptive or expressive language skills), and difficulty in internalizing language in the form of self-talk (talking to oneself that begins out loud for young children and eventually shifts to be an internal silent dialogue), which is the foundation of future self-regulation. They may also struggle to process or understand complex directions or complex language in conversations and may need adults and peers to slow down when speaking to them and to use short and simple sentences.
- *Attention and memory*. Often focused on scanning their environment for signs of danger, children with histories of trauma often pay attention more to nonverbal behavior (facial expressions and tone of voice) than verbal communication. This leads them to miss a lot of the information shared with them verbally. They can also have difficulty focusing, which makes it challenging for them to learn new skills, remember new information, and store information into memory for future recall.
- *Executive function skills*. Children who are impacted by trauma often have deficits in the development of working memory, attention, and inhibitory control skills or the ability to pause and control their behavior.

IMPACT ON PHYSICAL DEVELOPMENT

- *Sensory-motor development*. Children with histories of trauma often have both fine and gross motor developmental delays and sensory integration challenges (they are either sensory defensive where they are overly sensitive to sounds, textures in food, clothing tags, etc. or they are sensory seeking and seek stimuli e.g., crashing into people and objects, jumping from high places, licking walls, or drawing all over themselves). They often complain of somatic symptoms including headaches and stomachaches and may report what seems like an exaggerated amount of pain for minor cuts or falls or the opposite, not registering any pain when they are seriously injured or really sick. Most children with experiences of trauma struggle to go to sleep because of their hypervigilance, always scanning the environment for dangers, but also because the quiet brings a flood of memories and reminders of their traumatic experiences into their minds. They often ask a long list of questions, request repeated readings of storybooks, get up to use the bathroom, or use any other distraction to stop themselves from going to sleep. Because they live in a constant state of stress, they often sleep very deeply when they do fall asleep and it can be very challenging to wake them up with the other children during a typical nap time.

IMPACT ON SOCIOEMOTIONAL DEVELOPMENT

- *Attachment relationships*. Children who have disrupted or unhealthy early attachments learn that they cannot trust adults to keep them safe and take care of their needs. As a result, they feel like they need to keep themselves safe by being distant and not developing close relationships with adults and with peers.
- *Empathy*. The ability to have empathy develops from young children's early attachment relationships. When children are maltreated by their caregivers, they learn to expect that they will be rejected by others, which leads to neural connections that associate social connections with physical pain. They often have limited self-awareness of their own pain, little ability to self-soothe, and show little or no concern with the pain and distress of others. For example, they may step right over a peer who has fallen down and is injured as they do not have an internal feeling of wanting to soothe others when they are in pain.
- *Emotion regulation*. Two essential features of emotion regulation are identifying emotions and accessing effective coping skills (Kopp, 1982). Emotions such as pleasure or mild anxiety help to support persistence and continual engagement, while emotions such as anger, fear, extreme frustration, or high anxiety, which are often impacted by trauma, interrupt or disturb the child's ability to engage in a task.
- *Interpersonal relationships*. Children with trauma histories often develop internal mental models of the world as threatening and dangerous. They frequently misinterpret body language and facial cues, incorrectly perceiving negative intent by assuming an adult or peer is threatening or trying to criticize or harm them when this is not the case.

Spontaneous speech and verbalizing their thoughts and feelings can be challenging, which makes it difficult to form friendships and communicate with other children. They also struggle with self-awareness and learning to understand the consequences of their behavior.

IMPACT ON CHILDREN'S PLAY

- Trauma can significantly influence how children play. Many children are quite restricted in their range of play activities. Children who experienced trauma may be scared to explore, discover, and take risks. They do not feel safe and they are too frightened to take their attention away from the "here-and-now" because their brains tell them that their very survival depends upon maintaining a hypervigilant state and constantly scanning their environment for danger (e.g., tracking the adult to prevent their own abandonment, competing with other children for toys and materials). They are worried that if something happens to them, they may not have an adult who will protect them. This makes it very difficult for them to play, which is young children's primary format for learning and constructing knowledge.
- Infants may show very little engagement with toys and little interest in interacting with others in a playful manner. Toddlers' play often has a chaotic and purposeless quality. Preschoolers struggle to engage in imaginary play. They may be too scared to engage in imaginary play as children often embed their fears and worries in play but representing their own life experiences in imaginary play may prove to be too overwhelming and scary for them. If early relationships were disrupted, children may not have been able to use transitional objects and toys as symbols for significant people and experiences. They may need to initially stay involved exclusively with structured materials (puzzles, pegboards, water table, sand table) because these toys have a single purpose and do not require peer contact or communication. Other children have developed symbolic capacities, but they have no joy, adventure, story, or imaginative discovery in their play. Their imaginary play often repeats the trauma over and over with negative emotion and aggression as key elements in play that feels "stuck." In this case, they need teachers who can help them to think of alternative endings to their traumatic play narratives (e.g., instead of the girl dying in the story, she becomes the heroine who survives the scary fire that burned down her house) or they may need support to shift into engaging in different types of play in the classroom (moving from the dramatic play area into sand or water play).

Trauma Impacts Every Aspect of Young Children's Development and Ability to Learn (Craig, 2016; Osofsky, Stepka & King, 2017; Sorrels, 2015; Statman-Weil, 2018)

Trauma and Touch

Through touch, babies learn that they are safe, supported, cared for, and they experience a sense of belonging with others. Babies who live with trauma and toxic stress deeply need touch that is safe and nurturing. However, they may resist and avoid touch because of their experiences where touch from others, especially their caregivers, was scary, harmful, inconsistent, or in the case of neglect, not provided to them.

Children who resist and avoid touch will likely avoid eye contact. They may also arch their backs or kick and scream when picked up, grow stiff, and/or cry when someone tries to touch them. It is important that adults do not get angry and take a baby's rejection of their touch personally. It is also important that teachers not assume children do not need touch just because they are resisting or avoiding it.

Adults can offer gentle touches through play and in the context of daily routines, but they should always be responsive to a child. When a caring and supportive teacher offers gentle touches to a child, this will help them feel more comfortable with touch and over time as they build trust with the teacher, they will be less triggered by touch and learn that it can be comforting and communicate a sense of love and care.

Some children show the opposite pattern with touch as they are affectionate and immediately touch and want to be near any and all adults and peers. Sometimes this is a sign of sexual and physical abuse where children's physical boundaries were violated that they then transfer into their interactions with others. These children need adults who can model appropriate touch and then support them to learn the same.

The wide range of cognitive, social-emotional, and physical challenges young children with histories of trauma experience are the reason popular social-emotional curricula and/or classroom management approaches are often ineffective for these children. Many of the typical behavior management strategies used by early childhood teachers require children to use skills they either have not developed—due to developmental delays resulting from their exposure to trauma—or in other cases, they have developed the skills but cannot access them when their stress response systems have been activated, which for some children is continuous. For example, children may not have the expressive language, the memory skills, or the cognitive flexibility to engage in conflict resolution with a peer or to 'use their words', to describe how they are feeling and what they need when they have been triggered.

If a child is experiencing a trauma trigger in the moment, many of the high level and complex social and emotional strategies we teach will be ineffective. For example, let's look at Ahmed, a five-year-old child in Kindergarten:

A stranger walks into Ahmed's classroom. This stranger looks like a man that hurt Ahmed and his father. Ahmed becomes dysregulated (trauma trigger). He begins to punch and yell at the child next to him. The teacher is alarmed by his behavior being so hurtful to his friend and has no idea Ahmed is being triggered by the stranger in the classroom.

The teacher walks over and says to Ahmed, "we don't hurt our friends, can you use your words and tell me what happened." This strategy of "use your words" requires executive functioning skills. It requires regulation and a state of calm within Ahmed in order to access his thinking brain. With this trauma trigger, Ahmed is in his emotional (limbic) and brainstem (fight, flight, or freeze) brain. When Ahmed is in this level of emotional triggering, accessing his "thinking" and "solution mapping" is nearly impossible. What Ahmed needs are messages of safety, security, and calm regulation from an adult caregiver. A strategy that can be used is to assure him that the stranger who entered the classroom is not of danger and that he is safe and the teacher will make sure he is going to be okay. The teacher can stay calm and regulated which will help to calm Ahmed.

The use of typical social-emotional teaching skills in the middle of a trauma trigger are not effective strategies. Learning to use trauma-sensitive strategies that help children calm their trauma-impacted stress responses systems can help teachers support children who do not respond to typical "best practice" strategies.

This does not mean we cannot teach social and emotional skills to children impacted by trauma. It means we cannot teach children these skills when they are in a state of dysregulation. Often this is how children with trauma histories feel all day and night. If they are living in their brainstem (survival and reptile brain) scanning for danger all day, then it is nearly impossible for them to have the focal attention required to listen and learn. Safety, stable environments, and consistent caring relationships are the basic needs that are required for children experiencing trauma in the classroom. As children begin to feel safe and to develop a sense of calm, teaching social and emotional skills can become a part of a trauma-sensitive plan for the child.

Trauma and Young Children with Disabilities* and Special Needs

Children with intellectual and developmental disabilities (IDD)—**genetic** (cystic fibrosis, sickle cell, Tay-Sachs disease), **neuromotor** (cerebral palsy, spina bifida), **mental health** (depression, anxiety), **neurological** (autism, epilepsy), **intellectual** (Down's syndrome, fetal alcohol, fragile X), and **sensory** (vision and hearing, sensory-integration)—are at greater risk for trauma and adverse experiences. Children with IDDs are:

- Two times more likely to experience emotional neglect;
- Two times more likely to experience physical or sexual abuse;
- Twice as likely to be bullied;
- Three times for more likely to be in families where domestic violence is present (National Traumatic Stress Network, NTSN, 2016).

Because young children with IDDs are at high risk of trauma, teachers need to be continually asking whether the behaviors they are observing are the result of trauma versus only their disability. The NTSN (2016) provides an example of some of the complexities of working with children who have disabilities and histories of trauma:

> *P*atty Shure, Director of Child and Family Services at Las Cumbres Community Services in Española, New Mexico, recently recalled her work three years ago with a young toddler receiving care at the Conjunto Therapeutic Preschool at Las Cumbres. The treatment team believed that the child's developmental and speech delays were due to severe facial injuries she sustained in a car accident before she was a year old. Shure, a social worker who has worked for more than 22 years with children with disabilities and trauma, suspected that the girl's delays might also be related to unresolved traumatic grief over the loss of her mother, who had died in the accident. The family and the teaching staff were not convinced that her behaviors were a trauma reaction – until the grandmother, out driving with the child, had a minor fender bender. When she jumped out of the car to inspect the damage, her granddaughter, though unhurt, started screaming and was "inconsolable" for more than an hour. "That [event] was the clue for the family and the treatment team that, for her, the trauma was still very present," Shure said. "It wasn't solely her injuries that caused her inability to communicate and articulate words."
>
> *(p. 1)*

Until recently, there were no tools to support clinicians and/or teachers to distinguish between symptoms of trauma from behaviors related to IDDs. However, in 2016 a new tool, *The Road to Recovery: Supporting Children with IDD Who Have Experienced Trauma* (www.nctsn.org/print/1055), was designed with this purpose in mind. This tool supports adults working with children with IDD to take both trauma and IDD into consideration when considering the most helpful interventions to support the child and family.

Disabilities should be understood to be a combination of biological, psychological, and social factors, and not limited to biological terms.

Many children are diagnosed with disabilities—for example, autism, attention-deficit hyperactivity disorder, sensory integration disorder, speech and language delays, emotional disturbance or oppositional defiance disorder, intellectual disabilities, depression, and anxiety—when they are really suffering from trauma and the impact of traumatic stress on their brains and developing bodies.

What is a Trauma Lens in Early Childhood Teaching?

Many adults believe that a child cannot experience trauma because they are too young to perceive what is going on around them. The opposite is true. A young child is the most vulnerable to trauma and at risk of experiencing the adverse side effects trauma can cause. When faced with a single acute trauma, ongoing chronic or multiple traumatic events, the child is at higher risk to be impacted socially, physically, and emotionally in their current environments and in later years. A child's sensory system at a young age is more vulnerable to the impacts of trauma. As a result, the younger the child, the more likely internal feelings develop of utter helplessness and powerlessness. The intense stress, emotional charge, and chemical release during each traumatic event are stored in the children's central nervous system through sensations that were never released during the past traumatic incidents. Young children have very few options when experiencing a trauma to mitigate a traumatic event and release the stress from their body. Their only real choice is to shut down (Freeze), with almost no ability to run (Flight). When a traumatic event happens, there is a large release of stress hormones throughout the body and brain. Unlike an adult who can seek out external resources to talk, process, heal, and release the stress, a child is simply unable to do so. They often play out or act out their behavior in an attempt to process what has occurred in the past. As a teacher, what you may observe is challenging behavior that makes no sense. You might observe that a child may hurt others, cause parent complaints, disrupt learning, push your emotional buttons, and trigger in teachers a feeling of incompetence. This behavior often leads to poor outcomes for these most vulnerable children.

When teachers use a trauma lens in their practice, they strive to disrupt this pattern of negative outcomes for children who have experienced trauma in their young lives. A trauma lens begins with a commitment from teachers and caregivers to acknowledge the existence of trauma and traumatic stress in many children's lives and a desire to strengthen their understanding of trauma's impact on children's development and ability to learn. Developing a trauma lens means that teachers strive to understand the children they are working with including the stories they are communicating through their behavior and the underlying reasons why they are behaving the way they do. Using a trauma lens to inform work with young children, teachers have the following commitments in their teaching practice:

- They work hard to create a relationship and connection, so the child is able to re-learn that adults can be safe, attuned, and supportive.
- They seek to understand the meaning of a specific behavior in a specific moment for an individual child.
- They look for patterns of behavior for an individual child, including individual triggers that activate children's stress response system.
- They understand that what they perceive as "challenging behavior" is the child attempting to regain control as they carry with them previous experiences that left them feeling helpless and/or powerless. The child is sharing a story of what has happened to them and how they feel about it. They want the adults to listen to this story and respond with empathy and a desire to help them feel safe.
- They strive to create an environment that communicates to the child a feeling of safety and predictability.
- They engage in self-care so they may have enough restored energy and internal resources to support these most vulnerable children and re-build their sense of safety, to support their healing, and to create experiences that allow them to build resilience.

The Importance of Attunement

The most important intervention for trauma-informed programs is for children to be able to interact with a caring, responsive, and self-regulated adult who **attunes** to them. Attunement is seen when an adult focuses so intently in communication with a child that the child comes to believe that what she thinks and feels matters, she "feels felt" by the adult (Levine & Kline, 2007). The adult's interest in the child validates the child's presence and helps the child to feel a sense of belonging, safety, and protection. If an adult caregiver is curious about the child's thoughts, then the child in turn will come to value their thoughts and feelings as well. The experience of attunement begins in infancy through what is described as a **serve and return relationship**.

Serve and Return

The experience of attunement begins in infancy through what is described as a **serve and return relationship** between a young child and their caregiver (https://developingchild.harvard.edu/science/key-concepts/serve-and-return/). Young infants communicate how they feel and what they need, the "serve" (e.g., crying, smiling, turning their heads, verbalizing), and the adult responds to the baby in a culturally responsive manner through words and gestures (eye contact, tone of voice, pointing, smiling, picking them up, etc.), which is the "return." Through many repetitions of this serve and return cycle on a daily basis, babies learn that when they need something or someone, when they have big sensations and feelings in their bodies, and when they like or dislike certain things in their environment, their caregivers are aware and care about what they are communicating to them. When the serve and return patterns are healthy and optimally support children's neural development, the baby learns that she is loved, cared for, and will be protected by her caregiver. This communicates to the baby that she is an important member of the family/community and that her needs matter. These are the foundations for developing a positive sense of oneself and for building trusting and healthy relationships with others.

When children are living in chaotic or harmful environments with adults who do not respond to their cues, creating a sense of fear, uncertainty, and stress for children, the serve and return pattern is not developed between the young child and their caregiver. When a child in this type of environment cries, the adult may respond with an angry or yelling tone of voice and a touch that is rough and scary or they may not respond at all in the case of neglectful care or in the worst scenario of all for children's developing brains, they may be inconsistent, sometimes responding in a calm and supportive manner and other times in a frightening, harmful, or neglectful way. A child in this situation learns that their needs will not be met by their caregivers and that what they think, believe, and want does not matter. This not only negatively impacts their emerging sense of themselves but it also leaves a vulnerable child feeling that they have no control over their environment, that they cannot trust others to take care of them, and that the world they are living in is an unsafe, unpredictable, and threatening place. This sense of hopelessness can lead to impairment in children's brain development and a diminished ability to form healthy relationships with others.

Attuned interactions are the foundation for building self-esteem and a strong sense of self for the child. Tuning in to the child's perspective begins by taking the time to mindfully focus on the child and show genuine interest in understanding what their emotional state and/or behavior is communicating. Attunement is characterized by careful observation of children and responding to children's complex, puzzling, or challenging behavior by asking, what story is this child communicating to me about what how he feels and what he needs to feel safe? Attunement is supported when adults focus in on a child's emotional state, verbalizations, and/or nonverbal expressions and behavior without judgment or reactivity but instead respond with interest, curiosity, empathy, and a desire to provide support.

Attuned communication between adults and children is characterized by positive emotional exchanges between children and adults. With an attuned relationship, trust forms and feelings of safety are increased for the child, which can positively influence their ability to engage in the learning process. Additionally, confidence develops for a teacher who learns that she can regulate a distressed child.

The Importance of Co-Regulation in Supporting Children Experiencing Traumatic Stress

---

WHAT IS AFFECT ATTUNEMENT? WHAT DOES IT MEAN TO ENGAGE IN EMOTIONALLY ATTUNED INTERACTIONS WITH A YOUNG CHILD?

Affect attunement (Stern, 1985) is an interactive process that involves a responsive and aware teacher monitoring and regulating her own internal emotional state and behavior in order to communicate messages of calm, care, and safety to a young distressed child. By maintaining her own self-regulation, the caregiver supports the child to calm their nervous system (Als, 1982; Kopp, 1982; Schore, 2005; Schuder & Lyons-Ruth, 2004; VandenBerg, 2007).

When a teacher "attunes" to a child in this way and responds to a child's feelings of distress with caring, calm, and supportive messages, they help the child develop self-regulation skills and a healthy stress response system (Schore, 2003b, 2005; Schuder & Lyons-Ruth, 2004). In contrast, a caregiver who responds insensitively to children's distress will increase their stress, which can further disorganize their nervous systems and increase their emotional and behavioral dysregulation (Schuder & Lyons-Ruth, 2004). Caregivers who do not respond to children's distress with calm and regulated behavior will actually intensify children's traumatic stress and leave young children with the impression that adults will not be available to support them in their times of need.

It is vital for young children who are experiencing traumatic stress reactions to have caregivers who can support them to re-regulate their distressed bodies and dysregulated behavior. They are not able to do this on their own and need adults to support them through a process called **co-regulation**.

What Is Co-Regulation and How Does It Help a Very Young Child When They Are Experiencing Traumatic Stress?

Co-regulation refers to the assistance provided by a caregiver to soothe a child's emotional distress. As children learn to independently regulate their own emotions, they rely less on their caregivers for regulatory support. However, in the case of children who are easily dysregulated due to traumatic stress, it is important for teachers to demonstrate a willingness to assist them when their stress response systems are triggered. By staying with the child and communicating messages of calm, empathy, care, and safety, teachers support children to calm their nervous systems. In essence, the adults use their state of regulation to interactively guide a distressed child back to regulation. It is emotionally attuned interpersonal interactions with a reliable teacher that co-regulates children's arousal levels and generates a feeling of safety (Porges, 2011).

The quality of co-regulation is strongly influenced by the quality of the relationship between the child and the adult. When teachers and children are attuned with one another—i.e., when they are responsive to one another's emotional states and they interact back and forth in communications together—a caring adult can positively change a child's stress reaction and help them to calm their reactive brainstem and stop the release of stress chemicals in their body. Co-regulation becomes more challenging when children persistently experience fear and traumatic stress (Porges, 2011). Even capable caregivers may struggle to calm children when their stress response systems are on overdrive. This is because stress is contagious due to **mirror neurons** that are at work in our brains at a subconscious level, leaving us unaware of their impact (Cozolino, 2006). This explains why teachers who are effectively caring for typically developing children may be less regulated and supportive when caring for children whose stress response systems are continually triggered.

I learned the most curious thing as an infant and toddler teacher. I found out that if even in the slightest that I was feeling stressed or anxious, it impacted my ability to comfort an infant in my classroom. Some infants were more sensitive to my internal state of emotions than others. It is as if they picked up on my energy and could not be regulated until I had a state of calm. I have come to learn infants almost borrow my internal state of calm to help calm their own. Then when I am anxious or stressed they are the first to mirror back to me the internal world of what I am feeling.

(Jeffrey J., Teacher Aide, Infant-Toddler Child Development Center)

WHAT ARE MIRROR NEURONS?

Human beings are relational, and therefore, we absorb the emotions or affects of those around us. Our capacity to instinctively and immediately understand what another is feeling or experiencing is due to our mirror neurons. In this way, the mirror neuron system is the neurological foundation that supports humans' ability to empathize, socialize, and communicate our emotions to others.

Mirror neurons are activated when an individual observes someone else taking an action (e.g., walking toward them, gesturing that they need help) or when they observe someone experiencing an emotion (e.g., fear, anger, happiness, surprise) as they help us perceive other people's intentions (Acharya & Shukla, 2012; Conkbayir, 2017). That is, one person's emotional state is "mirrored" by the neuronal system of another as the mirror system of one person alters their emotional and physical state to match the emotional and physical state of the person they are interacting with. An example of this is when we see someone crying and feel sad knowing that they are hurting, or we sense someone is stressed and this creates our own feeling of internal distress. This process of taking-in another's emotional state happens at a subconscious level, which means individuals are neither aware of this process nor in control of it.

Mirror neurons play an important role in young children's social and emotional development. We see this with infants whose communication with others is primarily through eye contact, vocalizations, and movements or nonverbal gestures. Through the **serve and return** patterns of communication, babies observe and imitate their caregivers and learn over time to "read" their caregiver's cues (facial expressions, tone of voice, responsiveness to baby's expression of needs) to interpret whether they are safe or in a situation of threat and danger. The process of social referencing—where a child interprets an adult's cues to assess whether a situation is safe or dangerous—requires a healthy attachment relationship where a young child learns to trust an adult caregiver because the adult is predictable, caring, and responsive to the child's cues. If, however, the adult is not predictable or communicates messages of threat and danger to the child in facial expressions, tone of voice or physical action, the child's mirror neuronal system will not function optimally. When the adult-child attachment relationship is not healthy, the child will likely have difficulty learning to understand the intentions of others and will not have the healthy serve and return exchanges to help them learn how to express their own emotions (Conkbayir, 2017; Twardosz & Lutzker, 2010).

When very young children do not have caregivers who mirror safety, predictability, and care for them, they learn to shut down their feelings, push away memories of pain, and not to rely on relationships for protection, in essence, they learn not only to stop trusting and believing in others, they also learn not to believe in themselves (Levine & Kline, 2007). Adults can help children in this situation by mirroring messages of "repair" helping them to develop the sense of feeling felt where adults observe and attune to their emotional state and communicate messages of calm and safety.

What does this look like for children with histories of trauma?

The process by which stress is "contagious" begins with one neuronal system that mirrors another's neuronal system. In the case of a teacher working with a child in a traumatic stress response (e.g., a "fight" response where a child is kicking, hitting, and screaming) it is critical that the teacher remains calm. Children's mirror neurons will imitate internally what they see, hear, and feel, modelled by their caregivers (Levine & Kline, 2007). As a child's mirror neurons help them to subconsciously decipher an adult's intentions and emotions (through the adult's facial expressions and body language), adult caregivers must communicate to young children—especially when they are triggered and in distress—that they are cared for and loved and that the adult will work hard to help them feel safe and protected. Many children who have experienced trauma have not experienced attuned relationships with adults who will remain calm and relationally connected to them when they display stress behaviors, which is the number one experience they need to have repeatedly in order to heal. This is why it is so essential for adults to engage in their own self-care. Only by developing strategies to attend to the personal stress responses they experience when children express challenging behaviors can adults "mirror" for children emotional and physical states associated with love, care, empathy, understanding, support, and safety.

Co-regulation is a powerful tool in caregivers' toolbox that they can use to comfort and calm children who are triggered and dysregulated. Yet, to successfully co-regulate a distressed child, caregivers must actively work against the contagious nature of the dysregulated child's stress impacting their own well-being. Through the powerful influence of their own and the child's mirror neurons, caregivers are subconsciously influenced to "mirror" the child's stress and dysregulated emotions and behavior. Caregivers must remain keenly aware of their own sensory and emotional state. When in the presence of a distressed and dysregulated child, they can either follow

a child into dysregulation (mirroring the child's stress response system) **or lead the child back into regulation** (staying calm and influencing the child to mirror their own regulated state). Research suggests that having an attuned caregiver who can minimize the child's activation of neural pathways associated with fear and stress can literally change children's brains and lead these pathways to fade out/die due to their lack of use (Perry, 2002; Perry et al., 1995). This means that a child, whose experience of early trauma has impaired their brain development, can heal by developing new and healthier neural pathways when they are in the company of a consistent and supportive caregiver. Leading a distressed child back into regulation can be hard and very emotionally draining work. This is why self-care is so essential for teachers (a topic we explore in the final chapter).

ATTUNEMENT WITH YOUNG CHILDREN ON A DAILY BASIS

Three friends, Marcus, Rene, and Maria were playing together with shovels and buckets in the sandbox. Teacher Cynthia was monitoring from a distance but tuned in fully when they heard a scream from Marcus. When the teacher ran over to investigate further she found Marcus was hitting Rene and screaming "I hate you, you are stupid." The teacher recognized the pattern of triggers for Marcus. He grew up in a house with domestic violence. He witnessed violence against his mother. When he is faced with situations where he feels someone, particularly a girl, is being treated poorly, he becomes triggered. In this case, he perceived the other child not sharing the sand toys with Maria. Marcus was hyperventilating and the teacher could barely understand a word. His fists were clenched and she noticed his face looked scrunched up. The teacher just listened to him and stayed calm. She said to him, "you are safe here Marcus, no one is hurting Maria. We are here to help her and all the children stay safe."

She spent time with him and provided a soothing tone and calming space for him. After some time with the teacher, his speech slowed, he seemed more regulated. Once he appeared calm, the teacher said, "I can see in your body that you are calm now." She asked Marcus if he was ready to talk about what happened and Marcus agreed. She told him "I know you wanted to protect Maria but I can help you find other ways to help solve this conflict with your friends." "Are you ready to think together about other ways to solve this problem without hitting?" She gave Marcus a choice and he agreed to talk with the teacher and his friends. Cynthia helped Marcus, Rene, and Maria talk about what happened and to come up with alternative solutions to handle their problem. One solution they arrived at is Marcus or the other children can find a teacher and ask for help.

Cynthia used several strategies to support Marcus, one of which is called attunement. Can you describe how she used attunement? Here are some specific reflective questions to help you go deeper to explore how Cynthia used attunement strategies to regulate Marcus.

- Did the teacher try to learn the child's perspective? How?
- Was she aware of the physical signs that were visible with the child's body?
- Did she take sides as to who was right in the argument?
- Did she use punishment or threats to try to stop the behavior of Marcus?
- How did the teacher's attunement help regulate Marcus? Why?
- Did she help Marcus identify feelings and sensations in his body?
- Did she help him regulate his trauma trigger and intense emotional reaction?

All children who have experienced traumatic stress need caring and responsive caregivers who make them feel safe. The quality of the attachment relationship between the child and the adult who cares for them during and/or immediately after the traumatic experience and the adult's attunement to the child's traumatic stress response plays a central role in how children will cope with traumatic stress and whether they experience trauma symptoms. Secure attachments buffer children from traumatic stress and are critical for children to build their capacity for resilience and emotion regulation. In addition to the quality of care a child receives in response to trauma, other factors that influence a child's short- or long-term traumatic response include their age and developmental level (the younger the child, the more vulnerable they are), their physical characteristics and biological constitution (the biological makeup of the body), the intensity and degree to which the traumatic stress was prolonged and/or predictable (traumatic stress most likely to result in trauma symptoms if it is repeated, prolonged, and unpredictable), the degree to which the child had any control over the situation (the less control they have, the more traumatic the experience), the availability of social supports (extended family, friends, faith community, therapy etc.), and outlets for stress (art, play, sports, therapy).

Trauma-informed teaching for young children not only facilitates typical development but also changes the way children's brains respond to stress at the level of brain structure. Trauma-informed teaching consistent with neuroscientific research takes a long time and is effective only in an emotionally regulated and relational environment where adults provide children with physical and emotional safety and promote their emotional resiliency and adaptive coping skills.

Building Young Children's Capacity for Resilience and Healing

Resilience is the ability to adapt well to adversity, trauma, tragedy, threats, or even significant sources of stress.

(APA, 2011)

Any discussion of trauma should always be linked with a discussion of children's strengths, capacities, and resilience. The American Psychological Association (APA) defines resilience as "the ability to adapt well to adversity, trauma, tragedy, threats, or even significant sources of stress" (APA, 2011). Resilience is evident in young children when their development progresses positively despite being confronted with negative experiences including trauma. Research indicates that fostering young children's capacity for resilience is strengthened when children have access to **protective factors** within themselves (social-emotional competence), within their families (secure attachment relationship), and within their communities, especially the presence of **supportive relationships**, the opportunity to have **positive experiences**, and support that guides them to develop **adaptive skills** that enable children to respond positively to environmental demands.

The most important factor in supporting young children to develop resilience in the face of stress and trauma is being part of a consistent relationship with a supportive caregiver who is responsive to the child's needs. Adults who buffer the amount of stress a child experiences *and* guide them to develop self-regulation and executive function skills help children to learn to cope with the stressors and challenges they will undoubtedly face in life.

In addition to **providing supportive and caring relationships**, the following are ways a teacher in the field of early childhood can help build resilience for children and families.

Teach social and emotional skills to children. Skills such as emotional literacy, friendship skills, managing strong emotions, self-regulation, and problem-solving are all skills that if learned, can help children have the coping skills necessary to navigate day to day relationships and problems.

Provide stable, predictable routines and environments. Young children that feel safe in their environment can then focus and learn new skills. If a child feels unsafe, it impacts their ability for their sensory system to relax and for them to engage the focal attention necessary to learn.

Help children feel that they are part of a group; that they are valued, belong, and are an important member of the community. All children need to feel they fit in, can contribute something of value, and that adults value their contribution. Children need to feel heard, be listened to, and find meaning in how they can contribute to the well-being of those around them. Giving children important jobs, teaching them how to get along with others, and having them work as a member of the team, all give children a sense of value and purpose.

Provide education to children's caregivers on child development and strategies that support developing social and emotional skills. We cannot forget that children go back to their families every evening. If we can support families in learning strategies that will help build protective factors and resiliency for their child, this will help them grow up with a strong foundation. A family learning basic child development and strategies to develop social and emotional skills can build resiliency both in the home and at school.

Create community beyond the classroom. Find ways to bridge home and school by offering community bonding and building events such as trainings, potlucks, community action groups, parent groups, committees to provide input, and family engagement and involvement. When we create community it not only supports children, it reduces isolation for families and creates a connection of care, trust, and support.

Offer resources to support families. Every family needs support in times of stress or need. Sometimes the only person they can trust is the teacher that cares for their child. If classrooms had resources and referrals for families from basic survival needs (food and clothing) to counseling and support (therapy, support groups) to physical needs (medical, eye, or dental) and spiritual resources (church, synagogue, temple, mosque, meditation), the family can be referred for support from a trusted source. Some families even need help navigating the complexities of paperwork and the political red tape that comes with accessing resources.

Create strength-based environments and interactions. Teachers often feel overwhelmed with the paperwork, increased demands for quality, managing challenging behaviors, and juggling their own personal and professional stressors. With all the demands coming at once, it is hard to scan for the positive within the classroom and it seems easier to look around the room and address the "fires" or emergencies. Teachers often say, "I am putting fires out all day." How can the habit be changed and a teacher develop a new mindset? What if a teacher scanned the classroom for what children were doing well? What if they pointed out specifically the strengths of children? How would it make a difference for a child if you heard "you shared with your friend, that was so friendly or you were so helpful when you cleared your dishes after lunch or you used a tissue to blow your nose and that is being healthy and keeping germs from spreading." If a child hears corrections and directions and negatives more than they hear positive feedback about themselves this can inhibit rather than build a strong internal dialogue and self-esteem.

Although it is essential that teachers learn about how children's brains can be damaged by the impact of traumatic stress, it is equally if not more important to understand that children's brains have a remarkable ability to build new neural connections—to reorganize and rewire itself—when the child is able to experience supportive and nurturing environments. Because children's brains are developing most rapidly in the early childhood years, this is the time when the damage of trauma can be most significant but can also make the ability to restore and heal the impact of adversity most possible. This is why it is so critical that early childhood teachers create trauma-informed environments that build children's protective factors and support them to heal.

2

FOUNDATIONS OF TRAUMA-INFORMED PRACTICE FOR EARLY CHILDHOOD EDUCATION

How Can Teachers of Young Children Enduring Traumatic Stress Enhance Their Well-Being and Healing?

Key Topics Covered

- Trauma-informed foundational principles for ECE educators
- The impact of trauma on children and families
- Important key foundational strategies: building relationships and providing safe, supportive environments
- Children develop within an ecological context

In this chapter, we outline foundational principles that we suggest are used to guide early childhood educators' discussion of trauma and desire to build trauma-informed early learning programs/services for children and families. It is essential to consider the language used when referring to children and their experiences with trauma. We introduce these foundational principles by connecting them to a metaphor—a thriving coast redwood tree—that represents the image of a child whose health, well-being, and ability to grow and thrive are entirely dependent upon the adult caregivers and the environment around them.

The first necessity for healthy growth and development of any living organism is the overall **quality of the environment** in which growth and development take place. For children with histories of trauma to thrive, they need trauma-sensitive environments that are safe and predictable—that include consistent routines to reduce uncertainty and traumatic triggers—in order to support and buffer a child from toxic stress and promote healing and resiliency.

The second requirement for supporting healthy growth and development for living organisms are **deeply caring and responsive relationships**. If children grow up with caring adults who provide responsive and consistent love and support, they are more likely to build resiliency and develop tools that assist in coping with the negative impact of stress and trauma. In contrast, children who experience traumatic environments without caring and attuned adults are more at risk of not developing the tools they need to cope with toxic stress and trauma.

For individuals and communities impacted by trauma, traumatic relationships and toxic environments can lead to disruptions to their health, development, and well-being throughout their lives and contribute to a "trauma lens" where fear, terror, and traumatic stress impacts how they view the world and their place within it. The following is a table describing features of a healthy growth environment and features of a traumatic growth environment.

Healthy growth and healing environment	Traumatic and harmful environment
• Self-regulated adults • Balanced/centered/integrated adults • Relationship security • Strengths-based approach • Honoring child agency (can make choices and influence decisions that impact them) • Access to resources, supports, and referrals • Safe environments • Partnering with families and access to community resources • Use of reflective practices • Focus on the "whole" child and practices that promote social-emotional skills • Focus on justice and restorative practices • Awareness and integration of trauma-sensitive strategies • Focusing on child development versus child management	• Dysregulated adults • Chaotic/unbalanced/fragmented adults • Relationship insecurity • Deficit-based approach • Suppression of personal agency • Little or no access to resources, supports, and referrals • Unsafe environments • Disconnected from families and lack of access to community resources • Reacting in the moment • Little or no focus on the "whole" child and absence of practices that promote social-emotional skills • Little or no awareness of trauma and/or integration of trauma-sensitive strategies • Focus on control and punitive discipline

Developing in a healthy growth and healing environment not only protects children from the toxic stress experienced from trauma, it also prepares children to learn to build healthy relationships with others. This environment serves to both prevent trauma from occurring (fostering resilience), and also teaches the skills to heal from traumatic symptoms.

Why a Coast Redwood Tree? A Metaphor for a Young Child Experiencing Trauma

The coast redwood is a magnificent tree, known for its soaring heights, beauty, and longevity (Figure 2.1). Coast redwoods are some of the oldest and most sustainable trees on earth as they have been in existence and regenerating for 240 million years. Redwoods are resilient in the face of many potential threats to their health and longevity including insects, fungi, disease, and fire. One of the most impressive features of redwoods is how they continue to thrive in the face of devastating and frequent forest fires in their natural environment. The coast redwood's resiliency is due to a range of factors related to the environment in which they develop and grow:

- They reproduce in two ways—through seeds that drop from its cones and through "stump sprouting." At the base of many redwoods there develops a burl, or a mass full of dormant buds. Stump sprouting gives them a significant reproductive advantage because if the tree is damaged,

Figure 2.1 Redwood Tree.

Source: Jonathan Julian.

the buds sprout from the base of the tree and use the parent tree's root system for nutrients. *Babies come into the world with many competencies that bloom in interaction with the caregiving environment. Primary caregiving relationships provide the foundational need for an infant and child's safety, security, co-regulation, stress buffering, and the meeting of basic needs such as food, sleep, clothing, and responsive care.*

- They have an interdependent root system where the roots of baby redwood trees are intertwined with, and therefore protected by, the roots of the adult redwood trees around them. This intertwining is also essential to the redwood's ability to grow to soaring heights as their roots only grow five to six feet down into the ground, not providing the stability it needs without intertwining. *Babies' genetic predisposition and their ability to survive depends on the quality of the caregiver's interactions and resources. Young children thrive in the context of nurturing and responsive adult caregiving and relationships.*

- The bark is naturally resistant to insects, fungi, and fire because it is high in tannin and does not produce resin or pitch. The thickness of the bark, often up to a foot thick, provides protection and insulation for the tree, particularly the layer just beneath the bark called sapwood, which contains the nutrient system for the tree. *Babies have many competencies but by nature they are vulnerable and depend upon their caregivers for protection. Children have both internal temperament traits that can be resilient and also build resilience by being taught social-emotional skills in the context of safe environments and nurturing relationships.*

- The sapwood is the middle layer between the bark and the center of the tree, which is called the heartwood. Even if fire destroys the heartwood of a redwood, the protection of the bark still allows the sapwood to sustain the tree through its nutrient system, allowing it to continue growing and thriving despite its burned-out heartwood. *The containment and support offered to young children sustains them through hardship and trauma. Adults help to buffer traumatic stress for children by helping them build self-regulation skills, social and emotional skills, and a sense of self-esteem and self-efficacy.*

- Redwoods are critical participants in the environment. "Studies show that coast redwoods capture more carbon dioxide (CO_2) from [human emissions] ... than any other tree on Earth." In this way they are actively resisting climate change, as well as providing refuge for many endangered animals. *All children have strengths and collectively contribute to society. Environments that are safe, predictable, and supportive can help children thrive and provide essential buffering to toxic or traumatic stress.*

The coast redwoods unique features and impressive resiliency in the face of many threats to its well-being makes it a useful metaphor for young children's strengths and resilience, along with family and community assets and adaptability in the face of trauma. Below we link the foundational principles of trauma-informed practice (TIP) in early childhood with the coast redwood, emphasizing what it takes to create supportive, protective, and healing environments that promote—instead of disrupt and thwart—children's development.

Foundational Principles for TIP in Early Childhood

Children's primary attachments can provide a secure base to buffer their stress and support their development of resiliency. Young children learn through their primary attachment relationships with their parents and other adult caregivers whether the world is a safe place where they will be protected, their needs will be taken care of, and their emotions and behaviors will be understood and supported in a responsive manner. Parents and caregivers who form positive and secure attachments with young children can play an important role in buffering the impact of traumatic stress on their developing brains and bodies. Attachment has been described as the "emotional glue" needed for all future relationships (Perry, 2013, p. 1). This is because through attachment children learn whether they can build trust in relationships and whether the adults around them will provide physical and emotional security and protection. The goal of the attachment system is for a child to be near the parent/ caregiver (attachment figure) in time of stress, fear, or danger. In turn, the goal of the parent is to provide sensitive care and physical and social-emotional protection, through regulating the child's emotional state, often calming them through physical comfort and emotional availability and attunement (Bowlby, 1969/1982). When a distressed child has been responded to and is soothed and calmed, she is able to explore and engage in social relationships. For this to occur, the parent or caregiver acts as a **secure base** for the child to safely explore and engage, and to whom the child can turn to for safety and protection when upset. When a child's parent or primary caregiver is absent, early childhood teachers become their secure base, as young children rely on them to meet their needs and turn to them for comfort and safety when they are distressed.

In contrast, adults can be, and often are, the main source of traumatic stress for young children. They can worsen the consequences of trauma by compromising a young child's ability to form trusting relationships and influencing their young and vulnerable brains by predicting that they will not only continue to have negative and traumatic experiences, but that they are the cause of this trauma. Young children's brain development is profoundly impacted by the context of their first attachment relationships. Loving and attuned adults who are responsive to children's needs can significantly buffer children's stress and support them to develop resiliency in the face of traumatic stress. Early frightening experiences without the loving protection of a responsive caregiver are overwhelming and disrupt children's brain growth and emotional development.

Connecting this principle to the metaphor … *A young redwood is protected and supported by the mature adult redwoods around it.* Figure 2.2 shows a young redwood tree developing in a healthy environment and connected to the support it needs to grow, intertwining with an adult redwood. The "attunement" of the adult redwood provides the foundation this sapling needs to feel cared for and supported through relationships and connections with primary attachment figures over time. The intertwined roots provide critical support to the young tree and help to buffer the stress caused by outside threats (insects, drought, etc.) as the sapling's vulnerable development is supported and protected by the more mature trees that surround and nurture it.

A Young Redwood

Many of our youngest children experience trauma. It is our responsibility to acknowledge this truth even if it makes us uncomfortable to do so. It is very difficult for adults to acknowledge that so many young and vulnerable children experience trauma. Thinking about infants, toddlers, and pre-school and elementary school children in pain, harmed, terrified—and far too often, as a result of the actions of their own parents and caregivers—is a reality that too many adults do not want to confront. To reduce their anxiety and discomfort, many adults:

• Choose not to talk about the existence of trauma in early childhood, an injustice previously characterized as a "**conspiracy of silence**" (Craig, 2016, p. 12).

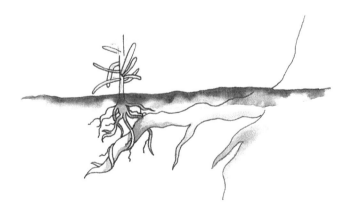

Figure 2.2 Young Redwood.

Source: Jonathan Julian.

- Others recommend **shifting the language to words and images that are less distressing** for them. For example, it is not uncommon to hear adults state, "I don't like to use the word 'trauma.' I prefer to use the word 'stress.'" Or similarly, "I like to talk about developmentally responsive practices instead of trauma-informed practices."
- Another pattern we observe is an assumption many adults have that **young children are too young to remember their traumatic experiences** or that children are "naturally resilient" in the face of adversity. As we discuss in this book, neither of these assumptions are accurate. To the contrary, brain research highlights that children are the most vulnerable and impacted by trauma. Even trauma endured in utero impacts young children's developing brains and bodies and can cause lasting damage throughout a child's life.

The first step in all societal change is to name and acknowledge a problem that exists. Trauma-sensitive early childhood education begins with an honest and transparent validation of *all* children's life experiences, including the large percentage of children who experience trauma in their earliest years. Trauma-informed early childhood programs and systems do not ignore or understate the painful and authentic realities of the widespread existence of trauma in children's lives. Bearing witness to children's pain and suffering without blaming or judging them for these experiences, and accurately and honestly acknowledging the consequences of trauma's impact, is a foundational principle of all trauma-informed work with young children.

Connecting this principle to the metaphor ... *A young child who suffers from trauma could remain "stuck in the flames" unless we acknowledge their traumatic experiences and actively work to support their healing.* If we imagine a young redwood sapling as a child, a forest fire could be a potentially traumatic experience that disrupts the young tree's growth and ability to develop into a healthy adult tree (see Figure 2.3). If a young redwood is exposed to fire before it is fully grown, it will likely not survive. However, as redwoods mature, they grow bark that provides a strong and protective fire-resistant shell that protects the tree even in the context of repeated fires. Unlike redwoods, children who grow up in a traumatic and harmful environment can remain "stuck in the flames," expressing traumatic stress behaviors and disrupted in their ability to find new growth in a field of ashes. By honestly acknowledging the existence of trauma—the forest fire(s) that engulf young children that often leave their inner spirits shriveled and vulnerable—we can provide supportive interventions that help them develop the protective bark they will need—coping strategies and resiliency—that will support them to heal and protect them from future fires.

Figure 2.3 Sapling Engulfed in Fire.

Source: Jonathan Julian.

A Young Redwood Sapling Engulfed in a Forest Fire

Neurobiological research on traumatic stress and resiliency is essential for early childhood educators to learn about and integrate into their practice. Although we now have decades of research on the neurobiology of stress and the impact that traumatic stress has on young children's developing brains and bodies, this knowledge is rarely integrated into traditional child development or early childhood college coursework. Nor is information on trauma and the neurobiology of stress typically addressed in professional development or coaching for the early childhood workforce. Instead, information about trauma and its impact on children has been primarily accessible to professionals working in clinical professions (e.g., psychiatrists, psychologists, mental health practitioners).

Given the prevalence of traumatic stress and adverse childhood experiences in young children's lives, a central principle of TIP is that high-quality early childhood training programs in institutions of higher education as well as high-quality early learning programs and services in the field must be trauma-informed. This requires that *all* **early childhood educators understand the impact of trauma on young children's learning and development**. Early childhood teachers and their directors need to understand that children who have experienced trauma focus on survival and often perceive that they are in danger, while they struggle to use the part of their brains that support problem-solving, planning, and self-regulation. Understanding young children's stress response systems is essential for responsive teaching and caregiving *and* for designing early learning environments that support children to feel safe and to heal.

Early childhood teachers who have learned about trauma and its impact on young children understand that all traumatic stress behaviors

have meaning and that these behaviors are automatically triggered by a child's "survival center" in their lower brainstem. They understand that children are not intentionally making decisions to have challenging behaviors, instead, their brains are in survival mode responding in the same manner they did during the initial traumatic experience. Because trauma is stored as implicit memories, children and adults are not consciously aware of why their bodies have the traumatic responses they do to certain triggers in the environment. A seemingly unexceptional daily event (e.g., the distant sound of a firetruck siren, a doorbell ringing, or a stranger walking into a classroom) can start a powerful cascade of stress chemicals that communicate to them, "You are not safe! You are in danger!" Children's emotional and behavioral response to this message is what we see as their traumatic stress behaviors; *it is the trauma story we need to be able to read in our work with children*. All behavior, especially the most challenging behavior in young children, is communicating a story to the adults caring for them.

Understanding the neurobiology of trauma allows teachers to observe children's behavior and listen differently. Trauma-informed teaching transforms how early childhood professionals regard young children with a traumatic history. Using a trauma-sensitive lens, children's impulsive and acting out behavior is understood as a result of harm from physical, emotional, or social maltreatment (Craig, 2016). Having this knowledge helps caregivers to understand that children with histories of trauma are communicating about something that happened to them, which left them feeling powerless and fearful, and what they now need from the adults around them to feel safe and secure in their care.

Children must be understood to be complex human beings and not solely defined by the trauma they experience. A central foundation of high-quality early childhood education is using a strengths-based (versus deficit orientation) perspective in discussions of children and their families and this remains true in discussions of early childhood trauma. Children must be understood as complex human beings and not defined entirely by the trauma they have experienced. This is why our discussion about trauma and toxic stress is always balanced with a consideration of the "whole child" *and* the topics of resiliency and healing. TIP recognizes the whole child by acknowledging that all children are complex individuals and have many aspects of their lives. When we talk about the "whole child" we are including consideration of children's **diverse:**

- Relationships
- Family, cultural, and community values and beliefs, routines, rituals, experiences, and memories
- Aspects of identity (race, ethnicity, gender, primary language, ability, etc.)
- Interests, likes/dislikes

- Temperaments
- Personalities
- Protective factors
- Support systems
- Strengths inherent in the child and that surround the child

A TIP approach acknowledges that although trauma impacts all aspects of young children's learning and development, defining a young child by their trauma is not acknowledging the full complexity of who children are as human beings. Our society is embracing the use of people first language in order to **place the person first** instead of defining individuals in language that is too generalized, stereotyped, or stigmatizing. For example, by saying "an individual with a disability" instead of "a disabled person" or "a child experiencing homelessness" versus "a homeless child," the person is placed first and the disability or condition of housing insecurity is no longer the defining characteristic of that individual, instead, this small but important shift in language communicates that these are one of several aspects of the whole person. This same consideration needs to be used in discussing trauma for young children. A child should never be defined by the trauma they have experienced. Trauma is a significant and impactful feature of their experience but it does not represent all of the complex aspects of who children are.

Another important element of not defining children by the traumas they experience is assuming that all children—including those with histories of trauma—have resources, personal characteristics, and relationships that can be mobilized to enhance their learning, development, well-being, and healing.

Trauma-informed practices never label or stigmatize children as "traumatized" and they are never used to diagnose children. Using a trauma-informed approach is beneficial for all young children and <u>essential</u> for children with histories of trauma. TIP is based on an assumption that understanding how trauma and stress impact children's development is essential for teachers to know how to be responsive and supportive in their interactions with children. This understanding informs how they arrange environments to minimize the chances that children will be triggered and feel unsafe. It also helps them understand the different behaviors that result when children's stress response systems are activated and the strategies they can use to help calm children's nervous systems so they can return to regulated emotional and behavioral states. As all children experience stress and a large percentage live in conditions of traumatic stress, TIP is effective without knowing what children's specific histories and/or traumatic experiences have been.

A Young Redwood's Growth Impacted by Fire
Continuing to Grow and Develop

Connecting this principle to the metaphor … *A young child who suffers from trauma can be deeply impacted by the experience but the trauma does not define who that child is. If we only focus on the trauma, we will fail to see the strengths, capacities, and resiliencies—the new growth—that are also significant aspects of that child's identity as a unique and whole human being* (see Figure 2.4). Holding a trauma-informed perspective is a balancing act where we see every child as inherently capable of health, resilience, and connection—the sapling developing in a healthy growth and healing environment—while honoring and validating that many children are, on the inside, struggling, tired, worn, stressed, scared, and disconnected—the shriveled sapling, engulfed in flames. It also means respecting the complexity of the whole child. This requires a view of the child developing over time, including their family, culture and history, new experiences to develop healthy attachments, trust and a sense of safety, and their ability to contribute meaningfully in constructing their future.

Children develop in an ecological context and their experiences of trauma, resiliency, and healing are impacted by these multiple spheres of influence including their families, their communities, and the larger society in which they live. Many factors influence young children's exposure to, and experiences with, trauma, including their family, culture, economic status, neighborhood and community, caregiving and educational

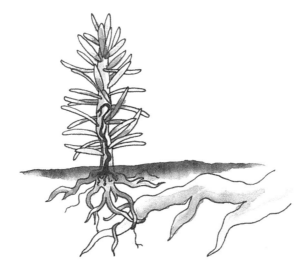

Figure 2.4 Sapling Impacted by Fire and Still Growing.

Source: Jonathan Julian.

environments, geographic region, and the political and historical contexts that influence their daily lives. Some children are more vulnerable to prolonged experiences of complex trauma and toxic stress in their earliest years because their families and communities are more trauma-impacted as a result of the existence of **oppression**, a form of injustice that exists in every country, culture, and society on earth. Oppression is the systematic and prolonged mistreatment of a group of people within a country or society. It is characterized by an uneven distribution of, or use of, power between groups where one group is privileged and engages in manipulation and control over the other. Oppression exists in socioeconomic, cultural, political, legal, and institutional contexts and is maintained through a variety of influences including societal norms, implicit biases and stereotypes, and rules and policies within governments and institutions that benefit some while marginalizing others. Examples of oppression include:

- **Racial oppression.** Genocide, geographic displacement (indigenous people losing their land), slavery.
- **Class oppression.** Economic or social positions based on income, wealth, property ownership, job status, education, skills, and power in economic and/or political contexts.
- **Gender oppression.** Sexism (mistreatment of women and trans*, gender-fluid, gender queer, or other individuals who do not identify with the male/female gender binary).
- **Sexuality oppression.** Mistreatment of anyone who is not heterosexual including individuals identifying as LGBTQIA+ (lesbian, gay, bisexual, transgender or questioning, intersex, asexual, or other individuals who do not identify as heterosexual).
- **Religious oppression.** Marginalization against a group of people for their religious beliefs (e.g., anti-Semitism).
- **Economic oppression:** Forced labor, labor trafficking
- **Institutionalized oppression.** Laws, customs, and practices that systematically include members of some social groups while intentionally excluding and marginalizing others. Examples include immigration laws that systematically reject all members of certain racial, religious, or ethnic groups or organizations that prevent individuals from promotion based on their gender.

- Oppression is the systematic and prolonged mistreatment of a group of people. It is built into our daily lives.
- Oppression extends beyond the actions of individuals. It shapes the systems we live and work in and the structures in society (e.g., education, health care, housing).

- Oppression exists within institutions and organizations at every level (e.g., harmful or inequitable policies, practices, interactions, and behaviors).
- Oppression impacts learning, teaching, leading, and decision-making.
- Addressing oppression and bias triggers strong emotions.
- Systemic oppression is the source of a lot of trauma in our society and impacts every aspect of children's lives whether they are advantaged or disadvantaged as a result of its existence.
- We all need to heal from the effects of oppression.

Source: National Equity Project, Oakland, California (www.nationalequityproject.org)

The effects of trauma are cumulative; the more severe, prolonged, and multi-faceted the experiences of traumatic stress, the more likely a child is to have lasting neurological damage. As previously discussed, the most important protection children can have from the negative consequences of trauma are positive attachment relationships with caring and attuned adults who can buffer their stress. If children live in families and communities with adults who are targets of one or more forms of systemic oppression (e.g., a child living in an economically distressed community where access to housing, nutritious food, healthcare, and quality education are all difficult to access due to institutionalized racism), the adults caring for them are likely to be trauma-impacted themselves. The multigenerational experience of trauma in families, neighborhoods, and communities can decrease children's opportunities for building strong and healthy attachments with adults and to experience relational buffering with their own stressors, which, in turn, compromises their ability to build resiliency and to heal.

To be trauma-informed requires that teachers think not only about a child, but also about the child developing in a larger ecological context. A child's experience of trauma is not isolated from the cumulative impact of the traumatic stressors that exist in the child's family and community. Children who have multiple traumatic experiences need early childhood teachers who understand trauma and their critical role in children's development. By developing a caring and attuned relationship with a child, they can be a critical adult who buffers their stress and in so doing, supports them to develop coping skills and to build resiliency.

A Young Redwood's Growth Depends on Several Environmental Factors Surrounding It

Connecting this principle to the metaphor … *A redwood tree on its own would not be able to withstand the dangers that it encounters in the environment*

Figure 2.5 Environmental Dangers.

Source: Jonathan Julian.

(see Figure 2.5). The coast redwood can grow to 350 feet or more, compared with the tallest of other trees that max out at 250 feet or less. In order for a typical tree to grow to great heights, it requires a deep root system to stabilize the growing tree. Without deep roots, trees are vulnerable to falling or being uprooted during high winds and floods, as well as dying out completely during fires. Although it might seem that a 350-foot-tall tree would need deep roots, the roots of a coast redwood are very shallow, often only 5 or 6 feet deep. Their strength comes from the width of the roots, which can extend up to 100 feet from the trunk. Redwood trees grow in thick groves where they can intertwine their roots together; they develop strength through their interconnectivity with other trees. A redwood tree on its own would not be able to withstand the dangers that it encounters in the environment, but the interconnection of roots makes redwood trees tremendously strong and sturdy.

Similar to a redwood tree, a young child requires relationships and connectivity with others for healthy development. Remember, a hallmark of a healthy growth environment is the ability to be balanced and centered with relationship security. A traumatic environment can disrupt a child's ability to form secure attachments, leaving them without a solid system of intertwined roots. Just as each redwood plays a role in supporting the stability and health of the others in its grove, each child needs caring and attuned adults surrounding him to provide him with support, stability, and protection from dangers he encounters in his environment. In certain families and communities where trauma is severe, prolonged, multifaceted, and across generations, the environment is more precarious for a young child. Some adults, suffering from the consequences of their own exposure to trauma, may not have secure intertwined roots of their own, leaving young children vulnerable to the dangers they may encounter in their environment.

Redwoods Thrive in Thick Groves Where Their Roots Can Intertwine

When they have relational support, young children can develop important coping skills and resilience (see Figure 2.6). In our efforts to care for young children enduring traumatic stress, it is important that teachers do not create additional harm by categorizing and stereotyping children. It is not unusual for teachers to work from a deficit perspective by focusing on children's challenging behaviors or the skills they have not yet learned. Teachers working from a deficit viewpoint may not observe that young children under stress often show significant strengths and develop a variety of coping strategies and capacities that, although not optimal for healthy functioning, are effective responses to significant stressors in their lives (e.g., suppressing their emotions, using distraction to shift their attention away from uncomfortable experiences).

Fostering young children's capacity for resilience begins with the child's ability to experience a caring relationship with a supportive caregiver who is responsive to the child's needs. Children with histories of trauma need at least one adult to provide co-regulatory support and help them build the foundations for future executive function skills. Even one caring and responsive adult can interrupt a child's stress response system from damaging their normal developmental processes. And one caring and responsive adult

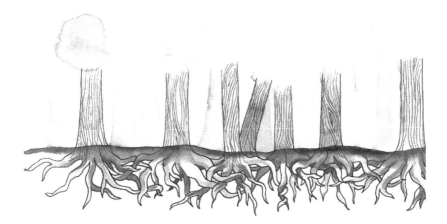

Figure 2.6 Thick Groves.

Source: Jonathan Julian.

can support children to shift from activating "survival" responses to stress and to learn healthy coping strategies that develop into adaptive social-emotional skills.

A Redwood's Bark Provides It With Protection

Resilience of the redwood. When faced with fires, mature redwoods are still able to regenerate and reproduce. Because the living part of the bark, the sapwood, is so fire resistant, the center of the tree, known as the heartwood, is able to be burned and the tree still thrives. Coast redwoods reproduce abundantly by forming sprouts around the base of parent trees. Even in the rare case that a mature tree is killed by fire, sprouts can still form around the base. Unlike coast redwoods, children who experience trauma—whose heartwood has been burned out—and do not have access to the elements of a healthy and healing environment, will most likely not remain healthy as they develop. Without access to caring, attuned relationships and trauma-sensitive environments, the effects of trauma may lead to complex physical and mental health challenges including anxiety, depression, ADHD, personality disorders, heart disease, breathing and sleep challenges, and/or early death (Figure 2.7).

However, with the proper support and access to elements of a healthy and healing environment, children and adults are able to develop a thicker sapwood, that is, build resilience and heal from trauma. When this is the case, though the heartwood is still burnt, the sapwood is able to help the tree thrive, and even produce new life at its base. For children with histories of trauma who have relational support, "new life at the base" is reflected in their ability to learn to form trusting relationships and to reduce their traumatic stress reactions as they go about their day playing, talking, singing, walking, and engaging with people and objects in their environment. For adults, "new life at the base" could represent the transformation of pain into a regenerated life. Many communities most impacted by historical traumas have developed significant resiliencies—there are traces of the impact of fire in their heartwood protected by a thick layer of sapwood, having transformed their pain into significant coping skills, strengths, and capacities.

Connecting this principle to the metaphor ... *A redwood's bark provides protection for the tree.* The bark of a coast redwood grows up to one foot in thickness and is the "heart" of the tree that provides it with insulation and protection from pests and danger. It is within this thick bark, called sapwood, that nutrients and water are "pumped" to the heights of the tree. The Redwood's bark forms a protective layer that makes it naturally resistant to insects, fungi, and fire.

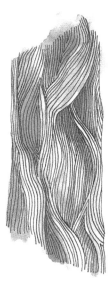

Figure 2.7 Redwood Bark.

Source: Jonathan Julian.

The Center of The Tree Can Burn and The Tree Will Not Die

Coast redwoods have survived for millions of years due to their adaptability and sustainability over time and in the face of traumatic environmental changes (Figure 2.8). Not only do they absorb toxins, they transform them into life-giving oxygen. By learning about trauma and creating trauma-informed programs, early childhood teachers can transform the toxic impact of trauma for children into coping skills and strengths that will help protect them with a thick and sturdy heartwood.

Redwoods Have Survived for Millions of Years. Even When They Are Severely Burned, They Produce New Life at The Base

Early childhood teachers and caregivers can model and encourage resilience. Imagine yourselves as a grown redwood in which the fire of trauma has burned out your heartwood. Your thick and healthy sapwood will still provide you with protection, allowing you to foster new saplings. This is similar to your own self-care: Thickening and reinforcing your resilient sapwood, while also attending to your own heartwood, will influence how attuned and responsive you will be to the children you are caring for. Only when you take the time to reflect on and acknowledge your own stress and history of trauma, will you be able to properly attune to, and support, the children you

Figure 2.8 Tree Will Not Die.

Source: Jonathan Julian.

care for. If a child is engulfed in flames, and teachers have not done their own work to attend to their own fire-riddled heartwood, they run the risk of being triggered and acting reactively with children. However, by becoming more aware of your own triggers, and doing your own healing work with your heartwood, teachers will be able to support new life and create healthy growth and healing environments for the children, or little saplings, in their care (Figure 2.9).

Healthy Growth and Healing or Traumatic and Harmful Environment?

They tried to bury us. They didn't know we were seeds.
(Mexican Proverb)

Young children, just like a sapling coast redwood, will only thrive and grow into healthy adults if we create developmentally supportive and healing early childhood environments. It is during this time when their brain development is most rapid and their neural networks most vulnerable to the quality of the environments around them. And when they develop their view of the world as loving and safe or cruel and dangerous. Key factors that

Figure 2.9 Life at the Base.

Source: Jonathan Julian.

impact healthy development include nurturing and responsive relationships, predictable and safe environments, promoting social and emotional skills, self-regulation, community supports, resources and referrals in times of need, family support and engagement, and identification and building upon strengths and resiliency.

3

TRAUMA-SENSITIVE EARLY CHILDHOOD PROGRAMS

What Are Important Trauma-Sensitive Teaching Strategies for Early Learning Environments?

Key Topics Covered

- Attuned and responsive relationships
- Self-reflection, self-awareness, and inquiry-based practices
- Identifying children's strengths
- Culturally responsive practice
- Creating predictable, safe, and nurturing environments
- Teaching social-emotional skills

The early learning environment is a critical time and place to introduce caregiving practices that promote young children's emotional resiliency. Trauma-informed caregiving and environments help children to feel safe. This is accomplished through the intentional integration of many trauma-sensitive supports including:

- Attuned and responsive relationships;
- Reflection and inquiry-based teaching practice to improve teachers' self-awareness and self-regulation;
- Using a strengths-based approach with children and families;
- Ensuring that the classroom curriculum, instruction, environment, and communication with children and families are culturally responsive;
- Predictable routines and schedules;

- Support for transitions;
- Use of visual aids;
- The introduction of sensory and emotional literacy;
- Direct teaching of social-emotional skills.

Building attuned and responsive relationships with children. Forming an attuned and responsive relationship with a child is the most important and foundational trauma-informed practice. As described in Chapter 1, the primary intervention for trauma-informed practices is for children's nervous systems to be able to interact with their caregivers in order to co-regulate their arousal levels. Emotionally attuned interpersonal relationships with a reliable and caring teacher help children feel safe and calms their stress response systems, which supports healing from trauma, buffers their toxic stress, and promotes their healthy development, including their ability to play, build positive social relationships, and engage in the learning process.

Trauma-informed early childhood teachers use their knowledge of child development and understanding of trauma to act as a secure base and co-regulator for children impacted by trauma, reducing their reactive behaviors (lower brainstem fight/flight/freeze response), and guiding children back to optimal levels of arousal. Using their own self-awareness and self-regulation to support attunement with children, teachers help to positively change young children's brain development by interrupting the over-activation of their stress response systems. Building attuned and responsive relationships with young children who have experienced trauma is the most important and life-altering strategy for early childhood teachers to focus on in their practice. **All trauma-informed practices begin with a caring, loving, and protective relationship with an adult caregiver.**

ATTUNED AND RESPONSIVE RELATIONSHIPS: THE MOST IMPORTANT TRAUMA-SENSITIVE STRATEGY FOR SUPPORTING YOUNG CHILDREN WITH HISTORIES OF TRAUMA

Three-year-old Alisa was playing at the water table in her preschool classroom when Jenna, another child in the class, arrived with her mother. Jenna immediately ran up to the water table and started playing with Alisa. While Jenna was engaged, her mother quickly left the room without telling Jenna that she was leaving. When Jenna turned around and soon learned that her mother was gone, she began crying for her mom inconsolably, "Mama, mama, where did my mama go?" A "disappearing mom" was a major stress trigger for Alisa—whose mother died unexpectedly when she was four months old from an appendicitis attack. Alisa immediately looked distressed, began itching her head, and finally when she couldn't handle the stress anymore, turned and ran to her teacher and collapsed into her lap with a shaking body. Her teacher reassured Alisa that she was safe, that the teachers would never leave without telling her first, and that her father was coming to pick her up as he always did at the end of the day. This allowed Alisa to calm down, to return to playing at the water table, and to stop itching her head. Later, her teacher shared her observation with dad explaining that if he saw Alisa itching, he could try providing her with some reassurance of her safety and his presence and that they would do the same at preschool.

Somatization: Stress-related aches and pains in children's bodies including headaches, stomach aches, itching, and body aches that result from traumatic stress (Gray, 2007). Alisa's itchy head was triggered by the trauma memory of losing her mother. Seeing her classmate, Jenna, so distressed when her mother disappeared from the classroom started a stress reaction in Alisa that her teacher observed in the head itching, running into her teacher's arms, and a full body startle response.

A secure base: Alisa's teacher acted as a secure base for her, a caring, attuned adult who responded to Alisa's attachment needs that immediately calmed her central nervous system and reduced her traumatic stress behaviors. After her attachment needs were met, Alisa was able to return to playing.

Using Self-Reflection to Strengthen Self-Awareness

Working with children with histories of trauma is very emotionally demanding. Teachers are continually observing individual children and noticing their emotional states and behaviors. They wonder what children are communicating to them through their behaviors and then use these observations to inform attuned and responsive communication. Being trauma-sensitive requires that teachers are emotionally available to children—especially when a child's stress response system has been activated. This is very challenging for adults to do and requires that they learn to identify their own triggers and emotional reactions to children's complex traumatic stress behaviors. **Self-reflection and inquiry** are practices that support teachers to remain emotionally attuned and available to children with histories of trauma.

Self-reflection is the process of stepping away from your day-to-day routine and taking time to think about your own reactions internally in order to improve the quality of your teaching and caregiving practice. Thinking about yourself may include reflecting on the following:

- How do I feel?
- How do others feel?

- How big are my feelings?
- If necessary, how can I pause or use a strategy to calm down and become more regulated emotionally?
- What are all the different ways I can handle a challenging situation?
- What biases and assumptions might be influencing my perceptions and actions? What additional information should I consider so I don't propose a solution prematurely?
- What consequences might result from different responses I could have in this situation? Who benefits and who is harmed with each solution?
- What do I need in this moment for my own self-care?
- How can I see the meaning behind the child's behavior?
- How can I support and regulate the child in the moment and to help them feel safe?
- What strategy will do the least harm to a child?

Through self-reflection, teachers have an opportunity to put on emotional brakes and take time to "think" before "reacting." Reflection can happen while teachers are caring for children (Reflecting "in the action" aka "thinking on your feet") or during other times when teachers are not responsible for teaching and caregiving (Reflecting "on the action"; e.g., before or after work, during breaks, throughout staff development, or professional learning experiences; Schön, 1983).

People like to engage in self-reflection in many different ways. Some examples include:

- Drawing a picture
- Writing in a journal
- Talking to a friend or trusted loved one
- Talking to a supervisor
- Walking
- Meditation and deep breathing
- Tuning in to how they feel and the intensity of their emotions

Can you think of ways you already reflect or other ways you might reflect? Can you think of ways you can press the pause button on the pressures of your life and just reflect on what you need, want, feel and think about yourself, your actions and your situation in that moment? What ways do you already pause, tune in to how you feel, and think before reacting?

Self-awareness is the ability to know yourself. The more you know yourself, the better you function in your professional and personal relationships.

Awareness of yourself can include the following:

- Your strengths;
- Your areas of growth and development;
- Knowing what you feel in a particular moment and the intensity of your emotions;
- Learning whether you react based on your emotional state or pause and wait until you can regulate and then think through solutions;
- Knowing what frustrates or triggers you;
- Knowing what brings you joy, calm, and/or happiness;
- Knowing what energizes and restores you and what drains your energy;
- Knowing your values and beliefs and how they impact your behaviors, interactions, and child development practices.

If teachers have strong self-awareness, the better able they will be to attune to the internal world of a child. An adult who is aware of their own range of feelings can in turn be aware of the range of emotions of a child. By strengthening self-awareness, teachers learn to tune-in to what triggers or upsets them and to use the tool of reflection to "think" about why certain things (e.g., children's actions or nonactions) lead to their own strong emotional reactions. Adults' strongest emotional reactions often stem from their family and values, perceptions, cultural beliefs, and from past experiences, including interactions that were intensely stressful or traumatic.

DEVELOPING SELF-AWARENESS: BELIEFS ABOUT CHILDREN'S BEHAVIORS AND EMOTIONS

Take a quick look at each of these questions and think about your values and beliefs. Over the course of your lifetime, what beliefs about children's behaviors and emotions have you developed through your family upbringing, culture, or community? Were there unspoken rules about how young children should behave?

- When you were a child, how did your parents/caregivers feel about you identifying or expressing emotions? Which emotions were children allowed in your family and which were not? How did they expect girls or boys to act? Was the expectation different? How many of your own family's beliefs have you adopted about the expression of emotions?
- Think of the following emotions. What did your family teach you about each one? Which were you allowed to express and how?
  - Anger
  - Frustration
  - Patience

- Sadness
- Happiness

Think of the following behaviors. How did your family respond to you when you did the following:

- Played quietly
- Played alone
- Talked loudly
- Talked quietly
- Interacted with others
- Were talkative
- Asked questions
- Expressed an opinion
- Acted shy or reserved
- Complained or whined

The way you were raised plays a large role in developing your mental framework—informed by your values, perceptions, and beliefs—about children and how they should behave. When faced with behaviors that push your buttons and bump up against personal values, you may find that you are more triggered. When triggered by certain behaviors, you can become more reactive, defaulting to strategies that are harmful. Increasing self-awareness about which behaviors push your buttons more than others, allows teachers to manage their reactions and associated emotions more effectively. Self-awareness can prevent adult unconscious and habitual practices with children that are punishing, punitive, yelling, blaming, threatening, and that cause more harm to children with trauma histories.

Emotional "Button Pushed" in a Reactionary Adult Caregiver = Unregulated Child

For a young child, the internal emotional state of their caregivers impacts their behavior and emotional well-being. This is why it is so important for teachers to develop self-awareness so they can identify, monitor, and regulate their internal emotional state.

We all have buttons that get pushed. The goal is not to eliminate the buttons that trigger us but to cultivate awareness and conscious management of those emotional reactions connected to the trigger. Managing our own reactions is a trauma-sensitive strategy for early childhood teachers. The following table lists behaviors exhibited by children in an early learning setting. Which ones "push your buttons" or "trigger" you emotionally? Choose the top five behaviors that trigger a strong emotional reaction in you. For those behaviors, list a word that describes a belief you hold about that behavior (usually learned in our families informed by our cultural backgrounds), how you feel when you see that behavior in the classroom, and what your typical response is toward a child with that behavior.

Behavior	Ranking top 5	Your belief about this behavior	How it makes you feel?	How do you typically respond?
Example: Yelling	1	I learned in my family that children should be seen and not heard. Yelling is unacceptable.	Angry	Stern lecture to them how disrespectful they are. Remove the child who is yelling. Tell them they will lose a privilege.
Biting				
Will not listen				
Cannot entertain self				
Tattling				
Swearing				
Hitting				
Demands attention				
Withdraws				
Cries a lot				
Cannot sit still				
Talks a lot				
Isolates or plays alone				
Easily distracted				
Aggressive toward others				
Whining				
Tantrums				
Talks Back				
Disrespect toward adults				
Destroys property				
Hurts self				
Other _____				

All teachers will be triggered on a weekly basis by certain behaviors. When teachers are triggered by a specific child's behavior, they are more likely to be reactive instead of attuned and responsive to the child. When emotionally triggered, teachers often default unconsciously and reactively by punishing, bribing, shaming, criticizing, correcting, or using rewards to try to stop the behavior. If a teacher is escalated, it increases a child's stress response system, which promotes dysregulated children with challenging behaviors. If teachers can remain calm and emotionally self-regulated, they are more likely to help children to calm their central nervous systems so they can be guided back to regulation. One of the most important foundations for trauma-informed practice is teachers' self-regulation as it leads to children's self-regulation. Children learn how to act and function in the world through mirroring adults' brain activity. **Because children mirror adults' internal emotional states, teachers should think of themselves as mirrors acting like they want the children to act, expressing the state of calm they want the children to display**.

Teachers' self-regulation supports and facilitates children's self-regulation. Any increase in adult reactivity and dysregulation, will result in increased reactivity, dysregulation, and then challenging behaviors by the child.

A few simple tools can support early childhood teachers to look inward (inside themselves) first before they look outward (at the child's behavior and internal state of emotions). Teachers must first become aware of their own internal emotional state and the need for self-regulation if they are triggered, or have their buttons pushed. Once they are self-regulated and calm, teachers are better equipped with the energy and patience to effectively tune in (attune) to the emotional state of a child. Any incremental increase in adult reactivity will exponentially result in increased dysregulation by the child. Increases in adult self-regulation and attunement will more likely result in a child learning to regulate.

Let's look at two examples ...

First, a teacher who has her "button pushed" but uses self-awareness to stop herself from being reactive; a skill that allows her to remain attuned with a child with the result being a child guided back to self-regulation.

Second, a contrasting example, where a teacher was triggered, did not tune-in with herself, had a reactive and dysregulated response to a child, which further stressed and dysregulated the child's emotional state and behavior. In both examples, we see the children mirroring the adults' internal emotional state.

1. Teacher Using Self-Awareness: Tunes-Inward → Regulates Self = Regulated Child

Child's behavior (triggering for teacher)	Child's feelings	Teacher's feelings	Teacher's healthy awareness and response	Child's response and thoughts
Hitting	Anger because their toy was taken away by another child. Responded by hitting that child.	Annoyed, frustrated, and protective of child that was hit.	Takes a deep breath to calm down. Asks self, "I wonder what this child who hit another child is feeling? What does he need from me right now to feel safe?" Tells child, "You hit someone. You must really want something. Let me help you figure out how to get it without hitting. Hitting can hurt but asking with your words could help. Let's do this together."	"You care about what I feel. You are helping me understand my big emotions. You want to help me get what I need. I feel safe. I can be calm again because an adult will help me figure this problem out." My brain feels calmer because you are staying calm.
Withdrawn in the corner	Scared because a stranger just walked into the room.	Worried.	Asks to approach child and sit with her. Tells him they care and see that their body is shut down. Wonders if they might be scared. Brings some paper over to color together until the child is ready to talk.	"I feel frozen and cannot talk with words right now but my teacher cares about me. An adult noticed me when I ran to the corner. She is not trying to make me talk and that helps me feel calm and safer right now."

In these examples, the teacher has learned that when a child is displaying challenging behavior, they are communicating that they need extra support from the adult/s around her. They need the teacher's help to support them to regulate and they need help learning how to communicate what they need and how to address frustrations and solve problems when they arise.

These examples highlight a teacher with an awareness of trauma-sensitive teaching practices. The teacher understands that in the first case, the child acts out when triggered by something in their environment. The second child withdraws when something upsetting happens and pressuring the child to come join the other children does not work if her stress response system has been triggered. This type of pressure only increases her withdrawal behavior. Instead of forcing or threatening this child to come to the group, the teacher knows that sitting close to her and doing an activity with her will help to calm her stress response system. Once calm, the teacher understands that the child will likely return to play with her peers.

Self-awareness is the foundation of this teacher's trauma-sensitive strategies. Although she feels a range of emotions in response to children's behavior (e.g., annoyed, frustrated, concerned), she does not allow her emotions to lead her to reactive and hurtful behavior that further harms children impacted by trauma. Instead, she acknowledges her feelings without acting on them. Her calm and regulated internal state allows her to attune to the children she is caring for and to respond to them in a manner that reinforces their safety and gently guides them to emotional and behavioral regulation.

2. Teacher Lacking Self-Awareness → Reactive and Dysregulated = Dysregulated Child

Child's behavior (triggering for teacher)	Child's feelings	Teacher's feelings	Teacher's unhealthy reaction	Child's response and thoughts
Hitting	Anger because their toy was taken away by another child. Responded by hitting their peer.	Annoyed, frustrated, and protective of child who was hit.	Yell at child Threaten to call parent.	Hits teacher "Fight" stress response "My brain is scared and I am not safe."
Withdrawn in the corner	Scared because a stranger just walked in the room.	Worried.	Leaves child alone until they are ready to come back to the group on their own.	Run for safety "Freeze" stress response "My teacher does not care about me. My teacher does not notice me. I know that no one cares about me."

In this second example, we see a teacher who has a quick reaction to a child by coming in and defending the child that was hit. She never considers that the child who hit his peer is also struggling and needs the support of a caring adult to bring him back to regulation. We also see a teacher who does not consider that when a child withdraws into the corner, they are not feeling safe and/or has some big emotions and needs the teacher's support. This teacher has asked the child to come join the other children in the past with no success. Now, the teacher leaves the child alone until he is ready to return to the group. The teacher has come to believe that the child is pouting because he did not get his way so ignoring the child is the best choice because this way the teacher does not reward the pouting behavior.

In this case, the teacher does not show evidence of self-awareness. The emotions she feels internally drive her reactive behavior (yelling, threatening, ignoring) reinforcing to already triggered children that they are not safe, the adults will not take care of them, and instead, reinforces their fears and stress and this leads children to internalize feelings of fear, shame, and self-doubt.

Self-Awareness Journals

Keeping a self-awareness journal can help teachers learn how to strengthen their own self-regulation skills so they are more patient and responsive to young children with challenging or dysregulated behavior. In self-awareness journals, teachers write about difficult interactions they have with children they work with and reflect on those experiences. Research on the use of self-awareness journals suggests that teachers improve at learning how to regulate their own emotions as well as the emotions of the young children they are caring for (Perez, 2011). Through thoughtful reflection about their own behavioral and emotional reactions to challenging interactions, early childhood practitioners can learn to cultivate their ability to co-regulate children who are stressed and dysregulated. Improving teachers' co-regulatory capacity allows them to better meet young children's regulation needs while also modeling for young children on how they can regulate their intense emotions.

The following is an example of a self-awareness journal from a toddler teacher, Suriya, where she describes:

- A triggering experience she had while caring for children;
- The feelings and thoughts she had in response to the situation;
- Personal beliefs that influenced her feeling/reaction to the situation;
- The intensity of her reaction on a scale from zero to ten (ten = highest intensity);
- The behaviors/actions she took in response to her internal thoughts and feelings;
- Whether she developed self-awareness that the experience was triggering for her before, during, or after the situation/interaction occurred;

- Coping skills and strategies she used to manage her emotions;
- How she would respond/cope differently next time.

Example of a Self-awareness Journal Entry

Suriya: Assistant Teacher	Date: May 20, 2017
Triggering situation: What happened?	I was playing with two children outside when suddenly they started arguing. One child took a toy out of the other child's hand. Both children started to hit each other. One child started to cry.
Identify your feelings and thoughts	I felt stress and I did not know how to handle the situation. My first reaction was to raise my voice and physically stop the children from hitting. My second reaction was to think about not saying or doing the wrong thing.
What beliefs explain what you were feeling?	I don't like to be in conflict situations. I don't know how to handle my own personal conflicts. I don't like not knowing how to approach a problem. I don't cope with stress very well.
Intensity scale 0–10	8
How were feelings expressed in actions/ behaviors?	Physically, my face turned red and my hands were sweaty. I felt tense and aware of my own body language and frustration. I wanted to raise my voice to take control of the situation.
Did you realize before, during, or after that the situation was triggering?	During and after.
Coping: What did you do?	I took a deep breath. I discussed the incident with my head teacher about how to support these two children. I thought about what I could have done better and how I could have prevented this from happening. I reflected throughout the day how I could have handled the triggering situation by offering them a toy or supporting the situation before it escalated.
What would you do differently next time?	Approach the children calmly and with confidence. Try to pay more attention to the children's cues and behaviors and regulate them before they get out of control. Regulate my own emotions by pausing and taking deep breaths before talking to the children. Speak respectfully and use firm limits and clear expectations ("we don't hit our friends"). I would encourage and model for the children on how to use their language to ask for the toy and to express concern over hitting our friends.

Trauma-sensitive teachers strive to increase their self-awareness. The more self-awareness they develop, the greater ability they have to attune to the internal world of the children in their care. Supporting children to become aware of how they are feeling and guiding them to effectively communicate their needs begins with adults learning how to "tune in" to their own feelings and strengthening their ability to notice these feelings but not react to them.

Inquiry: Asking Questions to Strengthen Teachers' Self-Regulation and Attunement with Young Children

When teachers engage in **inquiry**, they learn to ask questions about their daily practice in order to become more responsive and attuned to each individual child (Cochran-Smith & Lytle, 2009). Asking questions allows teachers to create a "pause" in their teaching practice that helps them to purposely slow down, strengthen their self-awareness, and think about, instead of act upon, their internal thoughts, feelings, and reactions. Through pausing, teachers learn to ask questions instead of making assumptions or coming to premature conclusions about children's behavior.

Using inquiry, teachers develop a habit to stop and wonder, "***What is this a case of?***" in order to explore the meaning of a child's emotions and/or behaviors so they can begin to consider what a child is communicating to them about what they need and how they feel. A teacher noticing a child beginning to scream across the room might pause for a moment and ask herself, "What is Adam's screaming and kicking communicating to me about how he is feeling and what he needs from me right now? How is his screaming making me feel inside? What do I need to do to remain emotionally available to support him and guide him back to self-regulated behavior?"

WHAT IS THIS A CASE OF? BECOMING A TRAUMA-SENSITIVE TEACHER BY USING INQUIRY

Using inquiry, trauma-sensitive early childhood teachers develop a habit to stop and wonder, "***What is this a case of?***" in order to explore the meaning of a child's emotions and/or behaviors. They understand that children's stress-related behaviors may require some detective work before teachers can identify what children are communicating about how they feel and what they need. Below is an example highlighting how Pam, a child care provider working in a private center, used inquiry to carefully attune to a young three-year-old girl named Paloma who became very distressed by a small hole in her shoe. Through mindful listening to Paloma and asking herself some questions (is this about the tiny hole in her shoe or something else? What is Paloma trying to communicate to me about what is worrying her?), Pam was able to identify Paloma's concerns. Although Paloma was crying about a small hole in her shoe, Pam discovered that the real worry was linked with the relational trauma Paloma experienced as a baby when she lost three primary caregivers before she was six months old.

January 3, 2015
Pam, a child care provider using inquiry to attune to three-year-old Paloma

Paloma began to cry today about a teeny tiny hole in the bottom of her shoe. She cried and cried and cried. I could not figure out what was worrying her and decided it was important not to assume I knew but instead, I asked myself a question, "what is this a case of? What is Paloma trying to tell me about how she feels and what is worrying her?" I said to Paloma, "You seem so sad about your shoe. Tell me what has you so worried about this tiny hole." She said, "I'm sad. I need new shoes. It has a hole. There is a hole in the bottom." I responded, "You can keep these shoes with the little hole. They don't have to go away Paloma. I wonder if you are worried about your shoes going away. Are you thinking about losing your shoes?" Paloma burst into tears. I thought to myself, she might be worried about losing things that she loves (I knew she loved her shoes), an experience that stems from losing a parent when she was young. She has traumatic stress reactions whenever she worries about losing people or things she cares about. I decided to acknowledge the fear she may have and to reassure her that she was safe. I said, "Paloma, when you were a little baby some people you loved went away and that made you very sad. I wonder if you are worried that other things you love are going to go away too? You are safe here and the teachers are going to take care of you. Your teachers aren't going to go away. Your family is not going away. The things you love … your toys, your clothes, your shoes … these things won't be taken away from you unless you say you are ready to share them with someone else." As I said these words to Paloma, her racing heart immediately began to calm down and her tears slowly stopped running down her face. She turned to me and said, "I don't want my shoe to go away. I don't want my family to go away." Asking a question, "What is this a case of?" allowed me to discover the connection between Paloma's early loss of her birth mother

and two foster mothers and her continuing fears of losing toys and posses-
sions she loves.

Without using inquiry, teachers may miss moments like these and not
"hear" the story a child is telling them about how they feel and what they
need to feel safe again.

Inquiry-based caregiving practice strengthens a teacher's **interactive regulatory capacities**. Through inquiry—asking questions about their own
behavior and emotions and their reactions to challenging interactions with
children—teachers can learn to use their own calm and regulated behavior
to guide children who are triggered back to regulation; modeling for them
how they can manage their intense emotions.

Interactive Regulatory Capacities. The teacher regulates her own emotional processes to match the child's emotions. Stern (1985) named this
interactive regulatory process affect attunement. The teacher's nonverbal
social signals of eye contact, facial expression, tone of voice, and body gestures are examples of affect attunement and communication.

**The power of inquiry: Creating a momentary pause to ask a question can
help teachers to**:

- **Gain self-awareness**: Learning to notice how they are feeling in a
  moment. After a preschool teacher observes one child kicking down
  another child's block structure, she "tunes in" to ask a question about
  how she is feeling (what do I notice in my body right now?) while she
  begins to walk over to the block area. She acknowledges her feelings and
  thinks to herself, "I notice that my heart is beating fast and I am feeling
  very angry and ready to explode and yell across the room. Why am I
  having such a strong reaction?"
- **Interrupt reactive behavior and maintain self-regulation**: Learning to
  acknowledge how they are feeling without acting out those feelings. The
  preschool teacher notices that she is really angry (her face is hot and her
  heart is racing) and wants to yell. While she acknowledges this feeling,

she does not act on it. Instead, she asks herself, "What can I do to calm myself down at this moment?" She decides to take five deep breaths to calm her stress response system.

- **Increase empathy for a child**: Learning to understand that all behavior has meaning. Pausing and asking questions can help teachers learn to observe children more carefully and try to understand the stories they are communicating through their behavior, through play, through their art and verbal and nonverbal expressions. Inquiry supports teachers to challenge their deficit assumptions or premature judgments about a child. For example, the preschool teacher might ask herself, "What is the meaning of this child's choice to knock down his friend's block structure? What is he thinking and feeling right now? What type of support does he need?"

- **Respond in a caring, trauma-sensitive, and effective manner**: Learning to ask for help if needed. After observing a child scratch and hit another child, the preschool teacher, noticing her internal reaction of anger and a desire to yell at the child, could ask her assistant teacher to step in for a few minutes while she took some deep breaths to avoid being reactive or hurtful toward others. She could also learn to pause for a moment and ask herself, "what are each of these children feelings? What do they need from me to feel safe in this moment? What new skills do I need to teach them?"

The act of pausing and questioning are micro-moments that allow a teacher to develop more empathy and attunement with children by monitoring their tone of voice, the words they use and the nonverbal behavior they display. This happens when teachers strengthen their self-awareness and interrupt their reactivity.

Micro-moments to pause and wonder are internal and very quick (split second reactions). Using inquiry in this manner does not disrupt a teacher from protecting children and keeping their classrooms safe. Asking questions becomes part of a teacher's disposition or stance in working with children and supports them to create a safer less reactive classroom environment for adults and for children.

Using self-reflection, self-awareness, and inquiry, teachers learn to manage the emotional intensity and complexity of working with children who have experienced trauma. By learning to pause and develop self-awareness about their personal triggers and internal stressors, teachers can become less reactive and increase their ability to respond with more empathy and attunement.

WHAT DOES IT LOOK LIKE TO USE SELF-REFLECTION AND INQUIRY IN TEACHING PRACTICE?

- **Adult Tunes INward First**:

Step 1: Reflective questions to ask yourself in order to gain perspective of how you are feeling in the moment.

- What do I feel and where do I feel it in my body?
- How big are my emotions?
- Am I regulated or reactive right now?

If you identify that you are dysregulated/reactive and have big intense emotions, then there is a need to pause and go to step 2.

Step 2: Regulation of intense emotions—When our buttons are pushed and emotions are heated, it is important to use healthy strategies to support the regulation of your emotions in order to move back into a more optimal state before progressing to step 3.

Here are some examples of behaviors that teachers can use to help themselves regulate:

- Breathing
- Listening to music
- Going for a walk
- Writing in a journal
- Talking to a co-worker, friend, or trusted confidant
- Asking for help

Can you think of other healthy strategies you use?

Once your body and emotions are calm, you can access the part of your brain called the pre-frontal cortex, which is responsible for logic, reasoning, and problem-solving. When emotions are intense and you are feeling out of control, this part of your brain cannot be accessed.

- **Adult tunes OUTward Next**

Step 3: Responding to the child with trauma-sensitive strategies and supports. Tuning outward to support the child comes after the adult is regulated and able to access the thinking part of their brain to map a responsive and sensitive solution to the challenge the child is experiencing. The adult can ask themselves the following reflective questions:

- How can I understand you (the child) better?
- What is your behavior communicating to me?
- What might have triggered your stress response system?
- How can I help you feel safe right now in this moment?
- How can I help you regulate your big emotions?

Using self-reflection and inquiry to strengthen self-awareness support teachers to strengthen their capacity for **self-regulation**. Self-regulation is just another term for self-calming strategies. Adult self-regulation involves the ability to find strategies or techniques to manage intense emotions BEFORE reacting or jumping to conclusions. When the right side of the brain is flooded with intense emotions, there is a greater chance of making impulsive decisions, hurting others, ourselves or property, and reacting to the intensity of how we feel versus thinking through how to make the best choices. Self-regulation can help teachers learn to manage their emotions and find various paths to calmness. When we are calm, the left side of our brain can start to function properly and help us think of better solutions.

Self-Regulation in Action

A kindergarten teacher finds himself escalated by a certain child's behavior in his classroom. Every time the child takes toys away from others, this teacher finds himself reacting strongly by making threats to call the child's parents, immediately taking privileges away, or by taking toys out of her hands just to show her "how it feels." These are reactive responses triggered from an emotional response in the teacher's lower brainstem. However, when self-regulated, this teacher is able to identify how intense he feels after observing his student's behavior. He may ask another teacher to take the lead in order to provide an opportunity for him to step back and wait until he calms down emotionally. After he calms down, he will be better able to objectively analyze the situation and perhaps identify what the child is communicating through this behavior. Now that he is calm and leveraging the left side of his brain, he realizes that his student has very limited vocabulary, does not really know how to ask for a toy with words, and really struggles to enter play with other children. With this new level of understanding, the teacher can better attune to this child and support her to develop some important new social skills instead of punishing her for acting out.

Adult Self-Regulation Facilitates Child Regulation

Young children have immature and underdeveloped brains. In fact, their brains continue to develop and evolve up to the age of 25. It is unrealistic to expect a young child to handle emotionally stressful situations calmly. If a child also has a history of trauma in their short life, it may be even harder for them to develop self-regulation skills. An adult who is regulated will have the energy necessary to support the regulation of the children they work with.

A Best Practice In Supporting Children's Self-Regulation Is If Their Adult Caregiver Is Calm And Self-Regulated

Children pick up on the adult's energy, especially anxiety, distress, or disappointment. Children who are sensitive may be impacted even more, and those who have experienced trauma are wired to continuously scan for danger around them. They develop this extra sensitivity in order to survive in highly stressful situations. Subsequently, a child impacted by trauma may perceive their teacher's escalated emotional state as dangerous, even if it is not. This is why one of the most important trauma-sensitive strategies in early childhood is for adults to stay calm, regulated, and to manage their internal emotional state. This will support children to transition to a calm state as well. Have you ever heard the saying that "yawning is contagious?" The same is true with self-regulation: **"calmness" is contagious when working with children.**

Teachers Need Support Too: The Importance of Parallel Process

*D*o unto others as you would have others do unto others.

(Jeree Pawl, 1995)

This quote highlights the importance of **parallel process** (Stroud, 2010), an understanding that the quality of relationships and communication between a supervisor and her staff can significantly affect the manner in which her teachers interact with the children and families in their care. Additionally, the way that teachers care for children can also influence how parents and families relate to their children (Heffron & Murch, 2010, p. 9). For example, if supervisors are critical, controlling, and punishment-oriented with their staff, teachers are likely to repeat these patterns in their interactions with children and families. Or, if supervisors build caring, attuned, and supportive relationships with staff, they are modeling the types of behaviors that are optimal for teachers to use in their interactions with children. If supervisors emphasize teachers' strengths and resiliencies, their staff will learn to do the same. Parallel process reminds us that the climate supervisors create in their interactions with the teachers they supervise can directly trickle down to the children and families.

Parallel process is rooted in self-reflection aimed at building self-awareness:

> *Providers who remain aware of their personal triggers and internal stressors, and who actively use self-care techniques, are more emotionally available to support families ... parents with a deeper understanding of their stress responses, personal triggers and parenting history can be less reactive and more emotionally available to their child ... and supervisors also need to reflect on their internal processes and develop self-understanding ... as knowing oneself is vital in the relationships one develops.*
>
> *(Stroud, 2010, pp. 47–48)*

If we want teachers to use self-reflection and inquiry to strengthen their self-awareness, they need to see these same processes being used and valued by their supervisors. They also need to have support to explore the complex feelings that arise in their work with young children, especially children who are trauma-impacted. Specifically:

Teachers need the support of a caring supervisor to buffer the stress they endure on a daily basis caring for children impacted by trauma.

Carving out space and time to think and reflect by themselves or with their colleagues and/or supervisor, is at the top of most teachers' wish list for professional learning. Trauma-informed early learning programs understand the importance of parallel process. In the programs, supervisors value support and practice self-reflection and inquiry in order to strengthen their self-awareness while coaching and supporting their teachers to engage in the same processes.

Parallel Process: The way we treat and interact with adults is the way they will be with children. The parallel process is reflected in the classroom by how you treat and interact with your supervisor, co-workers, and other adults that you work with. Essentially, how we treat others is how they will treat the children, and likewise, how you are treated is most likely how you will treat the children. Interactions with others create an energy within the workplace. When on the receiving end of kindness, we are in a better space to be kind and caring with the children. When on the receiving end of negativity, we will be more likely to act more reactive or treat children in a punitive or punishing way. The better you feel, the more energy you have to give to those around you. Being in an environment where you and your coworkers are kind and compassionate will create a more positive outcome for the children.

Here is a simple visual to illustrate this concept of **parallel process** where the child's behavior parallels like a mirror the emotional state of the adult caregiver.

If a child senses anger in an adult, then the child will have a fear response.

If a child senses safety with an adult, then this will reduce their fear response.

This chart illustrates examples of the parallel process: How an adult interacts with a child directly affects the child's internal state of regulation.

Adult feeling state	Adult reaction	Child feeling	Child reaction
Angry/on edge/ hyper-aroused	Punitive and stern with the child	Scared	Runs away and hides
Shut down/ frustrated/ hypo-aroused	Ignoring child	Agitated/feels alone	Hits another child
Calm/restored/ energized	Attunes to child, provides support, hears how they feel	Calm/it will be okay/feels safe	Back to focusing and playing with others

Remember

- When you are present, in the moment listening to another adult, tuning in to their emotions and story, it is regulating and calming. Adults being supportive to each other when they are under stress is a calming and regulating strategy.
- The right side of your brain houses the emotions and wants to tell the story and be heard in order to regulate and then allow for the left brain to be ready to map a plan/solution to a problem that does not hurt others, yourself, or property.
- When someone has shared their story (how they feel and what happened) and they feel regulated, calm, and like themselves again, it will be easier for them to engage in trauma-sensitive interactions with children.
- The way you are with other adults is the way you want them to be with children.

Reflective Questions

- Consider a time when you were so upset by something you could not think clearly. When you experienced this and your emotions were escalated, what sensations happened in your body? What feelings did you have? How were you with the children or other adults around you?
- Now think of a time someone really listened to and engaged with you when you had a big problem. Did their listening help? Why and how did it help? Did you feel more regulated? Did you calm down more easily?
- How often do you tune inward and think about what you feel and what you need? How can your own self-regulation and calming strategies help the children you care for?
- Think of a day when you were working with the children and you were not in a good place emotionally. Did you notice how the children responded differently to you when you were short-tempered or more irritated compared with when you are calm?
- The same may be true for you and your supervisor. If your supervisor comes in to talk to you rushed, short-tempered, controlling, critical, or in a bad mood, how does that make **you** feel inside? When your supervisor comes in to talk with you and she is calm, supportive, and listens to what you are saying, how does that change how you feel inside?

Trauma-Informed Teachers and Supervisors Use Self-Reflection and Inquiry to Strengthen Their Self-Awareness and Improve Their Self-Regulation

Engaging in self-reflection and asking questions instead of making assumptions will help early childhood professionals to:

- Build awareness about how they feel (their internal world);
- Learn to manage and calm their strong emotions;
- Increase their empathy for children's internal emotional worlds and the meaning of children's behavior;
- Engage their thinking brain (pre-frontal cortex) to identify solutions that are not reactive and harmful, but will provide quality interventions that can support healing from trauma and building resiliency;
- Strengthen their self-care and prevent them from experiencing burnout.

What Does Trauma-Sensitive Teaching Look Like? Does It Really Make a Difference?

Below is a scenario that includes handling a challenging situation in two different ways with two different outcomes:

- The first scenario shows a teacher and her assistant acting reactively and in a way that triggers the children and makes the situation worse.
- The second scenario describes the same situation where both adults use trauma-sensitive strategies to help the children feel safe, maintain their optimal levels of arousal and self-regulation, and gently guide them to participate in social interactions with their teachers and peers.

Scenario #1: Responding WITHOUT a Trauma-Sensitive Approach

Ms. Jarissa is a preschool teacher at Pacific Central Child Development Center. She is feeling particularly stressed today. Besides having some personal health issues that require an appointment outside of work, she just received a call from her son's school and learned that he is struggling academically. Back in her preschool classroom, she has two children with challenging behaviors that take much of her time and attention. The children are aggressive, can disrupt the learning environment, have hurt other children, and now several parents of other students are starting to complain that her classroom is not safe.

Right now, Ms. Jarissa is getting ready for an activity that she wants to do in small groups after circle time. She is teaching about rainbows, their colors and how rainbows are created because the children saw one yesterday while they were playing in the play yard. After their conversation together, she plans to guide the children to paint rainbows in small groups. She rings the chime to signal to the children to come and participate on the rug for circle time. All come to the rug except the two children, Alegna and Jeremy, the two children she describes as having challenging behaviors. Ms. Jarissa says sternly, "Alegna and Jeremy, you know you are not allowed to play with other things during circle, you need to come join us!" She then says to her teaching assistant, Monika, "please tell them to join us in circle."

Jeremy remained absorbed building a block tower in the block area. Alegna, on the other hand, started to throw objects into the circle area toward the other children. Monika responded to Alegna in an angry voice, "Look at all the other good children listening, you need to listen too!" Next Monika walked over to Jeremy and touched him on his shoulder. He did not turn or respond. Monika then took his hand and tried to lead him to the circle. Jeremy fell to the floor and began screaming. Both children's stress response systems have been activated, they are now outside of their optimal state of regulation and they are working from their reactive brains. Ms. Jarisssa has to interrupt what she is doing to come over and help Monika. Alegna is trying to throw objects at other children and begins to pick up the chairs and attempts to throw them as well. Jeremy is curled in a ball rocking back and forth crying and saying repeatedly to himself, "You are bad, you are stupid, you are bad, you are stupid."

Scenario #2: Responding WITH a Trauma-Sensitive Approach

The same classroom scenario could look very different if Ms. Jarissa and her assistant, Monika used trauma-informed practices including self-reflection and inquiry in their response to Alegna and Jeremy when they do not follow the others to circle time.

When they do not arrive for circle, Ms. Jarissa asks Monika to shadow Alegna and Jeremy and help support them to come join the group. Ms. Jarissa says, "Alegna and Jeremy, we really care about you and hope you can think about joining all of us for circle time. When you are ready, I am here to support you and go with you to circle." Ms. Jarissa then says to Monika (loud enough for the children to hear), "If Jeremy and Alegna are not ready, they can choose to play with something else, we will miss them but want them to feel safe and to decide on their own when they are ready to join us." Ms. Jarissa asked Monika to stay near both children and provide reassuring remarks and comments that help them feel supported and safe.

Jeremy stayed quietly absorbed building a block tower in the block area. Alegna played in the dramatic play area with the dolls. Monika said to Alegna in a soft and kind voice, "you are playing with the baby dolls and keeping them safe." She then went over to Jeremy and commented on what a tall tower he was building. Jeremy did not appear to listen or be responsive to her comment. He did keep looking over at the circle. Both children were not triggered and were in their optimal state of regulation. Jeremy then looked over at Monika and said, "Can you sit with me in circle?" Monika replied, "yes" and walked over with him to the circle. Jeremy decided to sit right outside but near the circle while holding Monika's hand. Alegna continued playing the rest of circle time alone with the dolls.

Reflect on the scenarios above:

- What were the triggers for Ms. Jarissa?
- What were the triggers for Alegna? Jeremy?
- How did Ms. Jarissa support each child individually and uniquely to feel safe and to stay in their zone of optimal regulation?
- What trauma-sensitive strategies did Ms. Jarissa and Monika use to provide support to Alegna? Jeremy?

Identifying Children's Strengths

Teachers need to find strengths in all children and families. This will take intention and commitment with many children who are impacted by trauma as their challenging and complex behavior could become the dominating factor that defines the child in a teacher's eyes. Statman-Weil (2018) describes how she supports teachers who are struggling with a child's

challenging behavior to maintain a strengths-based view of the "whole child."
She explains:

> *When I sit down to work with teachers who are struggling with a child, the first thing I want to know is, what does that child do well? I want to know what do teachers* **love** *about the child? Where and how are they able to connect with this child? What do they find inspiring about the child? Because from there, we can find ways to build on this child's strengths.*

Challenging behavior does not occur 24 hours a day. Although the challenging behavior can be so intensive and disruptive that to a teacher it may feel like "all the time." One important strategy is to observe when the challenging behavior is *not* occurring as this will help teachers learn about the strengths, needs, and resilience of a child.

Let's imagine a young preschool child Marta whose teacher, Betsy, describes a child who is regularly hitting other children in the classroom and a child who has difficulties playing with her peers without pushing, hitting, kicking, or pulling their hair. When Betsy was asked to document when these behaviors typically occur, she learned that they were most frequent during free play time. When Marta experienced a lack of structure and needed to enter the ongoing play of her peers, she struggled and the challenging behaviors emerged. However, through systematic observation and documentation, Betsy discovered that Marta's challenging behaviors did not occur during more structured times in the schedule that included clear instructions, clear expectations, and a defined activity. Betsy reported, "Marta does really well during small group activities because she sits in a defined space with a teacher and a few children and she follows the instructions and knows exactly what to do." Through this process, Betsy learned important information about Marta's strengths and capacities. She discovered that Marta does better with clear routines, structured-activities, and defined expectations. She also learned that free play time is triggering for Marta. Knowing Marta's strengths allows Betsy to support her more effectively in the classroom. She can adapt the classroom environment to reduce triggers (e.g., work with Marta to structure her free play time) and create the conditions for Marta to be successful (predictability, adult guidance, reduction of uncertainty).

Early learning environments that use children's questions, discoveries, and interests to inform the curriculum build in opportunities for children and their teachers to learn about children's strengths, their knowledge, and their capacities. Such child-centered environments also communicate to children that they can have agency (i.e., a sense of control) in their own learning process. Reinforcing to children that they have strengths and skills *and* that they have choice/control in what happens to them in the classroom are trauma-sensitive supports for young children. This is especially important for young children who live in families with adults who are not responsive to their individual interests and needs. These children will need lots of practice in learning that their ideas, their interests, and their needs matter. For their own survival, they may have learned not to express their interests and needs, and therefore, may struggle to make choices when offered opportunities to do so. Caring and patient teachers can start with small choices (e.g., do you want a blue crayon or a green crayon to draw your picture?) to help children develop confidence in making choices and expressing their needs in the classroom.

Strengths-based early childhood programs communicate to children that learning to regulate their emotions and behavior is a long-term process that requires practice, patience, and persistence. It is important that early childhood teachers normalize (that is, remove the stigma) from learning to regulate emotions and behavior. Teachers can support children by:

- **Acknowledging that it takes a long time to learn how to manage big feelings**. Reinforcing that adults are still learning how to do this!
- **Validating children's progress** (e.g., Tony, you are waiting patiently for your turn. It's hard work to wait your turn. Let's sing the ABC song while you wait. The time will go faster.)
- **Communicating that breakdowns happen and this is a normal part of the learning process**. When children struggle to regulate their emotions and/or behavior, teachers should not over-emphasize the breakdown. Instead, they can communicate that this is normal and *all children and adults need lots and lots of practice to learn to manage their big feelings*. Teachers can remind children that each day provides a fresh opportunity for them to keep practicing these new skills and that it is normal to take a long time to learn these skills: "You are still learning to take deep breaths when you feel angry inside your body." "We all need to practice, practice, practice. Even adults." "Tomorrow is a new day and we will keep practicing." "Let's try again." When adults communicate to children that learning to self-regulate is a normal part of growing up, children who struggle with regulating their emotions and behavior—often the case for children impacted by trauma—are less likely to begin to define themselves as "bad" and to internalize feelings of shame and self-doubt when they have self-regulation breakdowns.

This does not mean that all behavior—especially harmful behavior—is allowed in the classroom. Instead, it means that the teacher reinforces to a child who is struggling that:

- She understands that the child's behaviors represent significant underlying feelings and needs and that the child's behavior represents her best attempts to keep herself safe.

- She knows that the child may not currently have the skills and ability to express her feelings in a more appropriate manner.
- She can see "beyond" the child's behaviors and understands that her responsibility as the child's teacher is to support this child to develop and practice the social and emotional skills they need to succeed in her classroom.

Making Children and Families Visible Through Culturally Responsive Practice

The young child's capacity to experience, express and regulate emotions, form close and secure relationships, and explore the environment and learn. All of these capacities will be best accomplished within the context of the caregiving environment that includes family, community, and cultural expectations for young children. Developing these capacities is synonymous with healthy social and emotional development.

(Zero to Three, 2001)

In order for children to feel a sense of safety and protection, they need to be in early learning environments that value diversity and communicate messages of mutual respect and belonging. Supporting children and families to feel that they are an important part of the community is the central goal of culturally responsive early childhood practice that begins with teachers who acknowledge that cultural values, traditions, and learning styles have immediate influences on caregiving, teaching, and children's learning and development.

Culturally responsive teaching is more than including multicultural content into the classroom (Gay, 2010). Teachers understand that to support a child and family to feel a strong sense of belonging, they (the teachers) have a responsibility to learn deeply about the individual children and families they are teaching so they can use this information to help each and every child feel visible, valued, and represented in the classroom community so they hear on a daily basis that who they are matters to the adults around them. Culturally responsive teaching in early childhood acknowledges that cultural beliefs and goals for children's learning and development vary significantly across different racial, ethnic, cultural, and community contexts (Rogoff, 2003). Culturally responsive teachers communicate to children and their families that they believe diversity—in family constellation, immigration history, languages spoken in the home, cultural routines, goals for children's learning and development—is an asset for their classroom community. They also communicate that *all* children—especially those in nondominant groups whose cultural ways of thinking, talking, and behaving are different from the dominant culture norms—are capable learners (Villegas & Lucas, 2007, p. 31). Teachers who create culturally responsive early learning environments strive to create opportunities for children and their families to have their voices and input honored (informing the development of the curriculum, contributing to the environment, creating opportunities to learn about families' expectations, strengths, concerns, and dreams for their child, etc.; Ladson-Billings, 2009).

The infant mental health field created a shared set of guidelines for implementing culturally responsive practice that can be useful for teachers striving to create programs that respect and equitably serve all children in their communities (Seymour St. John, Tomas, & Noroña, 2012). Although written for infant-toddler caregivers, the following are examples of several of these principles adapted for use for all early childhood programs:

- **Self-awareness leads to better services for families**: Educators should reflect on their own culture, personal values, and beliefs, and on the impact racism, classism, sexism, ableism, homophobia, xenophobia, and other systems of oppression have had on their lives in order to provide diversity-informed, culturally attuned, services on behalf of young children and their families.
- **Recognize and respect nondominant bodies of knowledge**: Teachers must recognize nondominant ways of knowing, nondominant bodies of knowledge, sources of strength, and routes to healing within diverse families and communities.
- **Honor diverse family structures**: Families define who they are comprised of and how they are structured; no particular family constellation or organization is inherently optimal compared with any other. Recognize and strive to counter the historical bias toward idealizing (and conversely blaming) biological mothers as primary caregivers while overlooking the critical child-rearing contributions of other parents and caregivers including fathers, second mothers, foster parents, kin and felt family, early care and educational providers, and others.
- **Understand that language can be used to hurt or heal**: Recognize the power of language to divide or connect, denigrate or celebrate, hurt or heal. Teachers should strive to use language (including "body language," imagery, and other modes of nonverbal communication) in ways that most inclusively supports young children and their families, caregivers, and communities.
- **Support families in their preferred language**: Families are best supported in facilitating their children's development and mental health when services are available in their native languages.
- **Make space and open pathways for diverse professionals**: The early childhood workforce will be most dynamic and effective when culturally diverse individuals have access to a wide range of roles, disciplines, and modes of practice and influence (Ghosh Ippen, Noroña, & Thomas, 2012).

Families are critical to the educational experience and success of young children and building partnerships with families is an important foundation of culturally responsive practice. However, it is critical that teachers understand that parents and caregivers may also be trauma survivors and they may express their own fight, flight, and freeze survival responses in their interactions with teachers. It is important that teachers respond to any resistance or lack of engagement from parents with empathy, patience, and a lack of judgment. Teachers need to be prepared that it may take additional time to build trust with parents and families as the families own histories and lived experiences may lead them to struggle to build trust in relationships with other adults.

Reciprocity, trust, honesty, respect, and a sensitivity should also be the basis of a trauma-informed culturally responsive relationship with families. Culturally responsive practice with families begins with authentic listening, asking questions to learn from them, and having a genuine belief that all families have strengths and capacities that teachers can honor and integrate into their classrooms.

The Importance of Predictable Schedules and Routines

Consistent and predictable routines and schedules promote children's sense of safety as children feel less anxious when they know what to expect. It is helpful for teachers to create a daily visual schedule with the children and have it visible in the classroom for them to see. The schedule could include photos that the children take and that embed daily activities (see more in the "Visual Schedules" section). Using photos of the children and including children in developing the visual schedule will increase their interest, involvement and responsiveness to the schedule.

What Is the Difference Between a SCHEDULE and a ROUTINE?

Predictable schedule: Main activities completed in the classroom every day. Keeping the same predictable schedule every day with visual or auditory cues for each transition can help children. For children who become easily dysregulated, having a predictable schedule and limiting changes in the schedule as much as possible, can help create a sense of safety and reduce triggers in their environment. When changes are needed in the daily schedule, teachers should provide children with advance notice whenever possible with additional emotional support throughout the time of change. Using a visual schedule can help reduce children's triggers by providing support for children who are new to a program or when children feel anxiety. It is helpful if visual schedules are accessible at children's eye level and if they include photos for each activity that occurs during the day (e.g., arrival, circle time, free play, reading, small group activity, lunch, outdoor play, departure). Throughout the day, children can be guided to see what comes next on the visual schedule, which reduces uncertainty and helps them feel calm and safe.

Routines: The small steps followed in sequence associated with each activity included on the daily schedule. Establishing a routine for every activity with a sequence of tasks helps children understand what to expect during each event that occurs in the classroom. An example of one routine: clean-up time ⟶ transition ⟶ outdoor play. Understanding expectations can reduce anxiety and challenges associated with routines. When establishing a routine for each activity, it is wise to think of it as a story with a beginning, middle, and an end.

THE STORY OF ONE CLEAN-UP ROUTINE

Beginning: Teacher rings the chimes, begins to sing the clean-up song, and announces it is clean-up time. The auditory sound of the chime, verbal announcement, and song are cues for the children that it is clean-up time, which over time, they learn as the "clean-up routine."

Middle: Teachers walk around acknowledging children who are cleaning up and indicating how helpful they are. Teacher provides additional supports to children who may not respond to the beginning cue (chimes). She may get down to the child's level and provide a verbal cue ("it's clean-up time"), teach the child how to clean up by modeling and inviting the child to join her, or provide a visual cue showing a particular child who may need more guidance, such as a photo that shows them cleaning up.

End: Letting children know that every day they will go wash their hands and then go to the table for lunchtime after clean up. The teacher transitions the children in small groups or individually to go and wash their hands to avoid having them stand in lines for long periods of time. Additionally, she excuses small groups of children to join her at the hand washing station; a strategy that allows her to engage and support the children and reduce challenging behavior.

Visual Supports as Environmental Mediators

Visual aids improve children's daily transitions, reduce challenging behaviors, and assist children's self-initiated behavior. They do so by acting as **external mediators** to help individual children who need additional support to regulate their emotions or behavior (e.g., a child's placemat is used as an external mediator to facilitate self-initiated behavior of going and sitting at the table). Although teachers commonly use verbal prompts to get children's attention and prepare them for changes or transitions, not all children are responsive to verbal cues. An example of a verbal prompt for a preschool classroom would be "five more minutes" and an example for a toddler classroom may be "yes or no." The combination of visual and verbal cues more reliably focuses children's attention and helps them understand what is expected of them. Visual aids are helpful for all children, but in particular for children whose stress-response systems activate easily as seen with many children with experiences of trauma. Several examples of visual aids are shown below.

Visual Schedules

Visual schedules are one of the most common and helpful visual aids for young children (see Figures 3.1 and 3.2). A visual schedule can be helpful to children that do not respond to verbal prompts or instructions. It may be helpful to children who are new to your program. Additionally, it can help children with challenges or a trauma history to understand what is coming next and to develop a feeling of safety with a predictable routine. A visual schedule may be posted on the wall for all children or individual visual schedules may be

Figure 3.1 Example Classroom Schedule.

www.cainclusion.org/teachingpyramid/.

Figure 3.2 Example Daily Schedule.

www.cainclusion.org/teachingpyramid/.

created for one child. Visual schedules not only help children feel a sense of predictability by understanding what is coming next in their day, visual schedules can also reduce children's anxiety, tantrums, acting out behaviors, misunderstandings and miscommunication, and dependence on verbal prompts (Mesibov, Shea, & Schopler, 2005).

Some tips for making a visual schedule:

- Identify the skill or routine you want to teach.
- Break the skills or routine into small steps.
- Select the visual to convey the task. Using photos of the children will promote more engagement and personalize the visual in a way that is more meaningful than cartoon drawings.
- Teach children how to use it. Introducing it at circle is one helpful way or through a one-on-one conversation for an individual child. Teachers will find that some children will not need to use a visual schedule while others will feel safe and respond well by having this cue to remind them what is coming next throughout their day.

Figure 3.3 Five Minute Sign.

www.cainclusion.org/teachingpyramid/.

- Include a way for a child to show that a particular task is complete. One example is a moveable arrow that can be moved from one task to the next. Another example is the entire photo is removed from the schedule and placed into a "completed" bucket.
- Support the children to use it by referring to it throughout the day. Just placing it on a wall or in the room is not enough. It requires an introduction and active use through the day to make it meaningful for children.

Visual cues such as a five-minute visual photo provide individualized supports during sensitive transition times for children (Figure 3.3). For preschool children, you can teach them how to use the five-minute sign: one to two children can be given the job to go around the room with the sign and make sure each child visually sees it will be five more minutes until clean up. A teacher can also use this for the children individually who, with the visual, will have less anxiety and more success transitioning.

FAMILY ENGAGEMENT STRATEGY

Families can be encouraged to create visual schedules at home as well. It is helpful for teachers to partner with parents to talk about the importance of creating as much predictability in children's routines and schedules in both environments as possible. This will prevent the escalation of children's stress response systems and the release of harmful stress chemicals in their bodies.

This is an example of a visual schedule with activities that a young child would do at home (Figure 3.4).

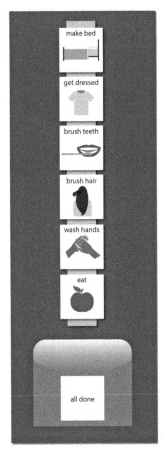

Figure 3.4 Example Visual Schedule.
www.cainclusion.org/teachingpyramid/.

Below is another type of visual schedule that can be made by a teacher and used to support children with their daily schedules and routines and as added support during transitions. There are three steps involved in creating it:

1. Using a medicine/pill organizing box, the teacher uses photos or drawings to represent the different activities in a child's daily schedule or the steps in a particular routine or transition process. These can be attached to the medicine organizing box using Velcro.
2. A puffy ball is placed inside each of the small compartments in the pill box.
3. As the child completes a particular activity, she can take the puff ball out of the pill box and drop it into a separate container (as shown below). Both the medicine box and container can be stored in a child's cubby or left out on a countertop (Figure 3.5).

Timers

A timer such as the one in Figure 3.6 allows teachers to use an external tool to provide visual expectations for a child. Children don't often understand the words "five more minutes" since their concept of time has not fully developed. When they can see the word five minutes and hear it verbally and visually, as well as seeing when the sand drops fully to the bottom, then it is time for a transition. Timers help to reduce challenging behaviors.

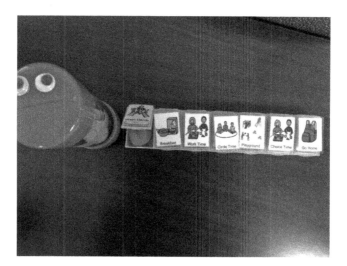

Figure 3.5 Pill Box Visual Schedule.

Karen Van Patten, El Dorado County Office of Education.

Figure 3.6 Timer.

www.cainclusion.org/teachingpyramid/.

"First-Then" Schedules

A **First-Then schedule** is a visual aid to help children with learning delays or behavioral challenges (Figure 3.7). It is a visual strategy that can support children to understand what comes first and then what comes next. Some children need visual aids to support their learning and understanding because instructions with words alone do not work. Teachers can take several photos of the child doing various activities and then laminate and use those photos for a personalized First-Then schedule. Using real photos of the child will help their engagement and involvement. The goal is to pair an activity that the child does not like to do (e.g., washing hands) with an activity the child would like to do (e.g., play outside). FIRST—Wash Hands/ THEN—Play Outside. With the help of these visual supports, the child has support to help him accomplish tasks the teachers would like him to participate in and to engage in the activities he wants to do. In this way, a First-Then schedule acts as an external regulator—supporting the child to regulate his frustration while learning how to delay gratification and wait without dysregulating. First-Then schedules help teachers to increase children's feelings of safety, reduce their anxiety, support visual learners, communicate clear expectations, and reduce challenges and triggers in the classroom.

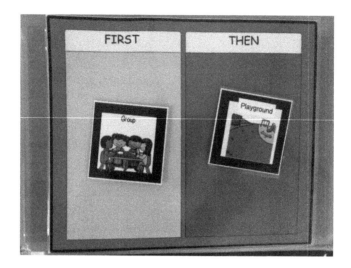

Figure 3.7 First-Then.

Karen Van Patten, El Dorado County Office of Education.

Footprints that Suggest Where to Stand When Waiting in Line

This is an example of creating a visual boundary in a preschool classroom to promote the concept of "personal space." Many children can become frustrated if another child enters their space, often escalating to disruptive interactions. This visually drawn boundary sets a clear expectation as to where children stand during an activity (Figure 3.8).

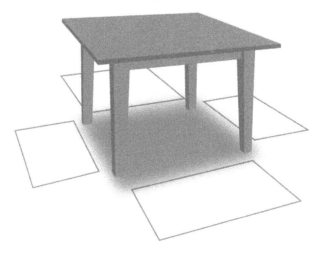

Figure 3.8 Footprints.

http://csefel.vanderbilt.edu.

Trauma-Sensitive Transitions

There are some key elements about transitions that are important to highlight that can minimize challenges in the classroom. First, minimize the number of transitions. Many challenges come during transitions. You can reduce challenges by reducing the number of times a child has to transition throughout the day. Next, think of each transition as a story with a beginning, a middle, and an end. If you write a story for every transition you have throughout the day, create a ritual and routine for each one. Children will begin to know what is expected when the beginning of the routine is introduced. For example, let's imagine a classroom that had a transition from circle time (beginning), to the handwashing (middle) station, to lunch (end). They passed out triangle, square, and circle shapes to the children and dismissed them one grouping at a time (squares first). They left in small groups to the teacher at the handwashing station. The teacher at circle time kept the children engaged until it was time to dismiss the next grouping (circles) while the teacher at the hand washing station was able to engage the children in conversation and humor while providing individual connection and attention. They were released to the third teacher at the lunch tables. This ritual and routine had several strategies. It minimized wait time and long lines and created a ritual for this transition. Children are also expanding their vocabulary and supporting their mathematical thinking by learning to identify different shapes.

Other rituals might be a clean-up song or a game to bring children from outdoors to indoors while calming down their energy level.

Transitions are a sensitive and triggering event throughout the day for children with experiences of trauma. Moving from the known to the unknown can cause an internal feeling of anxiety and loss of control. Adult caregivers must be mindful of these sensitive points and can take steps to mitigate the negative impact and promote a greater sense of safety and control for the child with a trauma history. Although it is important to reduce the number of times a child has to transition throughout the day, classroom changes are inevitable. There are many trauma-sensitive strategies to support children and keep their stress response systems calm during transitions:

- Clean-up songs that signal to children when a transition is coming. It is especially helpful if one song is used for the same transition each day. Repetition creates a sense of safety and predictability.
- Playing a game to support children's transition from outside play back into the classroom.
- Minimize the number of transitions especially unexpected transitions.

- Prepare for transitions with verbal and visual cues paired together to support unexpected changes or transitions.
- Adult one-on-one support during a transition to help the child feel safe moving from one activity to the next.

What do trauma-sensitive transition strategies look like in practice? The following are two vignettes describing preschool boys with experiences of trauma who each struggled with transitions in their preschool classrooms. Their preschool teachers used several trauma-sensitive strategies to support the boys to feel safe and to have some control over what would happen during transition periods at school.

Trauma-Sensitive Strategies to Support Michael's Transition to School

Michael, a three-and-a-half-year-old boy, started preschool shortly after a traumatic experience where he witnessed the police come to his home and arrest his dad. For several months after Michael joined the program, he would not talk. His first month at the center, Michael was found standing in a corner not interacting with the other children. The teachers observed that Michael would not move and would just stand in the corner immobile staring at others. After a month, he became more engaged socially, but still not verbally. His assigned primary caregiver, Ms. Crystal, would play with him every day. They did arts and crafts, played with cars, and built towers with blocks, his favorite activities. Michael would play with Ms. Crystal, but he would still not talk to her or any of his peers. He would point when he needed to communicate with others.

After three months, Michael shifted from playing with Ms. Crystal to beginning to play with some of the other children. When he played with his peers, he appeared happy and socially engaged but he continued to only communicate with them nonverbally. Throughout this time, Michael's mother shared with the teachers that Michael was very verbal at home with an extensive vocabulary. The adults decided that Michael's lack of verbal expression at preschool would only change when he started to feel safe in this new environment. As a result, they began to implement several trauma-sensitive strategies to support Michael to feel that his preschool was caring, safe, and predictable.

One strategy the teachers used to support him was creating a daily routine in the form of a visual scripted story. The book they made had photos and it described the sequence of activities he would participate in throughout the day and a list of things he liked to do while at preschool.

The book helped him know the schedule of the day and when his mother would return to pick him up. The book was made with photos that could be changed daily. It also included photos of Michael that made it very personal and motivating for him to use.

After one year in the program, and because of the patience and trauma-sensitive support the teachers provided to Michael, he began to speak at pre-school, first with his peers and later with the adult caregivers. When Michael left for kindergarten a few months later, Ms. Crystal introduced his new kindergarten teacher, Ms. Moore, to the book. Both teachers agreed to use the book to support Michael's transition to his new kindergarten classroom. Three months after Michael entered kindergarten, Ms. Crystal checked in with Ms. Moore to see how Michael was doing. Ms. Moore explained that his transition was smoother than she expected. Thinking back, she thought this was a result of several transition strategies that helped reduce uncertainty for Michael. Michael's mom arranged for the two of them to visit his new kindergarten classroom so he would get used to the environment and meet his new teacher before his first day of school. Michael played with his mom at his new school for almost an hour while also having an opportunity to talk with Ms. Moore.

After this visit, Ms. Moore sent a letter home to Michael with her photo and a picture of Freddy, the class frog, a stuffed animal that sits in their class. Ms. Moore stated in the letter that Freddy the Frog was eager to get to know Michael. The letter was written from Freddy who shared with Michael that he too was uncomfortable with change, reinforcing that Michael's feelings were normal. Freddy explained he also felt worried the first time he went to kindergarten. Ms. Moore explained in the letter that Freddy would help Michael feel safe and secure when he arrived at his new school and class-room. Ms. Moore also worked with mom to create a scripted story that she could read to Michael for two weeks before he arrived the first day. The scripted story explained his new routine—starting with waking up at home and the sequence of steps through his daily schedule in kindergarten all the way to pick-up time.

These strategies helped to reduce Michael's stress and helped him practice what to expect and to feel more in control of what would happen during his transition to a new school. Using Freddy as a transition object helped Michael feel safe along with visiting the classroom and meeting the teacher. The scripted story was an additional tool that helped Michael to understand the steps in his new classroom routine. Reading the scripted story over and over helped reduce his anxiety and prepared him to feel safe and secure. Transitions are sensitive points for all children. Transition strategies that reduce uncertainty and create predictability and a sense of control are essential for children with a history of trauma.

The following are some questions to guide your reflection on Michael and the trauma-sensitive strategies his teachers could use to support him:

- **What stress response do you observe with Michael (fight, flight, freeze)?**

  Michael was in the FREEZE response when he first entered the preschool. He would stand frozen and stare into space. He had almost no interactions or engagement with teachers or children. At home however, mom reports that he did not have these same responses.

- **What stress behaviors do you observe when Michael is triggered?**

  He was shut down, frozen, and stared into space.

- **What trauma-sensitive strategies did the teachers use that were helpful to Michael?**

  They did not pressure him to talk. They used hand gestures to help him communicate what he needed. They played with him to build a relationship. Then they created a visual schedule to help him feel safe, know what to expect, and to have a predictable routine. This helped him begin to expand from not talking to beginning to talk with peers and teachers. They used the scripted story and worked with his future kindergarten teacher to recreate it to support his transition to his new school. Also, the kindergarten teacher used Freddy the Frog as a transition object, she introduced herself, they visited the classroom, and he was able to become familiar with the environment, teacher, and routine before arriving the first day of school.

- **What adult reactions would not be helpful?**

  Pressuring him to talk and engage would have caused more anxiety for Michael.

  Pushing him to participate and make friends would have also caused him stress.

Trauma-Sensitive Strategies to Support Miguel's Transition from Home to Preschool

Miguel is a 4-year-old male child who lives with his two mothers who adopted him from foster care when he was 18 months of age after he was removed at age 16 months due to a history of neglect. He was reported by an anonymous caller who saw him sitting alone on the front porch with the door ajar and no visible caregivers. It was reported that, "The child was crying and looked unclean and scared." When the police arrived, they found Miguel crying with only a diaper that had not been changed in a few days and he was emaciated. It was unclear if he suffered any other abuse and stayed three days in the hospital for medical examinations. He had a two-month temporary placement until he was adopted by Charise and Melody. Charise stayed home the first year to care for Miguel. He was enrolled at Paraiso Child Development Center at age three years and has been there one year. Both mothers describe him as having minor challenges at home. They state he sometimes shows signs of neediness and is clingy. However, they have a regular home routine that includes a predictable schedule, minimal transitions, and few guests to reduce Miguel's anxiety. They are both calm at home and when he cries or becomes dysregulated, it is easy to hold him until he calms.

The teachers on the other hand have a different experience of Miguel. Transitions from either mom to school are very challenging because he typically cries for at least an hour after they leave. During the day, when other adults come into the classroom to sub or visit, Miguel withdraws and hides in the corner for several hours. The teachers report that they are busy and often leave him alone until he is ready to join his peers. They describe nap time as the most challenging because Miguel will not nap and needs to be with a teacher full time.

Also, the normal routine has changed recently and the teachers have observed Miguel shutting down, not engaging, and staring into space in a corner of the classroom. At other times, he responds with tears to loud and unexpected noises or movement, closing his eyes and covering his ears. When the teachers spend individual time with him, he responds and does better.

Miguel's teachers describe the following challenges:

- Cries for at least an hour when mothers leave
- Pouty and whiney throughout the day
- Withdraws from other children
- Plays mostly by himself
- When there is a sub or guest in the classroom, he clings to the adult teacher he knows well
- Difficulty with transitions and change, especially during nap time
- Stares into space for long periods of time
- Stays away from table, group time, circle time, or other activities with more than one child
- Shuts down, withdraws, hides, or closes eyes

Miguel's teachers and parents both describe his strengths commonly to be:

- Friendly and gentle
- Not aggressive
- Attuned to how others are feeling
- Sensitive and cries easily
- Plays well by himself
- Spends more time with adults than peers
- Helpful to adults

The following are some questions to guide your reflection on Miguel and the trauma-sensitive strategies his teachers could use to support him:

- **What stress response do you observe with Miguel (fight, flight, freeze)?**

  When he is stressed and triggered at school, Miguel moves from an optimal state of regulation to a hypo-aroused state. The triggers cause him to go into his FREEZE brain where he shuts down, withdraws, hides, cries, and closes his eyes or spaces out.

- **What adult behaviors trigger Miguel's stress response system?**

  Unexpected visitors to the classroom that are not introduced and are not familiar trigger Miguel. Other triggers are when adults leave him alone and do not support him to feel safe and secure when he shuts down. Additionally, when adults do not support him during sensitive transitions such as drop off in the morning, he becomes more distressed.

- **What stress behaviors do you observe when Miguel is triggered?**

  When stressed, Miguel consistently withdraws, hides, covers his face, and closes his eyes, spaces out, or cries.

- **What trauma-sensitive strategies can teachers use that would be helpful to Miguel?**

  Miguel responds well to predictable routines and minimizing unexpected changes. He is more regulated when adults attune to him and support him in feeling safe. An adult who is physically close to him who provides calming support is regulating. Adults can also help Miguel feel safe by supporting him in advance to understand that a change or transition is coming. Strategies can also be developed to support his drop off transition from home to the classroom. For example, a comfort toy that he can bring from home to school could help ease the stress of the transition for Miguel. A photo of his moms could be placed in his cubby to help him feel connected to his primary attachment figures throughout the day. Also, a visual schedule that shows a photo of each transition during the day could decrease Miguel's stress as it would help him to understand what to expect throughout his day in addition to seeing when he will be reunited with his parents. Knowing when he can see moms again can help Miguel feel safe.

- **What adult reactions would not be helpful?**
  Leaving Miguel alone or ignoring him causes Miguel more stress. Another reaction that is not helpful is when a teacher allows a visitor to enter the class and does not prepare the children in advance or announce and introduce the visitor and explain why they are there. Not supporting Miguel during sensitive transitions throughout the day is another adult behavior that does not help him.

- **What information did you gain from Miguel's parents that you could use as trauma-sensitive strategies in the classroom to support him?**
  Miguel's moms report that a regular home routine that includes a predictable schedule, minimal transitions, and few guests reduces Miguel's anxiety. They are both calm at home and when he cries or becomes dysregulated, they hold him to support him back to feeling calm.

Arranging Environments to Support Children's Optimal Regulation

The following are several strategies teachers can use to arrange early learning environments that support young children's emotional regulation. These are key strategies teachers can use to create an environment that is safe, predictable, and regulating for all children.

A Safe, Cozy, and Calming Space

Children who have experienced trauma at an early age fail to develop an internal sense of feeling safe and in control. As a result, they are left in environments that trigger them and cause extreme terror and fear. Their reptile brain kicks in and tells them to FIGHT, FLIGHT, or FREEZE for survival. Even though the trigger is often not dangerous to those around them, to a young child perceiving it through a trauma lens, it may leave them scared with no place to escape. Teachers are the best regulator. Through an adult, a child can begin to learn the world can be safe again. However, the environment can be the third teacher in the classroom when an adult is not readily available.

Carving out a safe and cozy space where a child can get away and feel safe, secure, and where they can calm their bodies is very important for children impacted by trauma. This is NEVER a punishment or time-out area. Time-outs will be terrifying to children with trauma histories. Being abandoned and sent away as a punishment will be more triggering. This is also not intended to be a replacement for an adult providing the necessary attuned caregiving to rebuild a child's sense of safety. Teaching children when they are calm to use a cozy section of the classroom to help them feel safe, secure, and re-regulate their internal emotional state is a trauma-sensitive strategy for early childhood environments. There are many ways to create a safe space in the environment. If teachers have room, they can carve out a special place designated to be a calming area or cozy corner. This is an area for children to take a **sensory break** (Figures 3.9–3.11).

These spaces are **not** to be used for punishment or time-out. The children are taught in advance to use it when they are calm and receptive to learning and practicing. This safe and cozy space should include objects that support a child coming back to optimal regulation. If there is not enough space in the room, a sensory basket or bag with items a child can use such as those listed below to support their regulation is a good alternative.

Sensory breaks are designed to create a "pause" for the child. When a child's sensory system is dysregulated, they need a break to find strategies to bring their body, mind, and spirit back to the present moment and to an optimal state of regulation. Sensory strategies are external activities, objects,

Figure 3.9 Cozy Space.

Los Medanos College Child Study Center.

Figure 3.10 Calm Down Chair with Pillows.

Los Medanos College Child Study Center.

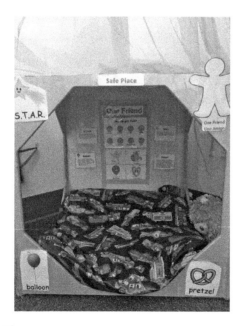

Figure 3.11 Safe Place.

Los Medanos College Child Study Center.

or people that can support a child coming back to a state of calm. As an adult, can you name one activity, person, or object in the environment that helps you in a healthy way to achieve a state of calm?

Materials for a Safe, Cozy, and Calming Space that Support Children's Emotional and Behavioral Regulation

Soft or hard pillows	Feelings check-in chart
Soft lighting	Sensory check-in chart
Art that is soothing	Stuffed animals
(e.g., nature photos)	Books that are calming including
Bean bag chair	feelings books
Blankets	Hands on the wall to push or
Books	footprints on the ground to stomp
Glitter jar	(if appropriate)
Bubbles	Paper to crumple and throw in trash
Pinwheels	A lotion bottle with a label on it that says
Coloring books	"calming lotion"
Family photographs	Playdough
Headphones with calming music or	Sand
guided meditation	Water elements such as a fish tank, a
	water table to play with, or nature
	photos of water to look at
	Chew toys

Some objects in your cozy corner can be calming and some can be stimulating energy for the child's sensory system. If a child is in the hypo-aroused or low energy state (FREEZE) there are options that are in the environment that can wake up or engage their regulatory system. Walking, coloring, climbing, rocking are examples. There are other options that calm the sensory system for children who are hyper-aroused (FIGHT). Things like sand, playdough, blowing bubbles, breathing to name a few examples. What is calming for one person may be stimulating for another. Giving children a choice and control is key to working with children impacted by trauma. Remember a child with a trauma history likely had a deep sense of losing control at the hands of an adult. The way teachers guide children to use the space must be gentle, provide agency to the child to make a choice, and teachers should avoid harsh words and frustrated or angry tones of voice that can be re-triggering. A child with a trauma history is often sensitive and scans the environment and your face, body language, and tone. They can easily be reactive to the slightest tone of disappointment or frustration. They look to the adults first to sense whether they will be safe and secure.

What Does A Safe, Cozy and Calming Corner
Space Look Like in Practice?

One classroom incorporated the book *Alexander and the Terrible, Horrible, No Good, Very Bad Day* by Judith Viorst and Ray Cruz. The teacher read the book to the children and then created a calming corner inside the room she called, "an island in Australia" playing off the theme of the book. This teacher described to the children, "Everyone has difficult days. We must all have a place to get away and calm down our big feelings." The teacher described to the children that only one child was allowed to be in the calming corner at a time but they can ask an adult for support while they were on the island of Australia that was created and named as their cozy area. The teacher and her assistant decorated the island with a lawn chair, umbrella, beach photos, and soothing music with headphones. There was also a thermometer that children could use to indicate the intensity or "temperature" of their feelings. The thermometer was made by teachers printing an image of a thermometer with green at the bottom, orange in the middle, and red at the top. The teachers laminated it and put Velcro on each color. Then they printed an arrow, laminated it, and put Velcro on the back. Teachers taught children about the intensity of emotions with green being calm, orange starting to feel intense emotions rising up in their bodies, and red was when you need a break because your emotions are too intense and you need calm before solving your problem or "thinking." Other items included a feelings check-in chart and a sensory body with images the child could use to identify the sensations in their body. There were books to read and stuffed animals to comfort them if needed. Finally, there were towels that acted as comforting blankets.

Creating a Safe, Cozy, and Calming Corner to
Support Children's Self-Regulation

- Can you think of ways you can create a calming area given the space you have?
- How would you introduce it to children?
- How would you teach using it throughout the day?
- What would you share with the parents and families about the calming area and why you use it?
- Do you have ideas about the types of objects you would place in the calming corner to support the regulation of children?
- What strategies can you use to make sure children and families do not view this space as a punishment or time-out area?

- Are you caring for children that would not find this space helpful? Why is this so?
- If you do not have room for a separate calming space, how can you use objects in the environment to support self-regulation?

Dramatic Play

In early childhood, the language is play and the role of the teacher is to provide a safe and creative space where playing becomes possible. During dramatic play, children tell their life story—how they feel about it and what they need and want. Young children's play also provides growth-promoting opportunities for them to develop crucial building blocks necessary for the emergence of self-regulatory and executive function skills such as cognitive and behavior flexibility, permitting them to consider various ways to solve problems and engage in prosocial behavior.

Play is one childhood developmental skill that is often delayed or severed for children with trauma. Play requires being present in the moment and letting go of control using imaginary and creative internal energy. Play is, and should be, imaginary and fun. Children with a trauma history have difficulty being present in the moment. They are often in a state of terror and internally scanning for danger frequently if not all the time. This internal hypervigilance causes them to not be present in the moment and have difficulty being able to play. As a teacher, you will see challenges for play with children who have been impacted by trauma in early childhood. As children begin to feel safe in your care, they will have the cognitive energy to focus on play instead of doing everything they can to keep themselves safe. Often sensory play (e.g., sand and water) are successful entry points into play for young children impacted by trauma.

Sensory Play

Sensory play is any activity that calms or excites the senses of touch, smell, taste, movement, balance, sight, and hearing. Sensory play introduces children to many new experiences, textures, and materials, and it facilitates exploration. Sensory play is calming for many children, especially if they are experiencing traumatic stress. Examples include playdough, bubbles, and sand and water play.

Expressive Arts

Expressive arts are activities that encourage young children's imagination through art, dance, dramatic play or theater, puppetry, and music. The expressive arts engage children across all domains—cognitive, language, social, emotional, and physical. Most importantly, children feel good while they are creating and the activity helps boost their self-confidence.

Manipulatives that Focus Children's Attention and Encourage Task Mastery

Young children's manipulative play includes activities where children move, order, turn, or screw items or "loose parts" to make them fit (Legos™, blocks, tangrams, etc.). This type of activity focuses children's attention and allows them to take control of their world by mastering the objects they use, experiences that are important for children with histories of trauma.

Introducing Sensory Literacy

Children experience a variety of sensations and feelings in their bodies when they are stressed and upset by a traumatic experience. A sensation is the way things feel in a person's body. Sensations in the body are described by how your body reacts to an emotional state. Hot, sweaty, heart pounding, shaky, antsy, cold, hot, tickly, dry, are all sensations your body can experience. Sensations like emotions change throughout the day. Here is a short list of examples of how sensations in the body can be described by a child. We have listed associated feelings so you can see how they are connected.

Sensation experienced in the body	Feeling associated with that sensation
Butterflies in my chest	Nervous
Bumble bees buzzing in my stomach	Anxious
A hammer in my head	Overwhelmed
A volcano erupting	Angry
Jumpy like a frog	Worried
Turtle	Scared
Prickly	Fearful
Sweaty	Stressed
Frozen iceberg	Numb, panicked, frightened

Cultivating sensory literacy helps children associate pictures with the sensations they are experiencing in their bodies. It provides children with the words to communicate what they are feeling internally when stress chemicals trigger a range of physical responses (e.g., rapid heartbeat, dizziness, tightened chest) in their bodies that children struggle to describe. Children with a trauma history whose stress response systems are activated often lose the ability to talk while they are triggered, which makes it hard to communicate to an adult how they feel and what they need. Providing children with a sensory vocabulary that helps them to name their internal sensory story and experience can be regulating.

SENSORY LITERACY HELPS CHILDREN COMMUNICATE HOW THEY ARE FEELING AND WHAT TEACHERS CAN DO TO SUPPORT THEM

As described in Chapter 1, past traumatic experiences that were not released as part of the normal, healthy recovery process are "stored in children's bodies" in the form of sensory memories. This trauma is imprinted at the time of the trauma into the body, especially if there were no caring adults to help them release the traumatic stressor and to provide buffers that promote healing from the event. When the memory is imprinted, it is stored in the sensory system. When a child is triggered in the future, the memories come flooding back as sensations and lack a coherent story with a beginning, middle, and an end. Asking a child to use their "words" is nearly impossible for a child when a traumatic trigger has them working from their brainstem (reptilian brain) and their neo-cortex (executive brain) is "out of business." Finding ways for children to express themselves by pointing to visual images or objects that identify the sensations they are feeling in their bodies can be regulating for them as the act of "naming" a sensation or feeling can "tame" or calm the child's stress response system (Siegel, 2003). This communication loop also provides a strategy that an attuned adult can use to make a child feel safe by being present and showing the child they are safe and being cared for.

Creating a list of sensory words that children can use to identify the sensations in their bodies will prepare them for the moments when they are triggered. If they can identify a sensory word by saying it or pointing to a picture or object that represents that sensation, children will communicate how they are feeling. This is a self-regulating strategy that will help children calm their stress response systems. If they have opportunities to practice using these sensory words on a daily basis (when their stress response systems are not activated), they will have a better chance of being able to use this strategy when they are upset and reacting in their reptile brain. Practice makes permanent and when you practice with children to communicate about sensations, it helps rewire their brains to develop a new skill. This new skill can be used to support a child in expressing themselves and releasing stress hormones associated with the triggering event in the moment.

Teaching Children to Describe the Sensations in Their Bodies

My heart feels **Jumpy like a Frog**
My head feels **Frozen** and my body feels **Cold**
My heart is beating **Fast like a Race Car**
My tummy feels like a **Roller Coaster**
My head feels like **Buzzing Bees**
My insides are **Twisty**
My legs feel like heavy **Rocks**
My insides are **Empty**
I feel **Cold** all over
My heart is **Heavy**
I feel like a **Volcano** ready to explode
My brain feels like a **Rocket Ship** ready to take off
My fists are **Tight**
My face feels **Hot** and **Sweaty**
My whole body feels **Loose**
I have **Scratchy** skin
My legs and arms are **Shaky**
My body feels like an **Iceberg**
My tummy is a **T-rex Dinosaur**
My mouth is like a **Cotton Ball**
My head feels like a **Roller Coaster**

Sensory Words Related to Children's Stress Response

Teachers could also think of sensation words for each of the brain survival responses (Fight, Flight, and Freeze) and help children to practice learning the words to describe their internal sensations.

- Children who respond to stress with a "**fight**" response could be taught to describe how they feel in their bodies as a "volcano," "hot and rumbly," or "fire."
- Children who respond to stress with a "**flight**" response could be taught to describe how they feel in their bodies as a "rocket ship taking off," "running," or "jumpy."
- Children who respond to stress with a "**freeze**" response could be taught to describe how they feel in their bodies as a "frozen," "tight," or "heavy."

FIGHT	FLIGHT	FREEZE
Volcano	Race car	Snowman
Lightening	Roller coaster	Frozen
Hot	Rocket ship	Cold
Rumbly	Shaky	Empty
Dinosaur	Loose	Tight
Fire	Fast	Heavy
Tight or twisty	Racing	Sweaty
Buzzing bees	Running	Scratchy
Rocky	Jumpy	

TEACHERS CAN CREATE A SENSORY POSTER WITH IMAGES UNDER FIGHT, FLIGHT, AND FREEZE

Start with four photos representing FIGHT, four photos representing FLIGHT, and four photos representing FREEZE and a silhouette of a laminated body (Figure 3.12).

Begin to introduce to children that when they experience intense emotions they also experience "sensations" associated with those feelings inside their body. Introduce each sensation word and practice placing the Velcro image on the laminated outline of a body.

Talk about the different sensations and how they feel in the body and support children to practice identifying where in their bodies they feel different sensations. Teachers can practice sensory literacy with children by reading books and asking how the characters in the story feel and the sensations they may have by pointing to different options on the sensation poster.

The photo shows a preschool child, Jeremy, who used the laminated sensory photos to place a frozen ice-capped volcano on the body. He told the teacher that he felt like "a frozen volcano." He put the Velcro picture of the volcano on the body part that showed where he was having the sensation in his body. In this example, **Jeremy said that he felt frozen in his heart**.

TEACHERS CAN CREATE A SENSORY BASKET WITH OBJECTS OR IMAGES THAT REPRESENT DIFFERENT SENSATIONS

This photo was taken by a teacher at a child development center in northern California who created a sensory basket with different objects that represented different sensations in children's bodies (Figure 3.13).

Sensation = _____

Pokie (sensation) = Shell

Fast = Race car

Jumpy = Frog

Bumpy = Cardboard image found in packaging materials

Twisty = Metal coil with no sharp edges

Heavy = Rock

Empty = Empty container

Tight = Chip clip

Shaky = Mini rocking chair

The teacher introduced each object to the children in her class and then read two books:

- *Gilbert the Great* by Jane Clarke and Charles Fuge; and
- *Tickly Octopus* by Ruth Galloway

Both of these books represent typical books that teachers can read to a child. You do not need a special book or one of these to teach sensory awareness. Most children's books have characters that experience a situation where you could ask children how they might be feeling and the associated sensations in their body.

The children practice guessing the sensations the characters may be feeling in their bodies. They also practice pointing to an object from the classroom sensory basket that represents how they are feeling inside their bodies. In this classroom, children are beginning to learn the difference between sensations and feelings. When the teacher reads a book, she focuses the children's attention on how the characters feel (e.g., sad) and what sensation object represents what they feel in their body (e.g., empty container). The children are beginning to learn through characters in books. Throughout the day, the teacher checks in with children wondering what sensation is in their body associated with the feeling they have. As time passes, children begin to naturally develop the habit of communicating sensations and feelings. When a child is faced with an intense emotion, they have the tools to communicate with an adult caregiver. An important consideration with children impacted by trauma is that approaching a child slowly with choices gives them a greater sense of control. Offering the sensation bag/basket or wondering is a better approach than "telling" them what they feel or are sensing. An example may be, "I wonder if the sensory basket would help you tell me how you feel" (versus "you need the sensory basket as you I see you are out of control)."

Garcia, G. (2017). *Listening to My Body*. Austin, TX: Take Heart Press.

This book can be used with young children to help them understand the connection between sensations in their body and feelings (Figure 3.14).

Here is an example of the way these connections are made in the book:

"When I pay attention and listen to my body, I notice many different sensations. Sensations are physical feelings we all have inside and outside our bodies. Cold, sweaty, and breathless are examples of some sensations. Have you felt these sensations before? Let's practice. Rub your hands together quickly for thirty seconds. What do you notice? Tingles? Sweat? Anything else? Those are sensations."

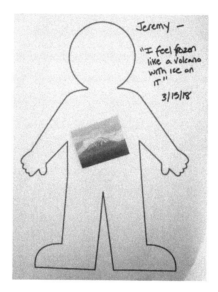

Figure 3.12 Jeremy Sensory Description.

Figure 3.13 Sensory Basket Figurines.

Lakshmi Padmanabhan, College Child Development Center.

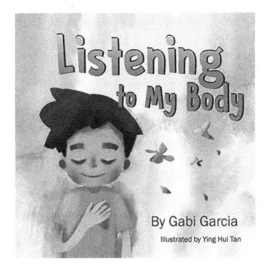

Figure 3.14

Garcia, G. (2017). *Listening to My Body*. Austin, TX: Take Heart Press.

Connecting Sensations with Emotions: Introducing Emotional Literacy

Emotional literacy is central to young children's social-emotional development. The ability to identify emotion words, to understand when you feel emotions, and to recognize the intensity of the emotion (how big the emotion is inside of you) is the foundation of emotional literacy and emotional recognition in oneself.

The child then can develop the ability to recognize emotions in others. They can be supported to read facial, body, and verbal cues and to recognize the emotional state of others, they can then begin to learn their own. Proactively building this toolbox of awareness by practicing is essential to developing this muscle.

SUPPORTING CHILDREN TO RECOGNIZE THE INTENSITY OF THEIR EMOTIONS

One strategy teachers use to cultivate children's ability to recognize the intensity of their emotions is to help them identify when their emotions are Green, Yellow, or Red. Using a thermometer, teachers help children learn to point to the color that represents how "big" the emotions are inside of them (Figure 3.15a).

A simple thermometer can be laminated and posted for children to use. Red is at the top, orange in the middle, and green at the base of the thermometer.

- **Green** represents "calm" and "I feel ready to talk through a problem"
- **Orange** means "emotions are beginning to rise up inside of me" or "my emotions are moving from intense toward the calmer zone"
- **Red,** the highest zone of intensity, means "my emotions are heated up" and "my feelings are very big!"

Teachers can also try using a laminated arrow with Velcro with the thermometer. Children can move the arrow up and down the thermometer to represent the different levels of intensity of their emotions.

Instead of thermometers, older children can identify their emotions across a continuum ranging from one to ten:

- **Small**: 1–4
- **Medium**: 5–7
- **Large**: 8–10

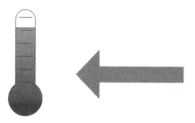

Figure 3.15a Thermometer and Arrow.

Create Environments that Support Children's Emotional Expression!

- Use feeling posters that depict emotions to help children identify and discuss various feelings throughout the day.
- Introduce children to various feelings in an age-appropriate way, e.g., by pairing a picture of a feeling face with the appropriate emotion.
- Act as role models by talking about their own feelings.
- Support children to build a vocabulary of feeling words and have opportunities to identify and label various emotions. Over time, their

vocabulary of feeling words will become a part of their conversations and daily practice with peers and teachers.

Teaching emotional literacy can be supported in several ways.

Proactive Teaching of Feelings

Mental Health consultant, Karen Van Patten, created this **Feelings and Self-Regulation** tool for teachers in the classroom she coached to use with children from ages two to six (Figure 3.15b). The teachers in this classroom did not have adequate wall space to hang these photos so they put them into an office plastic file folder. The teachers also shared that they wanted to keep their walls less cluttered so they did not overwhelm the visual sensory systems of the children. One important consideration in the environment is to minimize visual over-stimulation. Often teachers crowd the walls with photos and images. For some children, too many visuals can be over-stimulating to their sensory system. Eliminating clutter on the wall can support a calming and less triggering environment for children.

The left side of the folder displays several faces expressing different feelings. The right side of the folder shows children several activities they can choose to do to regulate their emotions. The feelings photos are kept in one plastic bag labeled **Feelings**. A second plastic bag labeled **Self-Regulation Strategies** includes pictures of the activities they can choose to calm their

Figure 3.15b Teaching Feelings.

Photo Credit: Karen Van Patten, El Dorado County Office of Education stress responses systems. Children choose from the Feelings bag to identify the feelings they have at a particular moment (e.g., frustrated) and Velcro it to the left side of the folder. Then, they choose a picture from the Self-regulation Strategies bag to communicate the strategy they choose to manage their feelings (e.g., draw a picture).

I Feel and I Can

Karen Van Patten also created the "**I Feel and I Can" tool** to help children identify their feelings and support their development of self-regulation (Figure 3.16). As with the tool above, Feeling Faces are kept in one plastic bag and pictures with different self-regulation strategies are in a second plastic bag. Children choose an emotion and a self-regulation strategy and communicate their choices by adding their selections to the folder. This child indicated that she feels "Angry." She also chose to get a ball from the self-regulation kit provided in the classroom. The strategy she chose to help self-regulate her angry feelings is to "Squeeze a Ball." Children can also indicate when they are Calm and Focused and ready to return to the group. This classroom understands that it is important to help the child

Figure 3.16 I Feel I Can.

Photo Credit: Karen Van Patten, El Dorado County Office of Education.

recognize when they feel calm and regulated. When they are regulated, the teacher chooses one of the following options with the child:

1. They may ask if they are ready to return to their activity.
2. They may ask what sensations are in their body or feelings they have now and help them see how their sensations/feelings changed.
3. They may ask how they might solve a problem they were having or what they might do next (mapping a plan).

All these strategies require the "thinking" part of the brain that is accessed only when a child is calm. They help the children think of solutions, map a plan or solve a problem only when they are regulated and can engage the executive part of their brain.

Cooling Off Posters

A cooling off poster shows several pictures of things children can do when they are very upset and need to "cool off" and calm their stress response system. Some examples of cooling off activities that can be included on a "cooling off" poster:

- Drawing
- Squishing playdough
- Walking with an adult
- Listening to calm music
- Playing with water or sand
- Going to a cozy area
- Counting to five or ten on their fingers
- Singing a song
- Bouncing a ball
- Holding a comfort object
- Talking to a teacher
- Playing with a glitter jar
- Taking belly breaths (see below)
- Crumple papers and throw them in a basket

Cooling Off Posters (Figures 3.17 and 3.18)	Glitter jar recipes are online or you can purchase one (Figure 3.19). A child shakes the jar and watches while the glitter falls to the bottom. It is intended to be calming and if a teacher helps a child to learn to breathe, along with the glitter falling, this is an additional strategy for supporting regulation.

Figure 3.17 Infant Toddler Cooling Off Poster.

Photo Credit: Courtney Vickery.

Figure 3.18 Preschool/Kindergarten Cooling Off Poster.

Photo Credit: Courtney Vickery.

Below the poster, teachers should have a box filled with all the supplies children will need to implement the choices included on the poster. For example, a tape player with music for dancing, a small ball, paper/pencil/crayons for drawing, and playdough for squishing. When children are just learning to use the Cooling Off Poster, adults can help them select a self-regulating strategy and do the action along with the child. For example, the child might point to, "Sing the ABCs" and the teacher and child would sing the song together. As children have more experience using the Cooling Off Poster, they will be able to use it by themselves; moving from co-regulation (with a teacher) to self-regulation (by themselves).

Figure 3.19 Glitter Jar.

www.calmingbottles.com.

Taking Belly Breaths to Calm Down (Sesame Street) Elmo teaches young children about taking calming belly breaths: www.youtube.com/ watch?v=_mZbzDOpylA Breathing deeply is an important strategy for children to learn and for their teachers to model for them. When people breath, they activate hormones (oxytocin) that inhibit the stress response system in the body and this is calming and promotes relaxation in the body. In addition to watching Elmo's video on belly breathing, early childhood teachers can teach young children to learn how to breathe deeply through play: blow bubbles or pinwheels or pretend to blow out a candle on a birthday cake or a hot bowl of soup.	Many teachers use a ball like this one to help children learn how to take belly breaths (Figure 3.20). Slowly open the ball having children inhale until the ball is expanded to its full size, then slowly close the ball having children practice exhaling slowly until the ball is as small as it can be. Repeat three to four times.

Emotion Posters

Once children have calmed down, they can be guided to look at an **Emotions Poster** that includes pictures of children with different emotions. Children can be asked to point to or name the emotion that is similar to how they feel inside.

Figure 3.20 Breathing Ball.

Using an Emotions Poster helps children to learn to label their feelings. Adults can model using an Emotions Poster with children when they have big emotions. This models to the children the process of acknowledging feelings and learning to name them as an important step in learning to calm down (Figure 3.21).

Labeling Emotions with Toddlers

Toddlers with a limited vocabulary will need support identifying their emotions. The natural setting of daily activities is the best way to teach toddlers how to express their feelings. For example, books on feelings are a resource to help teach toddlers about feelings in a natural, informal way. Also, caregivers can play a "Guess my Feeling" game with toddlers by taking turns making facial expressions and guessing what feeling is being shown.

Feelings should be talked about throughout the day, not only when they are intense. This can support children in gaining awareness about the range of emotions they have and the intensities associated with each of their emotions. Teachers can support children to practice "reminders" out loud as a foundation to developing self-regulation of their behavior. They can practice these reminders in front of a mirror:

- A young child who hit a classmate can hold up their hands and "talk" to them with a gentle reminder, "Hit pillows not people."
- Teachers can practice a reminder with a child who bites another child when feeling angry, "Bite chew toys, not people."

Figure 3.21 Emotions Poster.

www.carsondellosa.com.

With enough practice guided by adults, these "reminders" will become internalized by a child becoming their internal self-talk, an important milestone in the development of self-regulation.

Reinforce to Children That They Are Cared For and Loved When They Have Strong Emotions

Many children impacted by trauma worry that they must be "bad" because they feel such strong emotions so often. Because of this, teachers and caregivers need to normalize the experience of having strong emotions for these children. While reading books, teachers can point to pictures of a child or adult in the story and ask, "Do you think she ever feels angry? Do you think he ever feels sad?" This can be a good springboard for reminding children that everyone feels a whole range of emotions *and* their families, friends, and teachers still love and care about them. Talking together about how everyone feels emotions and hearing that they are still loved even when they have high-intensity emotions (especially anger) can be very calming and regulating.

A TEACHER OBSERVES A CHALLENGING BEHAVIOR: IT'S TIME TO TEACH A SOCIAL AND EMOTIONAL SKILL

Let's spotlight in on a three-year-old child named Antonio to think more about the concept of **TEACHING** a social and emotional skill versus punishing. Antonio is in the classroom and he sees other children playing cars. He seems interested in joining them but instead, walks up and takes some cars away from the children playing together. A teacher comes running over to Antonio and scolds him first saying "Why would you do something so mean?" She goes on to yell at him "Why did you treat your friends that way? That is not nice." She finally ends with "How would you like it if I took your toy away?" She takes the toy out of his hand and explains that he lost his privilege to play with other children because he could not play nicely with them. The teacher sent him to a quiet area where he did not have to interact with others to prevent him from getting into trouble again.

Reflective Questions about Antonio

- How do you think Antonio felt after his teacher questioned him and then sent him to the quiet area? What skills did Antonio learn from this experience?
- How do you think the other children felt observing this interaction?
- Can you identify what social-emotional skill Antonio struggles with?
- What skill could you teach Antonio instead of resorting to taking his toys away?

Reflections on Antonio: Antonio struggles with entering play with other children. This happens frequently where he enters play in a way that makes all the other children upset and they yell at him to go away or a teacher intervenes by sending him away.

- **If the teacher keeps punishing or removing Antonio, what will he learn about himself?** Likely that he is bad and always in trouble.
- **What social skill is the teacher helping him build?** She is helping him associate taking toys from other kids with punishment. So, he then may learn to take toys when the teacher is not looking. He may learn to negotiate verbally how he did not do anything. Will he learn from this punishment how to play with other children?

Consider the ways the teacher could help Antonio learn how to ask to play with the other children or how he can learn to ask for a toy. The teacher could recognize it is a strength that he seems interested in playing and prompt him to recognize it, **"You look like you want to play with the other children, is that right?"** If he agrees, the teacher can show him how to ask, **"Can I play with you?"** The teacher can teach another skill: learning how to play with the other children and take turns playing cars. If she helped him with this several times, Antonio would build several new social skills: how to enter play, how to share, friendship skills, and negotiation with other children.

Which outcome do you want most for Antonio? Which skills will help him most throughout his life?

All children will have challenging behaviors because of their underdeveloped and immature brains. Although teachers cannot eliminate behavioral challenges in the classroom, they can decide to respond to children's challenging behaviors by teaching them new skills. Teaching a new skill promotes the learning of a new and healthy social-emotional strategy while punishing creates fear, shame, and not learning a social-emotional skill. **Children impacted by trauma need teachers who will take the time to teach them and not punish them.**

Infusing social and emotional strategies into the classroom could also improve executive function skills and reinforce children's effort to practice inhibitory control of actions to achieve optimal arousal and attention regulation. We believe that regulating children's attention and focusing it toward their own internal sensations, body, and emotional states will enable them to recognize their own reactions and any strong emotions they may be feeling. Over time, the children could become better at regulating their own arousal levels and transition from reactive and impulsive behaviors to those that are more deliberate and thoughtful.

Strategies to Calm Young Children's Stress Response Systems

Visual	Auditory	Tactile

Dimming the lights
Reducing clutter on walls
Providing small
   enclosures where
   toddlers can hide
	Eliminate low-
	   frequency sounds
	Humming or singing
	Increase vocals/female voices
	   to support relaxation
	Playing instrumental music
	Playing white noise
	Playing nature sounds
		Patting or rubbing
		   the back
		Providing
		   textured blankets
		Swaddling
		Water or sensory
		   table

Vestibular
Rocking
Swinging
Bouncing
Swaying
Riding in a stroller
Taking a walk with
   an adult
Pushing the wall
	Proprioceptive
	Jumping
	Climbing
	Yoga
	Pushing heavy toys
	Trampoline
	Stress balls
	Squeezing objects
		Natural outdoor
		   environments
		Healing effects
		   documented
		   in research
		Rich sensory input
		Loose parts
		Wonder and creativity

Creating Trauma-Sensitive Early Childhood Programs

Early childhood teachers have one of the most important roles in a child's life—to *teach* life skills. There is no question that they will be challenged to work with children over the course of their career who have experienced some type of trauma. These children rely upon their teachers to work extra hard to learn about and practice trauma-sensitive strategies.

With the additional layer of early trauma, children experience prolonged toxic stress that changes the chemicals in their brain that can leave them in a constant state of arousal and hypervigilance where they are scanning for danger frequently if not all the time. This prevents children from being present in the moment and having the sustained focus and attention they need to access executive function skills necessary for self-regulated learning and social relationships.

In early childhood, self-regulation and executive function skills (behavior inhibition, working memory, and cognitive and behavior flexibility) emerge within a foundational context of positive caring relationships and conversations with teachers and caregivers through daily interactions. Initially, these skills are supported by co-regulation with adults but over time with support and practice, children learn to internalize what self-regulated adults model for them about how to manage their stress and emotions in productive ways.

Through relationships, safe environments, and actively teaching young children to strengthen their social-emotional and executive function skills, early childhood teachers can create trauma-sensitive early childhood programs that guide children from pain, stress, and trauma to healing and healthy development. Over time, the children develop into healthy functioning adults with strong social-emotional skills who can function independently, get along with others, identify and communicate how they feel, have empathy, self-regulate, and solve problems without hurting themselves or others.

SPOTLIGHT ON TIP IN PRACTICE

Angela Fantuzzi (Figure 3.22)
  Community College Child Study Center
  Scenarios

Melissa, age four, was in a Community College Child Study Center program. Her mom and dad were in a relationship that mom reported to the teachers was abusive. Mom shared with Angela that Melissa had witnessed domestic violence in the home including mom being hit by dad on several occasions. Mom chose to leave dad and they separated.

During this time, Melissa began to have a change in her behavior during preschool. When Melissa was involved in conflicts between children, she would shut down and run away to be by herself. She went to their classroom "safe and cozy corner" to hide. If Angela or her teaching assistant tried to speak with Melissa, she would shut down even more. When this behavior first started, Angela tried to rub Melissa's back but she noticed that this touching would trigger Melissa even more. It took time for Angela to observe Melissa and find the right strategy to support her regulation. Angela learned to let Melissa go to the cozy corner and hide when she felt stressed. During these times, Angela would make sure no one else went there for approximately five minutes. Then, after five minutes, Angela or her assistant would approach Melissa and at that time, Melissa would tolerate touch and often times she allowed them to hold her. Angela would sing a quiet song and gently rock with Melissa, sometimes as long as 10 to 15 minutes. Angela discovered that Melissa's hypo-aroused nervous system was calmed when she was held, rocked back and forth, and when the same lullaby or song was sung to her during this time. After about 15 minutes, Melissa would start talking about the worry she had that led her to hide in the cozy corner. Angela observed that Melissa would follow this

Figure 3.22 Angela Fantuzzi.

same sequence of events and timing each time she experienced conflict in her environment.

One example of an instance that triggered Melissa was when two of her classmates, Jacob and Tonya, were playing in the block area and Martoni, a third child in the class, approached them asking if he could join in and play too. Jacob and Tonya said "No" and Martoni proceeded to knock over their tower. Jacob and Tonya started yelling they were going to tell on Martoni to a teacher and that he would never be their friend ever again. When instances like this would happen, Melissa's body would become rigid, her eyes glassy, and she would start running to escape to her safe space. By creating a predictable routine to support Melissa over time, the teachers were helping her to learn: (1) coping strategies that she could use when she felt triggered or stressed, and (2) that adults would support her and guide her back to regulation. With predictable routines and her teacher's individualized co-regulatory support, Melissa slowly developed an increased tolerance for conflict in the classroom. She developed a stronger internal ability to regulate and calm herself rather than rely on the cozy area or a teacher to bring her back to an optimal state of regulation. This example highlights how adults can use consistent trauma-sensitive strategies with a child to teach them to calm their stress response systems over time so they are supported in learning how to shift from co-regulation (using the environment and teacher) toward self-regulation.

Teaching Tip: Building Resilience by Focusing on Young Children's Healing

Five-year-old Simon is eating lunch with his peers outside of his kindergarten classroom when he hears a siren from a passing ambulance. This triggers a freeze response and Simon's face turns white and his body begins to shake. His teacher, Alicia, observes his stress response and walks toward him. He starts to cry looks up at her and says, "It reminds me of Maria (his foster mom who died when he was in preschool)." Alicia, who knows about this traumatic experience in Simon's life, understood that the siren triggered his memories of the day the ambulance arrived and took his foster mom away, who then died in transport to the hospital. She acknowledged this experience for Simon and reminded him he was safe—"yes, it was very scary and sad when the ambulance came for Maria and she died. That was when you were only three years old. Now you are so much bigger as a five-year-old and you are safe here in kindergarten with all your friends and your teachers. It is my job to take care of you and keep you safe. That ambulance is going to help someone. You are safe here with me." Next, Alicia redirected Simon to focus on his strengths and resiliencies. "When you were a little boy you learned how to be strong and brave and you survived even though you had to go through such a scary and sad experience. Now you have a family who takes care of you so you don't have to be so brave. Now you can play because your teachers and parents are taking care of you." Simon listened quietly and then jumped up and said, "Yes! I survived! I'm strong and brave!" and then happily returned to eating his lunch and talking with his classmates. **We can acknowledge children's past traumatic experiences and also remind them that they are strong and brave, heroes and heroines of their life stories**.

PERSONAL REFLECTION

Teacher: Lakshmi Padmanabhan (Figure 3.23)
Site: Community College Child Development Center

Scenario:

I was at the writing table with a group of six children, all four and five years old. As I facilitated an art activity, I noticed one child, Ahmed across the room. He was under a low counter, all huddled up, holding onto his knees, and had his face to the ground as if he was hiding. I was at first uncertain what happened or what I might do.

I went over to him to check in and ask how he was feeling. I said that I was thinking about him and wondering where he was and if he was okay. The sensory items bag was within my reach. I offered for him to sit in my lap and I told him I was wondering what sensations he was feeling inside

Figure 3.23 Lakshmi Padmanabhan.

his body. I took the objects out one by one and named the sensations these children had heard me use when I introduced sensory literacy at circle time. First, I pulled out the frog and asked if he felt jumpy which he replied with a quiet no. The race car came out and I wondered if his heart was racing fast like a car. Still no response from Ahmed. Then I tried the rocking chair and asked might his body be rocky? After some thought, he pulled out of the bag on his own a small twisted coil. He began a conversation about what happened that made him feel twisted up inside like the small coil. As he spoke he shared how he was upset that the other children were making fun of him and telling him what to do. As I listened closely to his story, he began to shift from hiding and curled up in a ball in a corner, to coming back to a calmer state. He engaged with me in conversation about sensations in his body, how he felt, and eventually the story of what happened to him. He was gradually guided back to engaging with the group at the table in the activity.

Teaching Dilemma: I'm worried that using the word "trauma" is going to make things worse for a child who is already suffering? I don't want to cause more harm.

When supporting a young child, it is not necessary to use the word "trauma" directly with them, instead you will be supporting them by using *trauma-sensitive strategies* to support a child's healing. The most important thing with a child is using trauma-sensitive strategies. When you punish, withhold care, shame, make fun of, dismiss, ignore, provide rewards, and use other punitive strategies, this is the very thing that may cause more harm, not the word trauma itself. The following is an example of the use of a trauma-strategy that supported a child's healing by acknowledging the trauma a young boy was experiencing.

Jian and Serena were teachers at a preschool center, working together for the past five years in the same program. One of the children in the classroom started to develop behaviors that did not exist before. Marcus had been in the program for nine months and previously had no challenging behaviors. One day he arrived to the program with his dad. Usually, mom was the one who dropped him off. Marcus clung on to dad and started yelling "don't leave daddy." After dad left, Marcus stood by the window crying and was inconsolable most of the day. The teachers tried to comfort him. When they stood with him or held him he was able to be more regulated and calm. However, if a teacher walked away or was not holding or in close proximity to Marcus, he would begin to cry again. Jian pulled dad aside at pick up and expressed concern about Marcus and asked for any insight from dad that might help them. Dad said his mom had just died. They were divorced but Marcus was at home alone with mom and he kept trying to wake her up on the couch but she would not wake up. When grandma came by the house later she found Marcus with mom and saw she had died in her sleep.

Dad said he told Marcus mom was on vacation because he did not want to cause him more pain by saying she died. He said family was in and out of the house mourning but he thought maybe Marcus was too young to notice. Jian asked dad if he wanted support from a professional that might help him talk to Marcus about what happened and to support him during the process. Dad agreed and the program sent a mental health specialist to work with dad and Marcus. Dad began to read the book *When Dinosaurs Die—A Guide to Understanding Death* and *I Miss You—A First Look at Death*. The mental health specialist helped dad support the healing of trauma for Marcus. She also worked with the teachers on strategies to support Marcus, especially supporting him through transitions at arrival and departure and during transitions of adult caregivers, which triggered him more. The teachers and Marcus's dad learned that not acknowledging and talking about the trauma could intensify the triggers for Marcus. Allowing Marcus to name the traumatic loss he experienced through words, through play, and other means of expression including expressive arts, the adults supported a healing process for Marcus by allowing him a channel for communicating about his intense emotions, his fears, and the triggers in his environment that reminded him of the traumatic experience of losing his mother.

LOOKING THROUGH A CHILD'S EYES

When very young children experience trauma, as they grow up they often feel the trauma was their fault. This can lead them to develop an internal narrative of self-doubt and shame where they tell themselves that they are not lovable.

Four-year-old Sasha was severely neglected as an infant and now she struggles with internal feelings of shame and once or twice a day her preschool teachers hear her say, "I don't love myself. Nobody loves me" and when she is playing with the dolls she says, "Nobody loves her. She's a bad girl." Her teacher has noticed that Sasha has a perception that she is the only person in the world who makes "mistakes" and because she makes mistakes she can't possibly be "lovable." After observing this, her teachers started to "make visible" their mistakes for Sasha and the other children in the class. When they would make a mistake, they might say out loud, "Oh no! I just made a mistake. I accidentally left the cap off the marker and now it is dried out. I feel sad about making this mistake but I know everyone makes mistakes. I am going to forgive myself and 'try again.'" After modeling this for Sasha for several weeks, Sasha walked up to her teacher and asked, "Is that true? Does everybody really make mistakes?"

Sasha's teacher was using a **trauma-sensitive strategy to reduce her feelings of shame and self-doubt** by normalizing the experience of learning and making mistakes.

Interdisciplinary Partnerships and TIP

Tanisha is a three-year-old child enrolled in a Head Start program who lives in a neighborhood with a high level of community violence. Her teacher has been observing her imaginary play replaying themes of death with little resolution or change in the narrative. Tanisha's body is in a constant state of restless activity. She buries animals underneath plastic bins and inside block structures. She whispers over and over to herself, "Dead. They really are dead. Dead. Dead. Deeeaaaddd." This type of play has continued for several weeks and her teachers are concerned about Tanisha and don't know how to help her. Tanisha's teachers have asked the mental health consultant to observe Tanisha and to recommend strategies that they can use to support her in the classroom.

Mindfulness and TIP

This mindful activity draws a child's attention to the present moment. It helps them practice mindfulness in the moment and can help them feel relaxed and regulated.

Teachers can help children tune their attention to the present moment by becoming aware of sensations in their body and outside of their body. As you guide them through this activity, you can invite them to participate by focusing on the sounds, sights, and smells they notice for each of the following. Make sure the children are sitting comfortably in a circle. Tell them that this is an activity about noticing and observing. Set the tone by sharing that each may notice different things.

1. What sounds do you hear outside?
2. What sounds do you hear inside the room?
3. Pay attention to your heart, put your hand on your heart. Can you feel it beat? Is it beating fast or slow?
4. Notice your hands. Do they feel warm or cold?

5. Do you smell anything? What smells do you notice?
6. Now look around the room. Notice when you look around the room, can you find one object you like the most, maybe an object that makes you feel safe and happy.

Now take one very big breath in through your nose and breath it out of your mouth. Then we will be ready for our next activity.

Trauma-Informed Coaching

First: Connect to the Story and Emotions—
Second: Guide Toward Solutions

Frequently when you witness or listen to the painful events of another, it's natural to want to help by immediately suggesting a potential solution to help them feel better quickly. It's very difficult to allow others to express intense emotions and not "take action." It may feel like we are not supporting them by just listening, and when we offer a solution, it feels more like concrete support. However, the opposite is really the most helpful. Why? The right hemisphere of the brain houses our emotions, including those associated with a painful experience. All that right side of the brain needs is to unload the story and really be heard.

When someone shows care and concern and takes time to listen, this serves a very important function for the brain. Listening and showing compassion helps calm the emotional intensity within the right side of the brain. After a person is able to share their story and tell you about how they are feeling, and have an experience of being heard and supported, they will become visibly more relaxed and appear calm with increased regulation. These visual cues demonstrate that they are ready to move to the second step. During this time, their body softens, they will talk more slowly, they appear less agitated, and their emotional expression is less intense. These are signs that they may be open to a discussion around what solutions could potentially help solve their problem. The left hemisphere of the brain houses reason, problem-solving, and critical thinking, and this is the home of solutions. It is where our ability to think through alternate solutions and map potential outcomes to any given problem resides. The second step of guiding someone toward a solution cannot be accomplished until the right side of the brain is calm.

In summary, it is important the coach takes time to listen to the range of emotions a teacher has without correcting, directing, coaching, or teaching. Be a witness to their internal emotional world and the story they share before asking questions or making suggestions.

4

CASE STUDY

Infant and Mother Living in a Homeless Shelter

How Can Teachers Support a Mother and Her Infant Who Are Experiencing Homelessness and Have a History of Domestic Violence?

Key Topics Covered

- Mother and 11-month-old infant experiencing homelessness and past history of domestic violence
- TIP practices for supporting a hyper-aroused fight response in a young infant
- TIP family engagement strategies for communicating with, and supporting, the mother

Kara, a mother experiencing homelessness, and her 11-month-old female infant, Ava, have recently moved into a shelter after leaving the family home where Kara was domestically abused by Ava's father. Ava, who has been attending a child care program for eight months, is a socially responsive and happy baby who started walking at ten months and is typically developing. However, since moving to the shelter, Ava prefers to crawl and she cries and is fearful whenever Kara drops her off at the child care center and quickly leaves for work. At nap time, Ava takes a long time to go to sleep and needs Tasha, the child care teacher, to stay near her until she falls asleep. Soon after Tasha leaves her side, Ava wakes up crying and resists going back to sleep, often waking up the other infants and creating extra work for the care providers. Ava protests, cries, or becomes immobile whenever any unfamiliar adults enter the classroom, especially adult males. It takes great effort for the teachers to return her to a more balanced state of arousal, often leaving them, especially Tasha, who is assigned as Ava's primary teacher, exhausted and unavailable to the other children. The director is concerned that Ava is taking up too much of Tasha's time and the other infants are not getting their needs met, especially since they are short staffed at the program. Given the shortage of staff, there are a lot of new faces and continuous changes in the children's schedule and routines. Tasha frequently feels overwhelmed and has started looking for another job.

Application of Trauma-Informed Practices for Ava

Initial Inquiry Questions

- Are there resources and program-wide supports for trauma-informed care?
- Do the teachers know how to work with Ava who is regressing and responding to traumatic stress?
- Is there an understanding of the larger ecological contexts influencing Ava and her family (e.g., family's experience with homelessness and recent move to the shelter)?
- Is Ava reacting to separation distress when left at child care and at nap time?
- Does a referral need to be made for additional assessment, intervention, and/or supports?

Understanding Possible Factors Related to Ava's Traumatic Stress

- Domestic violence and a mother who is experiencing traumatic stress
- Separation from father
- The experience of homelessness and changes in living environment
- Changes in classroom routines and unfamiliar faces in caregiving environment
- An overwhelmed caregiver who is responding to Ava's trauma triggers

Identifying Traumatic Triggers that Lead to Ava's Stress Behaviors

- Transition from mother to child care
- Transition to nap
- When caregiver leaves her side during nap time
- Fathers picking up their children

- Unfamiliar faces in the classroom
- Changes in routine

Identifying Ava's Traumatic Stress Reactions

- Cries and acts fearful whenever she is dropped off at child care
- Cries and resists going to sleep at nap time
- Has difficulty sustaining her sleep
- Shows a regression in her gross motor skills, i.e., was walking and now prefers to crawl
- Over-aroused (cries) and/or under-aroused (immobile) when other fathers come to pick up their children or when new faces enter the classroom

Goals to Support Ava

- Support Ava during separations from mother to the child care center
- Help Ava during transition to nap time
- Regulate Ava when she is over- or under-aroused
- Restore Ava's walking and exploratory behaviors
- Support the caregivers' reactions to Ava's emotions
- Protect Ava from unnecessary exposure to traumatic reminders

Trauma-Informed Teaching Practices to Support Ava

- **Implement a plan to support Ava's transition from mother to child care center.** Tasha scaffolds the transition using several strategies including a regulating activity, looking for signs of readiness, and assuring Kara that Ava is safe and using attuned interactions with both Kara and Ava.
    - Tasha models a gradual transition for Ava from her mother to the child care center by supporting Kara to arrive early enough to engage Ava in a pleasurable and regulating activity such as reading her a story. Tasha and Kara look for signs that Ava is calm before Kara leaves for work.
    - Tasha discusses with Kara that quick departures reinforce Ava's distress and assures Kara that Ava is safe at the child care center and that her needs will be met.
    - Tasha uses attuned interactions with Ava throughout the day. These include looking at Ava with kind gestures, using a soothing voice to reassure Ava that her mother will be back and that she is safe, "I am here for you, what can we do to make you feel better?" and quietly humming or singing a lullaby to help Ava at nap time.

- Tasha works with Kara to identify a transition object that Ava can bring with her from her temporary home in the shelter to the child care center (e.g., stuffed animal, picture of mom). Tasha encourages Ava to use this object during the day to self-soothe and calm when stressed.
- Tasha develops empathy and understanding that Ava needs the physical presence of her teacher. Tasha explains to Kara that remaining close to Ava decreases her stress because she cannot call upon a mental image of her main attachment figure (Kara) as a form of self-soothing. This is because traumatic stress interrupts the development of symbolic thinking for young children So, for Ava, when her teacher moves out of her sight, Ava feels vulnerable and stressed as she perceives that her teacher has disappeared.

- **Use emotionally attuned caregiver interactions to regulate Ava's dysregulated behavior**
  - Tasha is aware that Ava is coping with her feelings of loss by wanting her caregiver nearby and that responding sensitively to her attachment needs by remaining close during transitions and nap time may be the kind of security she is looking for.
  - Tasha provides a relational and emotionally holding environment by being patient, emotionally present, attuned (responsive to Ava's needs), and communicating in a soothing tone of voice. She provides nonverbal affective communication through eye contact, facial expressions, tone of voice, and open arms that affirm Ava's emotions and initiate feelings of security and safety.
  - Tasha forms an emotionally sound relationship with Ava by being attuned, i.e., offering caring responses to regulate her emotional needs.
  - Tasha recognizes that nap time is an anxious time for infants with histories of traumatic loss and she makes sure not to reinforce Ava's distress by staying by her side until she is calm and ready for sleep.
  - Additional trusting caregivers, who can work with Ava when she is distressed without becoming dysregulated and upset, are identified for times when Tasha, Ava's primary caregiver, becomes overwhelmed.

- **Create features of safety in the child care classroom environment**
  - Protect Ava from exposure to traumatic reminders.
    - Reduce the number of unexpected guests and changes in schedule to provide Ava with a sense of control over the environment.
    - Anticipate the presence of fathers or other men picking up their infants. In these moments, allow Ava to see her caregiver and reassure her that she is being attended to and is safe.

    o   Provide Ava with an available caregiver and extra comfort and calming strategies during stressful times.

    o   Help Ava seek quiet safe spaces that provide sensory and regulating activities that modulate her arousal levels, such as reading, rocking, calming music, and lowering the lights.

    o   The caregiver recognizes her own stress reactions to Ava's trauma triggers and uses strategies like taking deep breaths, using a mindfulness strategy (e.g., pausing and reflecting or being in the moment), or asking for support from another caregiver when she starts to feel overwhelmed.

- Foster a feeling of safety with consistent routines, a predictable daily schedule, and a quiet area that includes family pictures, books, and comfort and sensory items (e.g., calming music, various textures to grasp) that calm and soothe Ava.
- Minimize unexpected changes in schedule (e.g., guests entering the classroom, absence of child care provider, fire alarms) and provide extra support such as a visible child care provider, visual daily schedule, communicating changes when possible in advance, and reducing the number of transitions.

- **Facilitate knowledge of typical child development**
  - Provide Kara with the knowledge that Ava is coping with all of the current changes in her life by staying close to her mother and her caregivers, and that she requires extra comfort when distressed.
  - Inform Kara that Ava's crawling reflects a regression that is resulting from the stress she is experiencing. Explain that the child care providers are working to create a safe and secure environment where Ava is encouraged to securely explore the environment and feel safe enough to try walking again. Reassure Kara that it is not unusual for children to experience regressions under stress and will regain her mobility when she feels safe and secure.

- **Integrate trauma-informed practices across the program**
  - Create a child care program culture of safety where the director understands and is responsive to Ava's needs and the child care providers' efforts to help Ava.
  - The center director recognizes and supports care providers who are overwhelmed and could be experiencing secondary traumatic stress by acknowledging the difficulty they are experiencing and seeking out trauma-informed training.
  - The center director models and encourages self-care among the staff, making sure the staff take their breaks at the appropriate time and eating healthy meals.

Reflecting on Ava

Talk through the following questions with a partner to strengthen your knowledge of trauma-informed practice and trauma-sensitive strategies early childhood teachers and caregivers can use when working with young and vulnerable infants:

- What was your first reaction in reading about Ava and her mom? What feelings and thoughts did you have when reading this scenario about Ava? Her mother? Her teacher?
- Identify your own reactions to Ava's trauma responses. Why might you have these reactions?
- What traumatic stress reaction does Ava use most often?
- What trauma-sensitive caregiver responses would be helpful for Ava?
- What kind of support would you offer to Ava's mother?
- Review the trauma-informed teaching strategies. How would you sequence them (e.g., what strategies would you prioritize)? Would you add any additional strategies that would build resilience and a sense of safety for Ava?
- What information did you gain from the case study that you could use as a trauma-sensitive strategy in your classroom?
- What culturally responsive interventions would you use with Ava to provide a sense of security and safety?
- Identify Ava's strengths and how you would use her strengths to build her coping skills during stress.
- List self-care strategies that Ava's caregiver could use to make sure she has enough energy to cope with the stress of caring for children and families impacted by trauma?
- Discuss program or school-wide support and community resources that could support Ava and/or her mom.

Teaching Tip

Infants and toddlers living in conditions of stress and trauma are likely to have difficulty with transitions, especially when they need to leave the care of their primary attachment figure. Building in time to scaffold these transitions by recommending gradual changes where the mother and child care provider sits with the child in a quiet area and engages her in a regulating activity such as reading, can reduce the stress of these experiences for everyone involved.

PERSONAL REFLECTION

Lynette Jones, Site Supervisor (Figure 4.1)
Parent Child Center, San Francisco

When Susan was about 13 months old, she was placed in the care of a teacher with two other children. This new environment was unsettling for both parent and child. Mom noticed that when she was approaching the classroom, Susan would become restless and clingy. By the time mom had entered the room and began signing in, Susan was distressed and crying. Mom reported that this occurred when they were separated at other times such as at playgroup. This pattern continued over a few days and it was apparent that we needed a strategy to ease mom and Susan's concerns about separation.

We discussed some options with mom and with her input planned to have both she and Susan arrive ten minutes before the other children arrived so that mom could spend some focused interactive floor time with Susan. After a few minutes, the teacher would join them on the floor and the three of them would interact. When Susan began to engage with the teacher, giving eye contact and allowing the teacher to respond to her with a gentle touch, mom would slowly and calmly say goodbye to Susan and gradually

Figure 4.1 Lynette Jones.

make her way to the door, waving goodbye and blowing kisses. The teacher would continue to wave and blow kisses at Susan and engage in the game.

The teacher noticed that although Susan initially cried when mom stood up, she would allow the teacher to pat her back gently. The teacher repeated the same words to Susan every day, "I am right here and I am going to take care of you." The teacher would calmly reassure Susan that mommy said bye-bye and would be back to pick her up.

When Susan calmed down, she began to insist that the teacher hold her throughout the day. In the beginning, the teacher held her. But the crying escalated when the teacher had to leave the room for breaks and lunchtime, leaving an alternate teacher in the room. With support from the mental health consultant, teachers began sitting on the floor near Susan rather than hold her constantly. Any substitute teacher that entered the room applied the same strategy of sitting on the floor near the teacher and Susan would engage in play with them. The primary caregiver would slowly stand and say goodbye to Susan and wave and blow kisses while reassuring her that she would be back in a few minutes.

This way of separating from Susan was repeated every day exactly the same way as much as possible. Mom reported feeling less anxious about morning drop offs and was enjoying the special time with Susan in the classroom. Transitions with the teachers were more challenging but we tried to have the same alternate teacher. After what seemed like weeks, Susan began to walk on her own, which gave her more independence and willingness to enter the classroom on her own. This new independence enabled her to control her entrance and she was ready for that.

Teaching Dilemma

What if there are no additional staff who can step in and provide support when a teacher is overwhelmed and needs a break?

Some programs may not have enough staff to arrange for alternate caregivers to step in and take over the care of a child when the caregiver is distressed, overwhelmed, or triggered in a manner that impacts their ability to provide attuned or responsive caregiving. In this case, it is important for the caregivers to examine their own emotional reactions to the most challenging behaviors and with practice and intention learn to manage strong emotional reactions. It is also important for the teacher to be supported by the supervisor for their efforts to stay calm and connected to dysregulated children who are experiencing traumatic stress reactions.

LOOKING THROUGH A CHILD'S EYES

When Ava is distressed—crying, refusing to go to sleep, or freezing in place—her brain is giving her messages that she is unsafe and in danger. These feelings are triggered automatically in her brain and body by something in her environment that reminded her of a stressful and traumatic experience she had (e.g., a father walking in reminds her of the screaming and violence in her family home). Ava's tears and behaviors are communicating an important part of her trauma story. Ava is telling her teacher, "I am scared and I don't feel safe. My heart is racing and my limbs are shaking. I need support and love from you, a trusting adult, even if I arch my back when you pick me up and it's hard for you to be near me because my screaming hurts your ears and makes you feel upset. Please be patient with me. I'm scared and this is the only way I can tell you about what happened to me and what I need. Please be patient, hold me gently, sing softly and tell me I'm safe and that you will take care of me. I will need to hear this many times over many days but every time you stay with me when I'm crying or upset instead of walking away or responding with anger, I learn from you that I can feel safe again."

Connections to Neuroscience

Ava reacts neurobiologically with intense fear that stems from her sympathetic nervous system (SNS). The SNS sends messages to Ava's brain and body to become hyper-aroused and to exhibit a fight response. Ava utilizing the fight response of crying is her attempt to communicate the need for the caregiver's protection. Other times, she reacts neurobiologically with intense fear that stems from her parasympathetic nervous system (PNS). The PNS sends messages to Ava's brain and body to become hypo-aroused and to exhibit a freeze response and to become immobile. Ava utilizing the freeze response of immobility is her attempt to communicate the need for the caregiver's protection and to tell her she is safe. According to brain research, Ava's behavior is under the influence of the lower brainstem with increases in both sympathetic and parasympathetic nervous system activity, with stress chemicals being released (e.g. cortisol). Young children who experience trauma see the world as a dangerous place and their nervous system needs to receive distinct cues from trusting adults that they will be and are safe.

Family Engagement Strategy

Tasha worked with Kara to implement a consistent and gradual transition plan during morning drop off. The plan allowed Kara to mitigate Ava's defensive behavioral strategies so they would not become conditioned. The objective was for Kara to arrive at the child care center early enough to engage Ava in a pleasurable and sensory regulating activity in a quiet area. Tasha helped Kara identify cues that Ava was calm and ready for the mother to leave.

Interdisciplinary Partnerships and TIP

In providing trauma-informed teaching practice, cross-disciplinary specialists such as mental health consultants or counselors could help teachers reflect on the meaning of Ava's behavior and that Ava's dysregulated states (hyper- and hypo-arousal) were traumatic stress responses. An infant mental health specialist could support the teachers to learn how to regulate Ava by responding sensitively to her stress behavior and communicating nonverbally with a kind face and talking in a soothing tone that affirms Ava's emotions.

LINKING TO POLICY

There are just over 20 million children under age 6 in the United States of which over 1 million are experiencing homelessness. That translates into 1 of every 20 American children.

Children are homeless in every city, county, and state—every part of our country. There are many efforts at a policy level to provide services for young children and their families experiencing homelessness. Two examples include:

Early Head Start/Head Start: As of the passing of the Improving Head Start for School Readiness Act of 2007, children experiencing homelessness are automatically eligible for EHS/HS services, even if those children do not meet EHS/HS income requirements.

Head Start is now required to:

- Mandate that children experiencing homelessness get priority for services.
- Increase administrative flexibility. Families are given a grace period to comply with enrollment requirements. They can enroll and attend for up to 90 days without required documentation, such as immunization records.
- Have 3% set-aside to hold spots for children experiencing homelessness.
- Coordinate with their McKinney-Vento Local Education Agency homelessness liaison, as well as other community organizations such as emergency housing providers, to identify and link families to comprehensive services (housing, employment, food, transportation, etc.).

CCDBG: Child Care and Development Block Grant Act of 2014

The CCDF Program provides funds to states to help low-income families pay for child care while a parent works or is in an educational or job training program. In 2014, President Obama reauthorized the CCDBG Act for the first time since 1996. The CCDBG Reauthorization now includes provisions specific to families experiencing homelessness. For example, states must establish procedures for enrolling children experiencing homelessness. They must use funds for providing training on identifying and serving children experiencing homelessness and conduct specific outreach to families experiencing homelessness. States must start collecting data on how many of the children receiving federal subsidies for child care are considered homeless. Identifying how many children and families fall into this category will allow policymakers to target services that better meet their needs.

Mindfulness Strategy for Tasha

Tasha can focus on herself for a moment and ask herself a question, "How am I doing right now?" bringing awareness to the sensations, thoughts, and feelings in her body and naming them in short words and phrases ("My heart is racing, my hands feel sweaty, and I am taking short breaths. I am thinking about how hard my job is. I feel tired and stressed.")

Then, taking a pause, Tasha can attune to herself and her current state and focus attention on her breathing while she takes three deep breaths: remaining aware of the movement of her body with each breath, how her chest rises and falls, how her belly pushes in and out, and how her lungs expand and contract. Finding the pattern of her breath and anchoring herself to the present with this awareness. After her three breaths, she can ask herself if she needs to choose a self-care strategy to reduce her stress so she can remain attuned to Ava. Tasha chooses to take her lunch break so she can restore her energy and be present to Ava.

TIP Coaching

A coach working with Tasha can provide several trauma-sensitive coaching strategies that parallel the same strategies that she would like Tasha to provide for Ava. When the coach is attuned to the internal emotional state of the provider, this can be regulating and calming of intense and reactive emotions. Creating a space for Tasha to reflect and talk through her emotions will support her to think through a plan for Ava that is responsive and sensitive and provides her with a sense of security, predictability, and safety.

Tasha's coach is using an approach that supports relationship building and emotional regulation first before she begins to directly teach or train Tasha on using trauma-sensitive strategies. She understands that when a teacher like Tasha is regulated and supported to reflect on her own practice to find solutions for her caregiving dilemmas, teachers are more likely to develop trauma-sensitive skills and confidence in practical application of those skills.

SPOTLIGHT FOR ADMINISTRATORS AND SUPERVISORS

When working with families who are homeless and have experienced domestic abuse, it is critical for site supervisors to model sensitive care for the caregiver when communicating with the families and guarding against judgment by not talking badly about the families.

5

CASE STUDY

Toddler with a History of Neglect and Three Foster Home Placements

How Can Teachers Learn to Accurately Interpret the Meaning of Children's Trauma Behaviors Rather Than Taking Them Personally and Becoming Reactive?

Key Topics Covered

- A 28-month-old toddler with an experience of severe neglect and a history of being placed in three different foster homes
- TIP practices for supporting a hypo-aroused freeze response in a toddler
- TIP family engagement strategies for communicating with and supporting foster parent

John is a 28-month-old male toddler who has a history of severe neglect and has lived in three separate foster home placements since he was removed from his biological parents at age 14 months. John has been in his third placement for the past six months and has been attending a family child care program for the past two months. When the foster mother, Megan, leaves John at the program, he is often subdued and shows little facial expression. His caregivers report that John is frequently tearful and silent except when he is aroused and protests if he has to wait his turn during meal times. Due to John's early experiences with neglect, he had many experiences of feeling hungry throughout the day and night as a newborn infant. Although he tried to communicate his hunger through crying, his cues were not responded to. These early experiences created a sensitization where he does not trust that his basic needs will be met.

Crystal, the primary teacher caring for John, says that he is often clumsy, bumps into things, and falls down without accepting help from her or the other teachers. When John cries and they try to soothe him with a reassuring tone of voice and positive facial expressions, he runs away and hides in a corner of the room, trembling and rejecting their comfort. When John does not accept Crystal's efforts to comfort him, she does not perceive this as rejection. Instead, she asks herself, "What is John trying to communicate to me?" The program director knows of John's history of neglect and foster care placements and works with Crystal and the other providers to support John during the transition from home to school and during meal times. The director and teacher meet regularly with Megan to discuss ways to support John at the family child care program and at home where Megan reports that John is often unresponsive and unable to communicate his needs. Crystal, the other providers, and Megan are committed to working with the program director and are optimistic about helping John.

Application of Trauma-Informed Practices to John

Initial Inquiry Questions

1. Are there resources and program-wide support for trauma-informed care in the family child care program?
2. Is John reacting to traumatic stress by running away and rejecting comfort?
3. Are the caregivers and the program director knowledgeable in trauma-informed strategies and are they able to apply a strategy that works for John?
4. Do you think John feels the environment is safe or his caregiver is trustworthy?
5. Is there an understanding of the larger ecological contexts influencing John (e.g., the neglect he experienced, the time when he entered the foster care system and the knowledge that he is in his third foster care home in 14 months, and information about his current placement)?
6. Does a referral need to be made for an additional trauma-sensitive assessment, intervention, and/or supports?

Understanding Possible Factors Related to John's Traumatic Stress

1. History of severe neglect
2. Loss of biological parents
3. Multiple foster care placements
4. Disrupted first and primary attachment relationships
5. Young age

Understanding Possible Factors Related to John's Traumatic Stress

1. History of severe neglect
2. Loss of biological parents
3. Multiple foster care placements
4. Disrupted first and primary attachment relationships

Identifying Traumatic Triggers that Lead to John's Stress Behaviors

1. Transitions from foster mother to child care or the absence of a primary caregiver
2. Meal time
3. Teacher helping John regulate his emotions

Identifying John's Traumatic Stress Reactions

1. Subdued and lack of excited, engaging, or happy facial expression when dropped off at child care
2. Generally silent and gloomy with few facial expressions during the day
3. Mostly plays alone
4. Clumsy and falls easily
5. Hides in corner and rejects comfort from caregivers
6. Distressed during meal preparation
7. Over-aroused (protests) and/or under-aroused (silent and expressionless)

Goals to Support John

1. Help John during separations from foster mother to child care
2. Support John during meal preparation
3. Reduce John's defensive behaviors (plays alone, sullen and quiet at drop off, runs and hides, etc.)
4. Re-regulate John's distress (Crystal uses a soothing tone of voice to acknowledge his feelings and stays close without touching John to reassure him that he is safe)
5. Build John's trust in his caregivers so that he can accept their comfort
6. Protect John from exposure to traumatic reminders (too many transitions, unpredictable adult caregiving, adult disappears unexpectedly)

Trauma-Informed Teaching Practices to Support John

1. **Implement a plan to support John's transition from the foster mother to the family child care program**

a. Crystal, her director, and Megan create a transition plan to implement during the morning drop off. They create a consistent and predictable morning routine for John and Megan, who takes the required time to help John engage in a pleasurable and regulating activity (e.g., Megan gets down on John's level and offers small toys to grasp and hold onto) and looks for cues (ready to explore the environment) that John is adjusted before departing. They all understand that it is important not to unintentionally reinforce John's distress by having Megan leave too quickly.

b. Megan and Crystal reassure John through maintaining close proximity but careful not to touch him, using kind gestures (smiles and reassuring looks) and a soothing voice that he is safe and will be cared for until Megan returns to pick him up.

c. Megan identifies a comfort item (e.g., a small square of soft material or small soft stuffed bear) for John to have available during the transition from home to child care that he can hold to soothe his distress and help to modulate his arousal to a more optimal alert state.

2. **Use emotionally attuned teacher interactions to re-regulate John's distress**

a. Crystal focuses on staying connected with John during stressful times such as transitions, between activities, and during meal preparation. She uses affect attunement (e.g., attuning to John's emotional feeling of distress by remaining present but recognizing that he needs his space) and interactive regulatory support (e.g., meeting John at eye level and using affective nonverbal and verbal communication) to reduce his fear and heightened levels of arousal.

b. Crystal provides a relational and containing environment for John by being patient, present, emotionally attuned, and communicating in a soothing tone of voice with nonverbal facial expressions that affirm John's feelings and initiate a feeling of security and safety for him.

3. **Create features of safety in the family child care environment**

a. Everyone works to protect John from exposure to traumatic reminders (e.g., experiences he had when his survival needs were not met, when there was no predictability or routines he could count on in his life as uncertainty, change, and chaos were common, and when adults including primary attachment figures would disappear). Preventing these traumatic triggers for John is supported through such strategies as:

    i. Implementing the morning transition plan discussed above to reinforce to John that his life can have a sense of predictability and routine that supports John to feel a greater sense of

        control and to reduce the amount of time John spends react-
ing to a stress response.

  ii. Providing John with a consistent teacher like Crystal that
offers him extra support and engages him in calming and sensory regulating activities during meal preparation.

  iii. Making plans for ways to modulate John's hyper-arousal
(overly active) and hypo-arousal (under-reactive, tuned out,
listless) levels by identifying strategies that work for John. For
example, including time for John to be in natural outdoor
environments, taking a walk, patting or rubbing John's back,
engaging John in sensory play (pouring with cups at a water
table, digging in/playing with sand), or supporting John to
participate in expressive arts (activities that emphasize the
process of creation or engagement instead of the final prod-
uct) including painting, dancing, listening to music, pretending, or acting out (e.g., pretending to be different animals).

  iv. Crystal learns to recognize her own traumatic stress reactions
to John's rejection for comfort. She understands how important it is that she not react negatively when John rejects her
initiation of connection and comfort (e.g., showing any type
of angry/rejecting behaviors toward John). If she does, she
understands that she risks retraumatizing John by reinforcing
his early memories of adults who were not safe, caring, and/
or attuned to his emotional state and needs. Instead, Crystal
expresses empathy and understands that his rejections are
protective as they reflect how his brain taught him to survive as a young infant being neglected. By learning to notice
their own traumatic stress reactions, Crystal and Megan can
develop their skills and ability to remain calm, regulated, reassuring, and attuned to John when he rejects them. This reinforces to John that despite his challenging behaviors, they will
continue to care and support him, to keep him safe, and to
meet all his daily needs.

e. The caregivers foster a feeling of safety for John with consistent
routines (arrival time, bathroom time, cleanup, departure) a predictable daily schedule (morning free play, snack, circle time, gross
motor play, lunch, nap, afternoon free play) and areas with sensory
and emotionally regulating activities (playdough, play and expressive arts, water and sand play, dress up) that provides a feeling of
calm and relaxation.

f. Crystal and her colleagues create a quiet area that includes pictures
of John's foster family, picture books that are familiar to John, and

at least one or two that relate to topics aligned with his interests, and comfort and sensory items (e.g., pillows, stuffed animals, pinwheels, chew toys, balls he can squeeze, etc.) where John can go to when he runs away from the caregiver, and where the teacher can quietly join him by being present, emotionally attuned, and communicating in a soothing tone of voice that acknowledges approval of John's strong emotions and initiates a feeling of security and safety.

g. Crystal forms an emotionally sound relationship with John by being attuned and offering caring responses to his needs.

h. Crystal understands that John reacts defensively to strong emotions and feelings of helplessness and fear by running away. When she consistently responds sensitively to his attachment needs, it will generate in John a sense of security and the expectation of an available caregiver in times of need.

4. **Facilitate knowledge of child development**

a. Crystal and Megan offer John social-emotional activities with feeling posters that help him identify his emotions both at home and at the family child care center. For example, Crystal introduces John to four basic emotions—happy, sad, mad, and scared—in an age-appropriate way by pairing a picture of feeling faces with the appropriate emotion. She then acts as a role model by talking about her own feelings and pairing the feelings with facial examples.

   i. Crystal and Megan introduce John to sensory literacy vocabulary to increase his ability to identify, understand, and express sensations that he is feeling in his body (e.g., energy charges that make him want to jump out of his skin) that stem from the trigger that his basic needs (hunger) will not be met or a physiological response such as a pounding heart. Crystal can focus John's attention toward his internal sensations and help him recognize the strong reactions he may be feeling and have him express them in a healthy way through movement, play, or art.

   ii. Crystal and Megan can both support John to practice self-regulatory strategies such as breathing.

Note: These social-emotional skills are not intended to be taught to John or any child when they are dysregulated. When a child is not regulated, they lose access to the executive part of their thinking brain and are unable to think and learn. Teaching social-emotional skills when a child is calm and in an optimal state of regulation is when a child is most receptive to learning new skills.

**BREATHING SUPPORTS SELF-REGULATION:
BREATHING ACTIVITY FOR TODDLERS**

Flower Breath

Imagine smelling a beautiful flower, breathe in through the nose and out through the mouth, releasing any tension. Stop and smell the roses, daffodils, daisies, or any other flower they like. This is a simple way to connect kids to their breath and how it helps them to feel.

Source: https://move-with-me.com/self-regulation/4-breathing-exercises-for-kids-to-empower-calm-and self-regulate/

---

    iii. John can be introduced to symbolic and language-based peer play experiences with Crystal who can mediate and foster his cognitive, language, and social development. For example, Crystal forms a small group of children to discuss the basic emotion "sad." She then creates and scaffolds a play where children identify something that makes them sad and then how they feel better. For example, I feel sad when I get hurt. But then I talk about it to feel better.

    iv. Crystal can create opportunities for John to engage in expressive arts, especially activities that integrate music and dance (e.g., "freeze" games to music), as they help John to improve his balance and gross motor skills.

5. **Integrate trauma-informed practices across the family child care center**

  a. The center director supports trauma-informed teaching practices and assists Crystal and her colleagues to create a trauma-informed classroom that facilitates an accurate feeling of safety with consistent routines, daily schedule, and relationship-based teachers. Crystal and her colleagues are supported for their efforts to develop an emotionally sound relationship with John. Reflective supervision from the director who bears witness/listens/attunes to her staff who will need to process the emotional labor involved in supporting John and not reacting negatively to his rejection of their efforts to connect with him.

  b. The program director values and teaches self-care strategies to the staff who are triggered and need time to regulate and de-escalate.

Reflecting on John

1. What was your first reaction in reading about John? What feelings, thoughts, and images did this case scenario inspire in you about John? Crystal and the providers? Megan, his foster care mother?

2. Identify your own reactions to John's trauma responses. Why might you have these reactions?
3. What traumatic stress reaction does John use most often?
4. What trauma-sensitive caregiver responses are most helpful for John?
5. What kind of support would you offer to John's foster mother?
6. Review the trauma-informed teaching strategies discussed above. How would you sequence them (e.g., what strategies would you prioritize)? Would you add any additional strategies that would build resilience and a sense of safety for John?
7. What information did you gain from the case study that you could use as a trauma-sensitive strategy in your classroom?
8. Discuss how you would approach teaching a young child who had a history of neglect and was placed in foster care.
9. What culturally responsive interventions would you use with John to provide a sense of security and safety?
10. Identify John's strengths and how you would use his strengths to foster resilience and a sense of safety.
11. List self-care strategies that John's caregivers could use to reduce secondary traumatic stress.
12. Discuss program or school-wide supports and resources that could support John.

Teaching Tip

Children who experience early relational trauma and neglect have emotional needs that may go unnoticed and unmet. These early experiences create implicit memories that can trigger defensive behavioral reactions (withdrawing or rejecting comfort) if adults try to console children when they feel threatened. In situations like this, it is important for teachers to take the time to build a relationship with the children so they can begin to feel safe and over time learn to trust that their emotional needs will consistently be met. Only then will the children be able to benefit from emotional co-regulation.

Teaching Dilemma

What if I don't know anything about the child's trauma history? I know one of the children in my program is living with a foster parent but I don't have any other history. How will I know what to do to support this child? This is an important question. This teacher is wondering if she can be effective in helping a child who is exhibiting traumatic stress behavior without knowing the child's history. A foundation of TIP is that you can support children without having a comprehensive knowledge of the histories.

A primary goal of trauma-informed teaching practice is for teachers to adopt an inquiry-based approach that questions whether the observed behavior is a traumatic stress reaction. To address this dilemma, the teacher could consider the context in which the behavior occurs, identify possible triggers, and choose teaching practices that respond accordingly to the child's strengths and use these strengths to build the child's capacity for resilience.

LOOKING THROUGH A CHILD'S EYES: WHAT STORY IS JOHN TRYING TO COMMUNICATE TO HIS TEACHER?

When I run away upset from my teacher who is trying to soothe me please understand that it is a defensive stress reaction of my nervous system that is misinterpreting my caregiver's efforts as harmful. Although my caregiver's affective exchanges (soothing tone of voice and positive facial expressions) have the potential to positively change my stress reactions and help me calm, my capacity to relate to others is compromised due to my adverse experiences and persistent fear. I see the world as a dangerous place and it will take time for me to feel protected and understood or held in mind by a trusting caregiver. Only then will I be able to calm and be receptive to positive emotional exchanges. Please do not give up on me. My nervous system depends upon your soothing voice and affective communication to feel safe and achieve an optimal zone of arousal that allows me to fully participate in social interactions. A state that I seldom experience.

Connections from Neuroscience

It is not uncommon for young children who have experienced unmet emotional needs to develop a sensitized neural response pattern to traumatic stress to withdraw and cognitively freeze when they feel anxious and out of control. John shows this behavior when he runs away and hides in a corner of the room, trembling and rejecting his caregiver's comfort. Sometimes this behavior is misunderstood as not wanting comfort when in fact, in this emotionally threatening situation, John is functioning in an alarm state mediated by lower brain centers at the dorsal vagal nerve with related increase in parasympathetic nervous system activity and cortisol levels that cause him to freeze.

Family Engagement Strategy

The director and Crystal met with Megan to discuss how to support John at the family child care program and at home. They created a predictable morning routine for John and Megan during the drop off and helped Megan identify comfort items to bring from home that John could hold onto during the day when distressed. Crystal and Megan offered John social-emotional activities with feeling posters that would help him identify his emotions both at child care and at home.

Interdisciplinary Partnerships and TIP

In providing trauma-informed teaching practice, interdisciplinary perspectives would help to understand John's behaviors. For example, an occupational therapist could assess whether John's subdued and limited facial expressions suggest difficulty processing sensory information and offer sensory-regulating activities to help John. A physical therapist could assess problems in John's gross motor skills (clumsy, bumps into things, and falls down) and offer strategies to improve his balance.

CHILDREN WITH TOXIC STRESS ARE BEING MISDIAGNOSED

"Trauma can affect hormones, the immune system, even the way DNA is read and transcribed. And it dramatically increases the risk of both behavioral and health problems in childhood and in adulthood. Toxic stress affects white kids, black and brown kids, rich, poor, urban, rural—in other words, it can affect anyone and it can happen anywhere. But right now, only 4 percent of pediatricians in the U.S. are screening for toxic stress. Most haven't received any training on how to identify kids who are at risk.

Too many children with behavioral symptoms of toxic stress are being labeled with ADHD and given stimulants without any identification of the root cause. Many kids show no behavioral symptoms at all. Yet they are still more than twice as likely to go on to develop asthma, autoimmune disease, heart disease and cancer – and their life expectancy can be cut short by decades."

Dr. Nadine Burke

Founder and CEO of the Center for Youth Wellness and author of *The Deepest Well: Healing the Long-Term Effects of Childhood Adversity.*

Source: www.pbs.org/newshour/health/opinion-too-many-children-with-toxic-stress-are-being-misdiagnosed

---

Mindfulness Strategy for Crystal

It would be helpful to identify one mindfulness technique to assist Crystal when she is feeling stressed or burned out. This strategy would be using breathing to support her own self-regulation and emotional reactions. Teaching her to use breathing techniques (mindful slow breaths in and out) can serve as a remote control for the emotional processing center in the brain. Slowing her breathing can serve as a simple strategy to manage and regulate emotional reactions and create a "thoughtful pause" for Crystal to support her through stressful experiences in the classroom.

TIP Coaching

A coach working with Crystal can help her to identify her own feelings and reactions to John's behaviors. Challenging behavior can be triggering and without a safe space to talk about it, it can impact Crystal's reactions unconsciously. Talking about how she is feeling can be regulating and will support Crystal in bringing awareness to her reactions, which can prevent her from taking any actions that would cause unintentional harm to John (using harsh tones or physical prompts for example).

SPOTLIGHT FOR TEACHERS/CAREGIVERS

It is important for Crystal to remember that John has only been in the program for two months. As a result, building a relationship with John is the most important strategy that she should focus on. Crystal should also focus on providing predictable routines, minimizing transitions and unexpected change, and providing attunement and connection with John in a way that feels safe for him. It is important for Crystal and her colleagues to stop themselves from using unintentionally harsh and quick movements. John will do best with soft regulating touch. Implementing these strategies will take time and the progress will likely be slow but these are critical foundations to build an attachment with John.

Spotlight for Administrators/Supervisors

Administrators/supervisors can help the teacher see what they do that already works! It is so easy to focus on what is not working. Caregivers rarely hear or see their own strengths reflected to them. A caregiver who is in the middle of their own "movie" cannot always see what works and the stress of trauma naturally focuses their attention on the negative. An administrator who scans for the strengths and reflects them back to the caregiver can help support the building of resiliency. The administrator can take some time to observe caregiver/child interactions and then provide thoughtful strength-based feedback.

6

CASE STUDY

Preschooler with an Undocumented Father who Suddenly Disappears Due to Deportation

How Can Teachers Learn to Care for Children Who Are Sad and Experiencing the Loss and Separation of a Parent?

Key Topics Covered

- Four-year-old experiencing loss of father due to sudden deportation
- TIP practices for supporting a withdrawn freeze response in a preschooler
- TIP family engagement strategies for communicating with and supporting her mother

Olivia is a four-year-old female child whose mother, Angelica, is an undocumented immigrant from Latin America and suffers from depression and traumatic stress. The family is experiencing a high level of fear and uncertainty over the sudden disappearance of the father, Manuel, who was deported without having an opportunity to say goodbye and whose current whereabouts are unknown. Olivia has been attending a Head Start program for the past year. The teachers report that she is a typically developing and a good-natured child who is friendly with her peers. Since the father was deported, Olivia has lost interest in eating her food and appears withdrawn and distressed when it is time to go to sleep. She often cries out in her sleep for her mother and the teachers are unable to soothe her back to sleep. They are reporting a steady increase in behavioral challenges during the transition to outdoor play. Olivia becomes hyper-aroused, hitting and snatching the other children's toys. Recently, when Olivia's primary teacher, Maria, ran after Olivia and tried to contain her, Olivia bit Maria's hand. Maria has noticed that Olivia is often upset and frequently hides in the corner when it is time to leave for the day. Other times, Olivia runs to the window and cries out "Papi, te quiero!" Olivia's teachers are concerned that they do not have the skills or knowledge to help Olivia. They have met with the program director, Daphne, to ask for training and ways that she can support them. Daphne is organizing a training on trauma-informed care and the Head Start family advocate is reaching out to Olivia's mother to offer support.

Application of Trauma-Informed Practices to Olivia

Initial Inquiry Questions

- What kind of program support and resources exist for trauma-informed care at the Head Start program?
- Do the caregivers know that Olivia's response to her fear and the traumatic reminders of her father's sudden disappearance may be evidenced in her loss of appetite, resistance to sleep, hiding in the corner, and increased expression of challenging behaviors?
- Is there an understanding of the larger ecological contexts influencing Olivia and her family? (e.g., the increased deportations happening in their community, the housing and food insecurity impacting Olivia's family due to the loss of the father's income)
- Does a referral need to be made for additional assessment, intervention, and/or supports?

Understanding Possible Factors Related to Olivia's Traumatic Stress

- Immigrant status
- Maternal mental illness
- Sudden disappearance of father due to deportation
- Disrupted attachment relationship with father
- Family is fearful and uncertain over father's current whereabouts

Identifying Traumatic Triggers that Lead to Olivia's Stress Behaviors

- Nap time
- Meal time
- Transition to outdoor play
- Teacher/adult running after Olivia and trying to contain her
- Departure from school

Identifying Olivia's Traumatic Stress Reactions

- Distressed at nap time
- Poor appetite
- Cries out for mother during sleep
- Difficult to soothe

- Hyper-aroused, chasing and pushing children
- Bites teacher's hand
- Upset and hides in the corner when it is time to leave school or cries out for father

Goals to Support Olivia

- Support Olivia during nap time
- Restore Olivia's interest in food
- Reduce Olivia's fear and regulate her emotions
- Help Olivia's transition to outdoor play
- Protect Olivia from exposure to traumatic reminders

Trauma-Informed Teaching Practices to Support Olivia

- **Support Olivia during nap time.** Maria, Olivia's teacher, recognizes that nap time is an anxious time for children with histories of traumatic loss. She implements several strategies to support Olivia to feel safe enough at the Head Start center that she can rest and/or fall asleep during nap time.
  - Maria looks for cues that Olivia is tired and ready to take a nap.
  - Maria creates a consistent and predictable nap time routine that prepares Olivia for sleep.
  - Maria works with the Head Start Family Advocate to make a plan for communicating with Angelica, Olivia's mother, to help them identify some comfort items for Olivia to have available during the nap time transition that would be calming and help Olivia soothe her separation distress.
  - Maria tries not to reinforce Olivia's separation distress, so she plans to stay by her side until she is calm and ready for sleep instead of abruptly leaving her and triggering her fear response.
  - Maria responds quickly to Olivia's cries for her mother by using a reassuring and soothing voice that communicates to her, "I am here for you and I will not leave your side until you feel safe." She hums the same tune quietly each time this happens allowing Olivia to eventually begin to calm her stress response system the moment she hears the humming begin.
  - Maria identifies additional trusting teachers who can support Olivia's routine for falling asleep when she, as lead teacher, is unavailable. All of the teachers follow the same routines and use the same strategies to support and calm Olivia.
- **Support Olivia's interest in food.** Maria recognizes that Olivia's loss of appetite is a traumatic reaction to the loss of her father, Manuel. With this understanding in mind, she identifies the following strategies to support Olivia.

- Maria allows Olivia to exercise and play outdoors before meal time to increase her appetite
- The teachers identify Olivia's favorite foods and make them available at meal time.
- The preschool staff cook foods that smell good and may stimulate Olivia's appetite.
- The teachers arrange for small meals and snacks to be available for Olivia to eat throughout the day. Making snacks available throughout the day may lessen the teachers' concerns that Olivia is not eating at meal time.
- The teachers support Olivia's health by offering foods that are nutritional and high in protein needed for her growth and development.
- The teachers recognize that "pressuring" Olivia to eat will cause her more stress.
- The teachers create calm environments and make sure that Olivia is in a calm state, which may increase her likelihood of eating.

- **Use emotionally attuned caregiver interactions to regulate Olivia's dysregulated behavior**
  - The teachers are aware that Olivia is coping with her feelings of loss by wanting her primary caregiver, Maria, nearby and that responding sensitively to her attachment needs by arranging for Maria to remain close during nap time, as well at the beginning and end of day transitions, are important types of security she is looking for.
  - All of the teachers are aware that Olivia reacts internally to traumatic stress with challenging behavior. They recognize that they need to provide co-regulation to modulate Olivia's behavior. For example, the teachers understand that the outside environment stimulates Olivia's arousal and they use reassuring words and close proximity to help Olivia transition to unstructured outdoor play.
  - Maria and her colleagues know that they need to approach Olivia slowly during outdoor play when she hits and takes other children's toys. They provide interactive regulatory support and positive communication to contain her behavior. For example, when they observe Olivia taking a toy from another child, Maria acknowledges that Olivia must want the toy and she calmly and warmly states, "Let me help you figure out how you can get the toy without hitting the other children. Hitting can hurt, but asking with words could help. You could tell [child's name], 'Can I have a turn with [name of toy]?'"
  - The teachers provide a supportive and relational environment for Olivia by staying connected with her—especially when she displays heightened levels of arousal (e.g., when she is hitting and snatching the other children's toys during outside play) and by being patient, present, emotionally attuned, and communicating in a soothing

tone of voice that affirms Olivia's emotions and initiates a feeling of security and safety for her.

- **Create features of safety in the Head Start environment.** The Head Start staff work together to protect Olivia from exposure to traumatic reminders.
  - o The teachers implement the nap time transition plan discussed above.
  - o The teachers understand and anticipate that departures from the Head Start program activate traumatic reminders for Olivia because the end of the day represents "loss" as Olivia experiences her caregivers and peers "disappearing"; an experience that triggers her memory of her father's loss. In these moments, her teachers understand how important it is that they provide extra support to Olivia, especially during transitions. They use reassuring language: "Mom is coming to pick you up. When you get home you will eat dinner, get ready for bed, and then sleep with your favorite stuffed bunny Sprinkles. When you wake up in the morning, mom will bring you back to our classroom where we will keep you safe and you will be able to play with your friends again. We will be here in the morning. You are safe." The teachers recognize Olivia's fears about losing the people and things she loves and they know that saying goodbye at the end of the day triggers Olivia to worry that people will disappear like her daddy did. To address Olivia's fears, the teachers offer her truthful, age-appropriate answers.
  - o Maria helps Olivia seek safe spaces in the classroom that have sensory and regulating activities that modulate her arousal levels (e.g., water table, playdough, bubbles, art table, calming corner with books).
  - o The caregivers reflect with their supervisor to gain awareness of their own reactions to Olivia's strong attachment needs. They are supported as a teaching team to create plans for attending to Olivia's intensified needs in addition to identifying strategies for their own self-care. For example, the director releases Maria and her colleagues for brief periods of time during particularly challenging days/times for Olivia so they can have a break and refresh themselves by engaging in self-care strategies (e.g., taking short walk outdoors, going in a car to listen to music, finding a quiet room to sit in, calling a close friend or family member to talk, playing a game on their phone).
- **Foster a feeling of safety with consistent routines, a predictable daily schedule, and an area that provides a sense of control over the environment.** For example, creating a quiet area with family

pictures, books, and comfort and sensory items where Olivia can go to instead of hiding in the corner and where the teacher can connect with her emotionally by being present, attuned, and communicate in a soothing tone of voice that acknowledges Olivia's loss and reassurance that she is safe and cared for.

- **Facilitate knowledge of typical child development**
  - Introduce a sensory literacy vocabulary that increases Olivia's ability to identify, understand, and express sensations that she is feeling in her body and to express them in a healthy way, i.e., an energy charge in the body that stems from a trigger or a physiological response such as a pounding heart. Helping Olivia express her emotions/feelings to an adult can help her regulate (e.g., she can point to an image or a feeling face, or express her feeling with words). If there is a feeling poster in the room, the teacher can take Olivia over to the poster and ask her to point to a word or facial image that represents how she is feeling. Alternatively, if the child is unable to identify her feeling, a teacher could say, "I am wondering if you are feeling 'worried' right now and if you might miss your dad?" This way the teacher is not definitively telling Olivia how she feels, instead, she provides a verbal scaffold to support Olivia to connect her sensory experience (pounding heart) with emotional literacy (feeling "worried").
  - Introduce social-emotional activities with sensory and feeling posters that help Olivia identify the feelings in her body and the related emotions.
  - Introduce self-regulatory strategies such as breathing.

BREATHING SUPPORTS SELF-REGULATION: BREATHING ACTIVITY FOR PRESCHOOLERS

Bear Breath: Imagine a Bear Hibernating

Breathe in to a count of three or four.
  Pause for a count of one or two.
  Breath out for a count of three or four.
  Pause for a count of one or two.
  Repeat a few times.
  This breathing exercise grounds and calms children. Use for restful, reflective time before nap, story time, or any creative activity.
  https://move-with-me.com/self-regulation/4-breathing-exercises-for-kids-to-empower-calm-and-self-regulate/

- Provide teacher-mediated peer play experiences where the teacher can help Olivia express her emotions and shift negative emotions to more positive ones that facilitate prosocial behavior. For example, Maria discusses with Olivia how it can be difficult for her to talk about her feelings when she is scared. The teacher adds, "When I feel scared, I know I won't stay scared forever. I also know that there are many things I can do when I feel scared to help myself feel better including asking for help, drawing a picture that shows how I feel, or talking about it with an adult."

> **Prosocial behavior** includes caring, helping, and behaving in ways that benefit others. During early childhood, parents and teachers model for young children prosocial behaviors that carry into their interactions and communication with peers. In turn, peer relationships provide opportunities for children to learn and practice prosocial skills, especially when teachers encourage children to share, act kindly, and help their peers. These types of collaborative interactions with peers strengthen the development of cognitive skills (e.g., perspective taking, self-regulation) that support children's prosocial behavior and contribute to successful classroom behavior and children's social competence. These prosocial behaviors are taught when children are calm and regulated and can access their prefrontal cortex responsible for thinking, planning, and practicing new strategies.

- Create areas that include expressive arts with music, dancing, and art.
- Provide Angelica, Olivia's mother, with the knowledge that Olivia is coping with the unexpected loss of her father and requires extra comfort when distressed. Encourage Angelica to realize that Olivia should receive prompt and accurate information about the loss (e.g., adults should not try to change the subject or otherwise deny the significant experience of her father disappearing), be permitted to ask all sorts of questions, and that she receive prompt and truthful, age-appropriate answers.

> ### Age Appropriate Accurate Information about a Loss when Communicating with Young Children
>
> - **Olivia**: Mom, where is my daddy? When is daddy coming home?
> - **Angelica** answers truthfully, "I don't know where daddy is but I am taking care of you and you are safe."
>
> An important aspect of trauma-informed practice is acknowledging the traumatic experiences that children have had in their young lives. Responding to children, however, should be done in a developmentally appropriate

manner. This means that adults should answer children's questions honestly but also only provide answers to the questions they ask (not additional information) and depending on the child's age, the answers should not be too detailed or specific.

As seen in the exchange above, Olivia's question opened up an opportunity for her mother, Angelica, to provide accurate and developmentally appropriate language that acknowledged the loss of her father while also reassuring Olivia that she was safely being cared for despite her father's disappearance.

- **Integrate trauma-informed practices across the program/center**
  - Daphne, the Head Start director, is organizing training on trauma-informed care and the Head Start family advocate is reaching out to Olivia's mother to offer support.
  - Daphne understands and supports the implementation of trauma-informed teaching practices and assists her staff in understanding the need to create a school culture of safety.
  - Daphne understands the importance of providing time for the teachers, especially Maria, to form an emotional relationship with Olivia. She works with her staff to make sure their program policies and practices are in alignment with the goal of creating safe classrooms within the context of a safe school culture. Their first goals are to work together to identify how Daphne can provide Maria additional supervisory support for her classroom during the most challenging times of the day for Crystal (e.g., drop off/pick up, shift to outside play, meal time, nap time) and also to ensure that Maria is not pulled outside of the classroom during these times to attend to administrative or other issues.
  - Daphne models the importance of self-care in her own life and provides a training to her staff to learn strategies to support their own self-care in addition to the signs of burnout and compassion fatigue. She also works with staff to consider how they can engage in self-care both at work and outside of work.

Reflecting on Olivia

1. What was your first reaction in reading about Olivia? What feelings, thoughts, and images did this case scenario inspire in you about Olivia? Angelica, her mother? Maria and the other teachers?
2. Identify your own reactions to Olivia's trauma responses. Why might you have these reactions?
3. What traumatic stress reaction does Olivia use most often?

4. What trauma-sensitive caregiver responses are most helpful for Olivia?
5. What kind of support would you offer to Olivia's mother?
6. Review the trauma-informed teaching strategies discussed above. How would you sequence them (e.g., what strategies would you prioritize)? Would you add any additional strategies that would build resilience and a sense of safety for Olivia?
7. What information did you gain from the case study that you could use as a trauma-sensitive strategy in your classroom?
8. Discuss how you would approach teaching a young child when there is sudden death or loss of a primary attachment figure.
9. What culturally responsive interventions would you use with Olivia to provide a sense of security and safety?
10. Identify Olivia's strengths and how you would use her strengths to foster resilience and a sense of safety.
11. List self-care strategies that Olivia's caregivers could use to reduce secondary traumatic stress.
12. Discuss program or school-wide supports and resources that could support Olivia.

Teaching Tip

The loss of a parent early on in life is one of the most unexplained and painful experiences a young child can suffer. The very person toward whom it is natural to turn to for comfort is no longer available. The loss gives rise to separation distress and to processes of mourning wherein aggression (acting out, strong emotional reactions), the function of which is to achieve reunion, plays a major role (Bowlby, 1980). Other aspects of mourning include protest, an urge to search for the person, anger, despair, and dissociation. A young child can follow a course of healthy mourning when favorable conditions emerge (Bowlby, 1980). The most important conditions are the existence of a living attachment figure (in this case Angelica) whom the child can trust and who comforts the child, and how the child construes her own part in the loss. Teachers can play a major role in helping a successful mourning process if children are permitted to ask all sorts of questions and receive prompt, accurate, and truthful, age-appropriate answers, and are encouraged to grieve the loss (Bowlby, 1980). It is critical that teachers do not misinterpret children's mourning as "anger or bad behavior" but rather as a natural reaction to loss.

Teaching Dilemma

I'm worried that if I provide prompt and accurate information about a child's traumatic loss, I will only make things worse for the child. I'm also concerned that I won't have answers to the questions a child may ask about their traumatic experience.

These fears are understandable and one of the primary reasons why children's traumatic experiences so often are a taboo topic and go unacknowledged by the adults who care for them. It is very difficult for adults to confront the terrible experiences that many children have. We want to protect children from trauma and allowing children to share stories of what has happened to them, and the fears they have as a result, can feel very scary for adults who do not know how to manage the personal emotions that result from hearing about children's pain and the very real concerns they have when they learn information that requires them in their roles as mandatory reporters to speak with Child Protective Services (CPS). It may be difficult to speak with CPS, especially if it is the first time that a teacher has to consult with this agency, but it is important to do as the number one factor is to always consider the protection of the child.

The reason it is important for teachers to acknowledge children's stories, to allow children to ask questions, and to provide developmentally responsive information about their experiences, is that this supports children to heal and build resiliency. Contrary to popular belief, research from such neuroscientists as Dr. Daniel Siegel highlights the importance of allowing children to tell their stories as an important strategy for helping to decrease the stress associated with traumatic experiences. This is because the right hemisphere of the brain houses our emotions, including those associated with a painful experience. When someone shows care and concern and takes time to listen to a child's story (told verbally, through drawings, or play), this serves a very important function for the brain. Listening to children's stories and showing compassion helps calm the emotional intensity within the right side of their brain. After a child is able to share their story and emotions in a context where they feel heard and supported, they will become visibly more relaxed, appear calmer, and more self-regulated.

It is important for teachers to understand the boundaries of their role. Teachers are not therapists and becoming trauma-informed in your practices as a teacher is not the same as providing therapy to a child. Instead, teachers learn to listen to children's stories to better understand children's concerns. With this knowledge in mind, teachers can then reinforce for children that they are safe, that the adults will take care of their needs while they are away from home/their caregivers, and that they have many strengths, skills, and capacities (e.g., the trauma they experienced is only one part of who they are). Whereas a therapist would promote healthy mourning development and support the grieving process in children who are experiencing the sudden loss and separation of a parent, teachers listen to children's stories to have empathy and attunement with a child so they can adjust their teaching and caregiving strategies to meet the child's individual needs.

Family Engagement Strategy

Maria is working with the Head Start family advocate and Olivia's mother to help the mother understand that Olivia's behaviors are a reaction to the loss of the father. They are also discussing with the mother that Olivia is being observed in the classroom by a mental health consultant who is helping Maria support Olivia in the classroom and recommending strategies that the mother can use at home with Olivia. They are also discussing with Olivia's mother whether a referral for family therapy is warranted.

Interdisciplinary Partnerships and TIP

Program administrators should refer children with Medicaid health insurance to behavior health services and those without to mental health specialists who work in private practice. Head Start programs have partnered with behavioral health services (county mental health) to provide classroom mental health consultation. It is important to make referrals to behavioral health services when a child is struggling with trauma-related or other persistent challenging behavior and emotional concerns. Waiting lists can be long so referring to resources before a child's behavior escalates is highly recommended. In the meantime, it is beneficial to observe a child and discover in the early stages trauma-sensitive strategies that support healing, skill building, and resiliency.

It is important to request that mental health providers include parents/caregivers in treatment and educate them about the impact of trauma on child behaviors and behavior management. For young children, seeing them alone can help but ensuring the parent/caregiver is learning strategies in the home is important as they support the child more than anyone else. It is also important to make referrals to mental health professionals who specialize in early childhood trauma.

Research shows that Latino citizen children with undocumented immigrant parents are at higher risk for several negative outcomes. Research demonstrates that undocumented parental legal status is a strong predictor of poor physical health, poor mental health, and compromised academic outcomes for Latino children. Children of undocumented immigrants face unique traumatic stressors including inaccurate associations of immigration with illegal status and ongoing fears about their family instability. The cumulative impact of this toxic stress on Latino citizen children leads to:

- *Higher* levels of anxiety
- *Poor* performance in reading comprehension, math, and spelling during middle childhood

- *Under-utilization of* most public services and programs their families qualify for

Research demonstrates that children of parents directly impacted by immigration enforcement through deportation or detention are at risk for many negative outcomes.

- *Mental health*. Higher levels of post-traumatic stress disorder symptoms.
- *Internalizing problems over time*. Higher levels of depression, extreme anxiety about physical symptoms such as pain or fatigue, and lower psychological and academic functioning.
- *Externalizing problems over time*. Behavior challenges reported by teachers.
- *Changes in father-child bonds*. Current deportation trends are leading to the prolonged or permanent separation from one's father, which impairs Latino father-child relationships, further impacting children's emotional well-being.
- *Economic instability*. Significant financial instability when a two-parent home suddenly becomes a single-mother home.
- *Housing insecurity, food insecurity, school and neighborhood relocations*, and disruption of other family support including child care.
- *Poor academic functioning and challenges learning*.

Source: Rojas-Flores, L. (2017). *Latino US-citizen children of immigrants: A generation at high risk. Summary of selected young scholars program research*. New York, NY: Foundation for Child Development. Retrieved from www.fcd-us.org/latino-us-citizen-children-immigrants-generation-high-risk/

Disparities by Race and Ethnicity in Adverse Childhood Experiences

*R*egardless of race/ethnicity, economic hardship and the divorce or separation of a parent or guardian are the most common ACEs reported for children. For white children, the next-most common experiences are living with an adult with mental illness, and living with an adult with a substance use problem. For black non-Hispanic children, parental incarceration is the next-most common ACE; for Hispanic children, the next most common are living with an adult with a substance use problem and parental incarceration. Black non-Hispanic children are the most likely to have experienced the death of a parent or guardian.

(www.childtrends.org/publications/prevalence-adverse-childhood-experiences- nationally-state-race-ethnicity/)

Mindfulness Strategy for Maria: Two Minute Breathing Space

- The first minute: Answer the question, "*How am I doing right now?*" while focusing on the feelings, thoughts, and sensations that arise and trying to give these words and phrases.
- The second minute: Focus awareness on your breath.

Source: www.mindfulnessexercises.com

TIP Coaching

The coach can support Olivia's teacher, Maria, by working with her to create a self-care plan. She can also help Maria to identify her triggers in the classroom and to learn to ask for help when she is dysregulated. Maria's colleagues and supervisors can be involved in this conversation. When Maria says to her colleagues or supervisor, "I need to take five minutes," a plan can be implemented to give her a short break. Even if she cannot step out of ratio, other teachers can take the lead in working with the child while Maria does something that keeps her in ratio but still gives her a mental break. The coach can help Maria identify self-care strategies she can implement during her short break to bring her emotional state back into optimal regulation. Also, the coach can help carve out reflective time with the other teachers in the center as well. Helping all of the teachers learn the key trauma-sensitive strategies for working with Olivia will help when Maria is absent or needs to take a break, easing the pressure on her.

SPOTLIGHT FOR ADMINISTRATORS

A supervisor/administrator can make sure there are other staff that can step in not just for required breaks but for time when teachers identify they are triggered and request a self-care moment. Should a break not be possible due to ratio and lack of adults who can step in, they can work with teachers to create a plan designating other teachers on the team to step in and take the lead. Having all teachers on the same page learning the trauma-sensitive strategies is important and helping teachers know it is okay to ask for help or identify if they are triggered is essential. If teachers feel safe and supported in this way by their administrators, they will be more likely to feel open to sharing how they feel and what they need in the moment. Regulated teachers have more restored energy to support the challenging behaviors they face with children.

7

CASE STUDY

First Grader who Recently Witnessed a Drive-by Shooting While Playing at School

How Can Teachers Work with the School Psychologist or School Counselor to Support Children in the Classroom?

Key Topics Covered

- Six-year-old exposed to community violence
- TIP practices for supporting a withdrawn freeze response in a first grader
- Beyond classrooms: Strategies for extending TIP across an elementary school

Application of Trauma-Informed Practices to James

James is a six-year-old first-grade child who attends an elementary school in an urban public school district. He recently witnessed a drive-by shooting of an older high school age student who was walking by the school while James was playing on the schoolyard. The teacher, Monique, describes James as a highly motivated and bright child who gets along well with his peers and teachers. Since the incident, his behavior has changed. Now James comes to school tired from sleeping poorly at night and his mother, Kim, states that James cries out in his sleep that he is scared. Monique reports that James shows little interest in the classroom activities and has become quiet and withdrawn while he is at school. At other times, he is over-aroused and yells and screams at his classmates when they attempt to engage with him, "leave me alone!" When James hears a loud noise, he runs and hides under a desk, burying his face into the floor. If Monique approaches him quickly and asks him to come out from under the desk, either James does not respond or he manages to run away to a quiet area of the classroom, quivering and crying. He often refuses to go outside for recess or lunch, unless Monique or the classroom aide holds his hand and stays nearby. James will cry or become immobile when there are unfamiliar adults approaching the school or coming into the classroom. In these moments, it is very difficult for Monique to help calm or re-regulate James into a more optimal state of arousal.

Application of TIP Framework to James

Initial Inquiry Questions

- What kind of program support and resources exist for trauma-informed care at the elementary school where James attends?
- Is James reacting to traumatic stress as evidenced by his disturbed sleep, loss of interest in his classroom activities, fleeing behavior when stressed, and freezing behavior when it is time to go outside and when in the presence of unfamiliar adults?
- Is there an understanding of the larger ecological contexts influencing James and his family? (E.g., living in an environment with high levels of community violence?)
- Is James able to detect accurately if his school and classroom are safe and his teacher Monique is trustworthy?
- Does a referral need to be made for additional assessment, intervention, and/or supports?

Identifying Traumatic Triggers/Reminders that Lead to James' Stress Behaviors

- Loud noises
- Teacher approaching James too quickly
- Going outside to play without an adult's support
- When peers come too close to him
- Unexpected and unfamiliar adults approaching the school

Identifying James' Traumatic Stress Reactions

- Disturbed sleep – cries out "I am scared"
- Lacks interest in any school-related activities or lessons. Hypo-aroused as evidenced by his quiet and withdrawn behavior
- Hyper-aroused as seen with his yelling and screaming at his classmates
- Fleeing behavior seen when he hides under a desk and runs away quivering and crying

- Freezing behavior when he refuses to go outside and when he is immobile in the presence of unfamiliar adults

Goals to Support James

- Protect James from exposure to traumatic reminders
- Improve James' tolerance for loud noises
- Support James' transitions to outdoor play
- Restore James' interest in his classroom activities and lessons
- Improve James' trust with his peers so that he can accept their friendship
- Reduce James' defensive behaviors and feelings of helplessness
- Help James express his feelings and have a place he can talk about what happened

Trauma-Informed Teaching Practices to Support James

- **Create features of safety in the school and classroom environment**. Monique, her classroom aide, the principal, and other school staff work together to protect James from exposure to traumatic reminders.
  - Monique anticipates that loud noises could trigger fear in James who has been exposed to the noise of gun shots. Monique understands and reminds others at the school that loud sounds trigger fear for James and an automatic "flee" response as he runs and hides in an attempt to find shelter.
  - Monique understands that she must approach James slowly rather than quickly so she does not further activate his fear response. She also speaks quietly and calmly when he is hiding under the desk. She looks for cues (e.g., eye contact and movement toward Monique) that he is ready to come out from under the desk and communicates empathy and reassurance that he is safe at school. ("James, it looks like you might feel worried from the ambulance with the loud siren that just drove by our classroom. I know that in the past you heard a loud sound when someone was shot and that was really scary and sad. Right now you are safe at school in our first-grade classroom. The sound you heard was a siren telling cars to move over so they can take someone who is sick to the hospital. I am going to stay here with you James until you feel ready to come out from under the table. Nothing bad is going to happen to you. Your teachers are going to keep you safe while you are here at school. You are safe. Let's take two big breaths together.")
  - In stating the above to James, Monique is using attuned interactions and acknowledging that James is feeling scared but is safe right now.

It is useful for the teachers to help James to differentiate his past experiences from the circumstances of the "here and now." When James' brain hears the loud sound, it immediately starts his stress reaction telling him that his body is in danger—reminding him of what he felt like in the drive-by shooting—and it is hard for him to distinguish the difference between the two situations. By creating a time-register for James (the scary event was back then, this is now and you are safe), Monique is preventing James from being re-traumatized by associating all loud sounds with the fear response in his body. By staying close to him and calmly reassuring James and helping him breathe, she is supporting James to interrupt his body's stress response to the environmental trigger.

- Monique makes plans for different ways she can help to modulate James' arousal levels by identifying strategies that work for him. For example, by having at least one adult who understands and anticipates James' traumatic triggers and is consistently available to him to reassure him about his safety at school, to engage him in calming activities (e.g., blowing bubbles, playing with water or sand, breathing or mindfulness activities, playdough), expressive arts, or listening to calming music with headphones.

- Monique recognizes her own traumatic stress responses to James' reactions to loud noises (she feels worried that she won't know how to support James and her heart races and she feels the desire to flee the classroom and have someone else support his de-escalation process). Monique realizes that it may take a long time for James to build a tolerance for loud noises and that it is important to attune to his emotions and needs even if she does not immediately see how her efforts are leading to his healing and progress.

- The teacher and school staff work to reduce the number of unexpected guests who arrive in the classroom. They explain to James in advance if a new adult will be coming into the classroom, what the purpose of their visit is, and how long they will stay. They stay by his side during the adult's transition to and from the classroom to provide additional support. They also keep an eye out for adults who are walking outside the classroom on the street who may worry James anticipating his fears and reassuring him of his safety: "It looks like you are noticing that man walking outside. He is taking his dog for a walk. You are safe. Remember, you are here with us in your first-grade classroom and we are keeping you safe and taking care of you until your adult comes to pick you up at the end of the day."

- Monique and the staff provide extra support for James to negotiate any changes in his daily routine/schedule. Understanding that predictability and reduction of uncertainty help James to feel safe at school, the school staff work with James and his mother to prepare him for any changes to his school schedule. This includes providing him—as much as possible—with advanced notice about his *teachers' absences* and reinforcing that they will return ("Teacher Monique has a cold and is home resting today. You will have a substitute teacher named Ms. Priya who will take care of you until Ms. Monique feels better and comes back to school. If you are missing your teacher, we can make her a Get Well card today"), preparing him for *field trips or special school assemblies* ("Today we will be going to see a play in the lunch room after recess. The play is a story about … I know that sometimes having changes in our schedule is hard for you. You can sit next to me during the play"), and providing advance notice about or exemption from disaster preparedness routines (e.g., fire, earthquake, tornado or other disaster preparedness experiences can be very frightening for young children like James. Active shooter drills could be extremely traumatic for a child such as James).

- Monique fosters a feeling of safety for James with consistent routines, a predictable daily schedule (posts a visual schedule for the students to see when they enter each morning), and an area that provides a sense of control over the environment (e.g., water and/or sand table, playdough) or an art area that supports open-ended and creative expression.

- Monique includes a quiet area in her classroom with pictures of the students' families including photos James can see of his mother and extended family members, one or two of James' favorite books, some comfort items including one that James likes to hold when he is worried or upset. In addition, the classroom includes access to sensory regulating activities that James can go to when he is feeling scared rather than hiding under the desk and where Monique and the teachers can quietly join him by being present, emotionally attuned, and communicating in a soothing tone of voice that they are taking care of him and he is not alone, initiating feelings of security and safety.

- Monique is aware that using a stern tone may be triggering for James and she actively works to maintain a calm and positive tone of voice to help him feel safe.

- **Support James' transitions to outdoor play**. Monique recognizes that the transition to recess can create concerns for children who have experienced traumatic events like a drive-by shooting. The lack of structure and routine at recess and the unpredictability of children's behavior at this time can increase anxiety for a child such as James. Monique implements several strategies to support James to feel a sense of control and safety during his play time outside:

- Monique and the school staff understand that revisiting the location where a violent event occurred is a traumatic trigger that produces intense anxiety for James. They also understand that James would benefit from an adult who is consistently available to him during the transition to the outside play yard. This adult reassures him on a daily basis that despite the stress responses he may be feeling in his body, he is safe and his teachers will take care of him ("I know your body might be feeling scared about going outside on the playground, but you are safe with me right now").

- Once outside, Monique and the school staff understand that it is important that James can track the teacher who is monitoring the children on the play yard so that he feels seen, attended to, and can co-regulate with this adult to feel safe. He may need to stay close to this adult for a while. He might also need to have alternative activities available (reading a book, playing with manipulatives—blocks, puzzles, etc.) if he feels too scared by the sudden, unpredictable, and/or loud movements of the children's play during recess.

- **Use emotionally attuned caregiver interactions to regulate James' dysregulated behavior**

  - Monique is aware that James reacts internally to his fear by yelling and screaming at his classmates to leave him alone. She attunes to his emotions and uses reassuring words to reduce his heightened levels of arousal. She also acknowledges that James gets scared when his friends come too close. She teaches him to say, "I need my space" and "I will play with you when I am calm and ready to play."

  - Monique forms an emotionally sound relationship with James by being patient, present, emotionally attuned, and offering caring responses to his needs. In doing so, she helps James feel a sense of security while he is in his first-grade classroom. She helps him to develop an association in his brain between having a need or a worry at school and experiencing that a caring adult will be available to support him.

  - Monique understands that she should not be afraid to help James tell his story about the shooting. Allowing him to do so won't make his distress worse, instead, allowing him to tell his story through words, through expressive art, through play, or another format will support James to calm his strong emotions, to differentiate the past from the present, and to have control and agency in his life again.

Helping James tell his story. Monique encourages James and a small group of children to share their feelings and fears through storytelling. She reads *When I Feel Scared* by Cornelia Spelman and uses the story to talk with the students about how it can be difficult to identify emotions that are unpleasant but there are many things they can do when they feel scared including talking about their worries or asking for help. Monique then guides James and his classmates through a role-play activity where the children practice expressing their fears through play. Each child in the group identifies something that makes them scared and one thing that makes them feel better. For example, "I feel scared when I hear a loud noise or when I have a bad dream. But then I can go and talk to my mom about it or cuddle with my blanket to feel better."

- **Facilitate knowledge of typical child development**
  - Monique offers James social-emotional activities with feeling posters that help him use words to identify his emotions and how he is feeling about the shooting. She also introduces some storybooks to help James identify his feelings and learn some strategies for managing big emotions. For example, *When dinosaurs die: A guide to understanding death* by Laurie Krasny Brown and Marc Brown or *A terrible thing happened* by Margaret M. Holmes, a story for children who have witnessed violence or trauma.
  - Monique introduces a sensory literacy vocabulary into the classroom to increase James' ability to identify, understand, and express sensations that he is feeling in his body and to express them in a healthy way. The energy charges/physiological responses in his body that stem from the environmental triggers (loud sounds) that remind him of the initial traumatic event. For example, James learns to describe the feeling of his pounding heart as "a wild volcano" or "hot lava."
  - Monique introduces James to self-regulatory strategies such as breathing, especially bunny breathing when he is triggered and breathing so fast that he can't catch his breath.

BREATHING SUPPORTS SELF-REGULATION: BREATHING ACTIVITY FOR CHILDREN WHO ARE TRIGGERED, BREATHING FAST, AND CAN'T CATCH THEIR BREATH

Bunny Breath

Just three quick sniffs in the nose and one long exhale out the nose.

Invite children to pretend to be bunny rabbits, sniffing the air for other bunnies, smelling for carrots to eat, or looking for danger so they can keep themselves safe. Children can use bunny breaths as a cleansing breath. Use bunny breaths with children who are very upset and can't find their breath. It will help them quickly inhale and then exhale. This will get oxygen in their brains and calm their stress response systems so they don't cycle into dysregulation.

Source: https://move-with-me.com/self-regulation/4-breathing-exercises-for-kids-to-empower-calm-and-self-regulate/

- Monique will support James to engage in play experiences that can foster prosocial peer interactions. She and her teaching assistant can help James to accurately assess the safety of his classroom environment and guide him to shift his fearful responses and/or negative emotions when he perceives a threat to more positive accurate assessments of the context he is in. For example, she could lead the class to play freeze dance together but before they start, she will make sure James is in close proximity to her and that he has ample room so the movements of his classmates do not accidentally touch him. If, however, a peer does touch James while dancing, she can calmly respond and decrease any perceptions of danger, "It looks like you both need more space for your fancy dancing moves. We want to make sure you can each dance like a star but also freeze like a statue without touching each other."
  - **Integrate trauma-informed practices in James' classroom and across the school**
    - o The principal understands that the shooting was traumatic for many students on campus and she is working with the district to arrange for a training on trauma-informed care for her staff and some ongoing technical assistance/coaching on how to implement trauma-informed practices across their school site. Because funding is limited, she arranges to share the cost with principals from two neighboring schools who are also interested in this professional development opportunity.
    - o The principal uses her increased knowledge of traumatic stress to work with a small task group of staff to create a school culture (policies and practices) that reinforce safety and belonging for the children and families.
    - o The principal understands that it is critically important that she considers how she can support Monique to develop an emotionally sound relationship with James. She takes this into account when she is considering staffing decisions throughout the year.

    o   The school counselor (e.g., mental health counselor, therapist, consultant or school psychologist, behaviorist, interventionist, early interventionist) is available to speak with James about the shooting event and his traumatic stress, and if needed, can refer James for additional counseling support.

Reflecting on James

1. What was your first reaction in reading about James? What feelings, thoughts, and images did this case scenario inspire in you about him? Monique, her teacher?
2. Identify your own reactions to James' trauma responses. Why might you have these reactions?
3. What traumatic stress reaction does James use most often?
4. What trauma-sensitive caregiver responses are most helpful for James?
5. Review the trauma-informed teaching strategies discussed above. How would you sequence them (e.g., what strategies would you prioritize)? Would you add any additional strategies that would build resilience and a sense of safety for James?
6. What information did you gain from the case study that you could use as a trauma-sensitive strategy in your classroom?
7. Discuss how you would approach teaching a young child when there is a sudden death or loss of a primary attachment figure.
8. Identify James' strengths and how you would use them to foster resilience and a sense of safety for him at school.
9. List self-care strategies that James' teachers could use to reduce secondary traumatic stress.
10. Discuss school-wide supports and resources that could help James.
11. Discuss the type of referral that could be made outside of the school if determined to be appropriate for James. How would you know when it is time to refer a student? Does your school/program have access to outside resources such as counselors that specialize in trauma?
12. Talk about how you would talk with James' family. How would you partner with his family to identify and implement strategies to support James?

Teaching Tip

All children who experience trauma need teachers to create classrooms that are predictable throughout the day. When teachers know in advance that there will be a change in the schedule, they can share this news with the children and invite them to plan for these changes. For example, they might support the children to create a visual schedule with pictures showing the sequence of activities that will happen during the day with the adjusted schedule (e.g., on a day with a field trip, a special assembly, or school event). This not only helps children to have a sense of control over their environment, it also models for the children a strategy they can use to calm their stress response system by reducing the uncertainty associated with a change in their routine.

Teaching Dilemma

I can support my students to feel safe in my classroom and while they are at school but I have no control over the community violence they witness and live with in their neighborhoods. What can I do to support my students who live with a significant amount of traumatic stress?

That is right. The creation of a safe and predictable environment for children in the classroom does support their healing and buffers them from the traumatic stressors they experience in their community. If you help the children to feel safe, they build a resiliency that helps them to be more equipped to withstand the impact of toxic stressors they experience outside of the school.

LOOKING THROUGH A CHILD'S EYES: WHAT TRAUMA STORY IS JAMES REVEALING WHEN HE SCREAMS AT HIS CLASSMATES?

From a teacher's perspective: "Other times he is over-aroused and yells and screams at his classmates when they attempt to engage with him, 'leave me alone!'"

From James' perspective: " Ever since the drive-by shooting, I feel like I'm in danger all the time. I don't feel safe being near any adults because I worry that they might have a gun and shoot me. Every time my teacher or anyone tries to get near me, I feel like a volcano is exploding inside my body and I start to scream. What I wish my teacher would understand is that my sense of safety and trust was shattered and the only way my brain knows to keep me safe is to make sure nobody gets close to me. My brain has a 'fight' response whenever other children attempt to talk or play with me. My yelling and screaming is my way of telling everyone, 'I'm scared you will hurt me. I don't want to be hurt or killed. Go away!'"

Link to Brain Development/Brain Integration

Strong emotions are contagious and frequently transmitted beneath levels of consciousness from adults to children. The process by which this occurs begins with the child's neuronal system mirroring the adult's neuronal system—i.e., what we call "mirror neurons." In this way, the child "takes in" the emotional state of the adult caring for her. Neuroscientific research shows that mirror neurons exist in parts of the human brain critical for the recognition of facial expressions and emotional behaviors (Iacoboni et al., 1999). The mirror system alters the limbic (emotional) and bodily (physical) states to match those the individual is seeing. In the case of a teacher working with a child who is in a fight response (acting out and screaming), it is critical that the teacher remains calm so that the child's stress response system can eventually take in and "mirror" this calm state and resonate with the teacher.

Family Engagement Strategy

James' teacher could work with the school or district psychologist to talk with Kim, James' mother, about his fears about sleeping at night. The psychologist can explain to Kim why James might be scared about sleeping—how the scary memories and thoughts might flood his mind in the dark and quiet. In addition, the teacher could share some ideas about how Kim could support James at home with some of the same strategies they are using at school (e.g., stay by his side when he is falling asleep, remind him that he is safe while he is sleeping, and provide him with a stuffed animal who, along with his parents, will watch over and keep him safe). Kim could also remind James that he will see her when he wakes up (helping him to predict reunion with his main attachment figure). Lastly, to reduce his fear of going to sleep, Kim could be consistent with a bed time routine that includes reading a book about a topic James loves before he goes to bed, singing the same lullaby each night as he falls asleep, and using white noise or soft music to reduce his fears of quiet in his room.

Interdisciplinary Partnerships and TIP

James could be referred to work with the school counselor or school psychologist to talk about the trauma he experienced witnessing the shooting. This mental health professional would work with teachers to observe James and develop a trauma-sensitive plan with strategies that will support his trauma triggers and promote safety and security and re-engagement with his peers.

LINKING TO POLICY: ARE LOCKDOWN DRILLS TRAUMA-INFORMED?

There is an increasing focus on zero tolerance policies and an expanding number of schools across the country—including preschools—mandating that children engage in Code Red drills also known as Lock-Down or Active Shooter drills. When teachers hear an announcement for the drill, lights are turned off, curtains are drawn closed, and children practice curling up in quiet little balls in the corners and closets of their classrooms. Although teachers remind the children that these are "just for practice," as Stephanie Kennelly recently described in a blog post titled, *Are lockdown drills trauma informed?* we cannot reason with the amygdala. Even though the school librarian may be the person walking through the hallway to check that all the doors are securely locked, the sound of someone touching the door can be a terrifying and triggering experience for many young children, especially those with histories of trauma. As Kennelly reminds us, this is because the amygdala, the part of the brain responsible for survival, goes into action before our thinking and reasoning cortex can tell us not to worry because it is "just a drill."

For young children, this means that their brains activate a Fight/Flight/Freeze response. Because children are required to stay still throughout the drill, their only option is to "Freeze," the response that is the most harmful to their brain development and their long-term health. When children have a Fight or a Flight response, the intense stress energy streaming throughout their bodies in response to the activation of their stress response systems (and the release of stress chemicals) can be discharged through running, shaking, kicking, hitting, and hiding. When children have a "Freeze" response, this energy has nowhere to go except to remain within their central nervous systems; which, if repeated over time, is what leads to the most concerning and detrimental adverse outcomes for children.

It is important that policies to support school safety be trauma-informed and developmentally appropriate for young children. There is no reason to practice Active Shooter drills to prevent children from being harmed in a future shooting while repeatedly undermining their health and safety by triggering a traumatic stress response in their brains. As long as these drills are going to be a reality in our schools, Kennelly provides recommendations for making these policies less harmful and more trauma-sensitive:

Step 1: The Huddle

*W*hen students assume the huddle position, cue them into the Child's Pose. With the head below the heart and a curved *spine, this position naturally relaxes the body. Take long, deep breaths to activate the relaxation response. Another benefit to this pose is the elimination of the visual stimuli that can cause hyper-vigilance (i.e., waiting for the door handle to shake, sounds in the hallway). Practice when children's bodies and minds are calm so that they know what to do during high-stress moments like lock-down drills.*

Step 2: Release

*I*t is critical that children are given an opportunity to "release" after a lockdown drill. The best option is to tap into the "flight" response and run a lap around the school. If that is not possible, encourage the children to shake and jump to discharge the stress hormones released during the lockdown drill.*

Step 3: Re-Integrate

*G*uide the children back to a relaxed state. Encourage the children to bend forward two to three times as this will help to calm their central nervous system. To transition back to learning, use a breathing ball and take ten belly breaths.*

Source: Are Lockdown Drills Trauma Informed? Stephanie Kennelly on ACESConnection (www.acesconnection.com)

Mindfulness: Body Posing

Encourage your students to practice making superhero poses, which can help them feel strong, brave, and happy. They find a place in the classroom where they feel safe. Then practice two poses:

- Superhero #1: Students stand with their feet just wider than the hips. They clench their fists, reach their arms out, and stretch their bodies out as long as possible without falling.
- Superhero #2: This time, students stand tall with their legs wide. They place their hands or fists on their hips.

Source: Mindfulness Exercises Library (p. 31)

TIP Coaching

A teacher like Monique's says to her coach, "I do not have time to implement any extra supports for James as I have 25 other children to manage in my classroom." This is a common reaction from a teacher and a very real concern for her. It is important to validate how she feels and to acknowledge how hard this is. The coach can help regulate the teacher's initial reactions just by listening and naming her feelings as this can help to disarm the teacher's intense emotional reactions. When the teacher is regulated and calm, the coach can help her think of a plan that is manageable in small steps. For example, the coach can help the teacher think of how she can receive support from other adults at the school to help James reduce his traumatic stress behaviors. The coach can also help the teacher think of other strategies that don't take too much time such as proactively building a relationship with James, *avoiding using a critical tone of voice or punitive verbal strategies*. The coach can help the teacher see that staying calm is also a strategy that can support James to optimal regulation. If the coach can help the teacher break down the teaching strategies to support James into small steps, it will likely feel more manageable for the teacher to implement.

Tone of Voice

The teacher can be aware of their tone of voice and the words they use to communicate with a child. A teacher that uses a stern tone can trigger a child or may increase their escalated state. A stern voice might not be the exact words you use but the underlying tone associated with the words. If a child "senses" disappointment or frustration from an adult, a child with a history of trauma may respond with an increased level of reactivity. Children with trauma histories are especially tuned in to their adult caregiver scanning for micro facial expressions that may pose a danger or threat. A comment can be made with a calm tone but still have an underlying note of frustration or disappointment with the child. An adult can reassure the child by maintaining a calm composure and use words that assure safety such as "we will work this out together" or "everything will be okay, I will help you through this," or "what happens feel scary but I am here to help you and keep you safe."

SPOTLIGHT FOR TEACHERS/CAREGIVERS

Children organize the daily experiences that confuse, overwhelm, frighten, surprise, anger, and excite them while they are pretending. Through imaginary play, children often reverse the reality of their lives—where it is common for them to feel a lack of control and little ability to influence decisions that affect them—by placing themselves in roles where they are both powerful and in control. We see this with young children who pretend to be the doctor giving a shot to another child or a doll instead of being the patient experiencing the injection. Or when children respond to a natural disaster (hurricane, tornado, flood) in their community by re-enacting the experience positioning themselves as the "helpers" who rescue people and pets from danger. When children have the opportunity to engage in imaginary play, they not only have a chance to shift from feeling vulnerable and frightened to heroes and heroines with strengths and resiliency, the experience of integrating their worries into their play is calming for their central nervous systems. Children who experience trauma may need to replay the situation in pretend play repeating it over and over many times to allow their brains to make sense of the experience and create it into a story that is predictable with a beginning, middle, and end. By making the traumatic memory into a predictable narrative that they have control over, children can often reduce the activation of their stress response systems and reduce the likelihood that stress chemicals will cause lasting damage to their brains and bodies.

Many teachers and administrators do not understand the critically important role of imaginary play in children's social-emotional health, especially for children with histories of trauma. Because of the focus on school safety, many children are no longer allowed to explore certain themes in their play including death, violence, loss, and fear, even though decades of research provide evidence that this play is beneficial for children's development. This reasoning is developmentally incongruent. Because children experience so much trauma in our contemporary world, more than ever they need opportunities to communicate what has happened to them and how they feel about it. They also need safe places to work through the intense fears and worries the trauma leaves in its wake. Imaginary play provides these opportunities for children by allowing them to process their fears, to communicate with the adults around them how they feel and the types of reassurances and supports they need, and to develop coping skills for managing their fears and traumatic stress.

Spotlight for Administrators/Supervisors

Having compassion for how teachers feel when they work with children displaying traumatic stress behaviors is essential. Too often administrators and coaches approach teachers with directions and corrections and flood them with overwhelming emotions. Yet, they often have little knowledge of the emotions teachers are feeling and the reality that many teachers who work in communities with high cumulative risk factors are more vulnerable to the impact of vicarious trauma. If administrators and coaches approach teachers only directing and correcting or critiquing them when they are already emotionally exhausted and/or feeling a lack of confidence in work-ing with the child, then implementing any new strategy will be difficult. Providing emotional and psychological support and a safe place to talk about how they feel, as well as supporting their co-regulation by remaining calm and present, are essential steps in supporting teachers. When a teacher feels calm, she will be better equipped to access the "thinking" or execu-tive part of her brain to talk through strategies and to construct a plan for supporting James.

8

THE IMPORTANCE OF SELF-CARE IN TIP WORK

Taking Care of Yourself in Order to Prevent Burnout, Compassion Fatigue, and Secondary Traumatic Stress

How Does Self-Care Help Teachers Provide Trauma-Sensitive Strategies to Children Enduring Stressful and Traumatic Situations?

Key Topics Covered

- Preventing burnout, compassion fatigue, and secondary post-traumatic stress
- The importance of self-care
- Creating a healthy brain map for quality self-care

Early childhood teachers have very demanding jobs. They work long days on their feet with constant demands on their energy and patience—whether they are holding and rocking infants, reading storybooks to toddlers, engaging in imaginary play with preschoolers, or building problem-solving and self-regulation skills with kindergarteners. Despite the intense workplace demands early childhood teachers face on a daily basis, they do not receive the compensation, benefits, professional development, and support they need (Lieberman, 2018). Unfortunately, most teachers and child care providers continue to earn poverty-level wages and almost half qualify for public support programs (Whitebook, Phillips, & Howes, 2014). Head Start teachers, the nation's largest preK program, has significantly increased the number of the teachers with bachelor's degrees with a specialization in early childhood education (74% as of 2015). Despite the demands Head Start teachers have faced to earn their degrees and the increase in quality resulting from having a better-educated workforce, Head Start teachers in many states have seen a *decrease* in their compensation over the past ten years. Such conditions have led to significant stress and high turnover rates for early childhood teachers (Kaplan & Mead, 2017).

Working with young children is complex and challenging work. Teachers' ability to develop high quality attuned and responsive relationships with children is the most important factor in trauma-informed practice. Even the most committed and skilled teachers may be challenged to care for children well if they are worried about paying their bills and continually exhausted from the increased policy mandates leading to a range of requirements to increase the quality of early childhood programs.

We also know that working with children who are impacted by trauma can take on the professional and personal toll on the lives of teachers, putting them at risk for burnout, compassion fatigue, or secondary trauma (Perry, 2014). When teachers' stress system is activated for long periods of time, they are exposed to several stress hormones, including cortisol. As previously discussed, having prolonged exposure to stress hormones creates a toxic and harmful impact on the body (Cozolino, 2006; Pally, 2000; Stein & Kendall, 2004) resulting in a variety of health problems including: anxiety, depression, digestive problems, headaches, heart disease, sleep problems, weight gain, and memory and concentration impairment. This reinforces why it is essential that adults learn to manage the multiple stressors in their lives.

As described throughout this book, traumatic stress also negatively impairs the developing brain of a child. Knowing this allows teachers to have a deeper understanding of why their own self-awareness and self-regulation is so essential. Remaining positively attuned to a child, especially when they are triggered, responding to young children's cues, and supporting them by co-regulating their distressed states is a critical responsibility of teacher. Only by attending to their own self-care and working to prevent or minimize their own triggering experiences in the workplace, will early childhood teachers be able to guide children to overcome unhealthy responses to traumatic triggers and support them to rewire their brains to develop positive stress response systems.

Compared with other caring professions like nursing or social work, teachers—and particularly early childhood teachers who have so few professional development opportunities in comparison with their K–12 counterparts—receive little or no training to understand trauma and recognize its impact on the children in their care. Further, training in the importance of "self-care" for teachers and strategies for directors showing them *how* to support the integration of self-care into their early learning programs is also very rare. Trauma-informed early learning programs acknowledge the significant relationship between teachers' self-care and their ability to work effectively with young children impacted by trauma and they ensure that teachers, administrators, and all adults interacting with young children and families learn about trauma *and* self-care.

Preventing Compassion Fatigue, Secondary Traumatic Stress, and Burnout: Restoring Your Energy

Self-care is not selfish. You cannot serve from an empty vessel.

(Brownn, 2014)

Burnout is described as a "reaction to job stress in which the focus is on the physical, emotional, and mental exhaustion caused by long-term involvement in situations that are emotionally demanding" (Pines & Aronson, 1988, p. 73) and a "psychological condition that involves a response to chronic stressors of the job" (Leiter & Maslach, 2004). Workplace conditions—workload, poor supervision, negative work environment, poor benefits or pay, difficulty with co-workers, or excessive work demands and a lack of social support, have a cumulative effect and slowly develop into burnout over time (Gottlieb, Hennessy, & Squires, 2004; Maltzman, 2011). Burnout impacts individuals physically, emotionally, spiritually, and/or mentally and results in emotional exhaustion and reduced feelings of personal effectiveness and accomplishment (Gottlieb, Hennessy, & Squires, 2004; Maslach & Jackson, 1986).

Burnout can be avoided if:

- Teachers learn to recognize the warning signs and symptoms of burnout
- If they actively plan for and engage in their own self-care

---

Burnout impacts individuals physically, emotionally, spiritually, and/or mentally and results in emotional exhaustion and reduced feelings of personal effectiveness and accomplishment.

Warning signs of burnout include

- Feelings of negativity
- Feeling a lack of control
- A loss of purpose or energy
- An increased detachment from relationships and/or feeling estranged from others
- Feeling unappreciated
- Having difficulty sleeping
- Difficulty concentrating, continually feeling preoccupied
- Feeling trapped
- Difficulty separating personal life and work life

Source: Gottlieb, Hennessy, & Squires (2004)

Burnout that is not addressed may turn into **compassion fatigue**. With prolonged stress and a lack of self-care activities in an adult's life to restore and buffer their stress, an individual may begin to suffer from compassion fatigue symptoms (O'Brien & Haaga, 2015). Compassion fatigue results when adults become overwhelmed by the suffering and pain of those in their care (Figley, 2002; Lipsky, 2009; Ray, Wong, White, & Heaslip, 2013). Individuals with high levels of empathy for others' pain or traumatic experiences are most at risk for compassion fatigue (Adams, Boscarino, & Figley, 2006; Figley, 2002).

Although compassion fatigue symptoms vary for each individual, there are common behaviors that emerge when stressors are not mediated by self-care strategies. Compassion fatigue symptoms include but are not limited to: feelings of depression, grief, anxiety, being short tempered, more reactive emotionally, socially withdrawn and angry, having nightmares and sleep challenges, difficulty concentrating, loss of hope, and irritability (Mathieu, 2007; O'Brien & Haaga, 2015). While compassion fatigue primarily impacts the individual providing the care, these symptoms can be transferred to the caring professional's family members and significant others (Mathieu, 2007; Ray et al., 2013). Some adults respond to compassion fatigue behaviorally with self-numbing strategies including the excessive use of drugs, alcohol, or overeating. Other adults direct their behavioral symptoms of compassion fatigue outward with aggression, irritability, short temper, and/or reactivity toward others or even the environment (punching the wall or kicking the furniture). The toll of compassion fatigue will be socially, emotionally, physically, and/or spiritually. Research on compassion fatigue also relates this condition with poor decision making, crossing ethical boundaries, and at times, actions that result in hurting ourselves and others.

When early childhood teachers suffer from compassion fatigue they are at risk of losing their ability to have empathy, compassion, and desire to help the children and families they serve. Compassion fatigue can lead caring professionals to lose sight of the original reasons they entered into their work, to help others, and in the case of early childhood teachers, to love, care for, and support the development of young children and their families.

It's very important that we re-learn the art of resting and relaxing. Not only does it help prevent the onset of many illnesses that develop through chronic tension and worrying; it allows us to clear our minds, focus, and find creative solutions to problems. We will be more successful in all our endeavors if we can let go of the habit of running all the time, and take little pauses to relax and re-center ourselves. And we'll also have a lot more joy in living.

Thich Nhat Hanh, Zen Master and Mindfulness Expert (Source: Schnall, 2017).

WARNING SIGNS FOR COMPASSION FATIGUE

- Feeling helpless and hopeless
- Having a sense that one can never do enough
- Hypervigilance (heightened sensitivity to stimulus in the environment—lights, sounds, comments or actions of others, facial expressions)
- Decreased creativity
- Losing compassion and the ability to empathize
- Inability to embrace complexity
- Chronic exhaustion
- Inability to listen
- Dissociative moments
- Lack of efficacy in one's life
- Guilt
- Fear
- Anger
- Addictions
- Decreased sense of importance (impacting self-esteem and sense of value in the world)

Source: Lipsky (2009)

Secondary Traumatic Stress refers to the effects of being exposed to another person's reaction to their traumatic experience. This type of stress can result from working with children or families who experience traumatic symptoms. When teachers are working with others on a daily basis who have experienced trauma and display trauma triggers and behaviors, it is difficult not to absorb into your own mind and body the traumatic stress and the intensive feelings they are displaying in their communication with you. When teachers attune to another human being, they can easily be affected by the others' internal emotional state even when they are not directly experiencing any trauma. Over time, hundreds or thousands of these experiences can profoundly affect us and put us at risk for several outcomes.

- **Feeling overwhelmed and stressed out.** It is not uncommon for those in the caring professions—like early childhood teachers—to internalize the stress and trauma from the young children and families they are working with to a level that leaves them feeling totally overwhelmed and incapacitated by their own stress. The result may be an impact on your personal and professional life including a decreased ability to manage your daily tasks, focus on your job, impact on relationships, or the ability to attend to the needs of others in a consistent and trauma-sensitive way.

- **Becoming numb or harmful in our interactions with the children and families we serve**. Becoming numb is a survival response many professionals who work closely with individuals and communities that are strongly trauma-impacted have when they observe and witness trauma stories daily. This survival response may look from the outside like the caring professional is losing compassion and the ability to "respond," which may look like shutting down emotionally, calling in sick frequently, avoiding children or families, or giving up on a child or family (perhaps because of the feeling that every strategy you have tried is not working). A lack of response, a dissociation from the present moment, and shutting down and ignoring can cause additional harm to the children and families that need our support healing from trauma.
- **Becoming short-tempered and reactionary in our interactions with children and families we serve**. Becoming on edge, short of temper, or reactionary is another survival response professionals may have as a sign of the impact of secondary traumatic stress. Behaviors such as blaming, being short-tempered, yelling, critical, or being punitive (punishing children instead of regulating, supporting, or teaching) become the behaviors that can cause more harm to the very individuals that seek our help and healing.

Without intentional self-care strategies and an ongoing routine of restorative activities, the risk to teachers' own self-suffering, burnout, compassion fatigue, and secondary traumatic stress increases. The result of poor self-care then trickles down to those teachers that care for children and families each day. The outcome is that no one is well-served and well-intentioned caring and passionate professionals, including early childhood teachers, can actually become part of a tragic scenario where they further traumatize young children and/or families. **For this reason, self-care is not just a nice thing to do, it is a critically important professional responsibility of all in the early childhood profession.**

Secondary Traumatic Stress Can Lead to Harmful Interactions with Children and Families: An Example in Context. This is an example of a family advocate answering calls from parents and supporting them in completing their required annual paperwork for your program. One parent calls asking why it is required. The Family Advocate reactively states, "Do you want your child in the program or not?" The family advocate is unaware that the parent is overwhelmed and worried that their personal information might lead to the family being deported. In this situation, the family advocate's response may be due to her own stress and poor self-care that is preventing the advocate from having a more thoughtful and less reactive response. An example of a more regulated response would be to ask the family to express its concerns and whether providing the information is too much or inappropriate. The advocate would ask how to support the family to make sense of the paperwork and help the family to feel safe. The family would be reassured that the information is for funding purposes only. Lastly, the advocate offers to meet in person to help fill out the information to meet minimal requirements.

What is Self-Care and Why is it Important for Early Childhood Teachers?

Self-care is defined in many different ways. The National Association for the Education for Young Children (NAEYC) Focus on Ethics Column (September 2015) described the importance of self-care in our profession and defined it in the following way:

> Self-care is identified as self-regulation of ones needs—physically, emotionally, cognitively, and socially. It is the ability to recognize and identify when you are not having your needs met and planning a course of action that will support you in changing your behavior or circumstances. Why is it important? As one early childhood educator shared, self-care is how you assure that you bring your whole self to your work in the classroom and community in early childhood education.

What is keeping early childhood educators from enacting self-care in their daily lives? Research suggests that in early childhood, the personal and professional self are interconnected (Osgood, 2012). What this means is that it can be challenging for an early childhood educator to separate their personal life from their professional life. Here are some simple questions to ask yourself:

- Do you take work home with you?
- Is it difficult for you to stop thinking about what happened at work when you get home?
- Do you carry the stressors from your personal life into the workplace?
- When work is stressful, is it hard to shake the emotions you feel when you get home?
- If you have personal life stressors, do you take those to work? Are you more on edge at work and quicker to be reactive with others?

The two worlds of home and work are difficult to separate. They both are connected and can strongly impact one another. Too many stressful experiences in one or both worlds can impact whether you bring your highest and healthiest self that is filled with renewed energy for giving or the self that is drained, depleted, and burned out with little energy left to give to others.

Teacher Amit complains to his co-workers that this year they have so many more children with challenging behaviors. In particular, he states there are two that are "out of control." Every day, he feels the stress of having to manage these two children, Sharla and Jon. Amit states that "Sharla disrupts circle time, hits and bites other children and Jon cries and whines for him throughout the day." He sacrifices his break and lunch to help the other teachers because he is the only one that knows strategies to calm both children. The two children are only comforted and responsive to him. He finds himself continually behind on required paperwork and his supervisor just reprimanded him and told him that he is facing disciplinary action if he does not turn in his required documentation by week's end. The supervisor has no idea that he is prioritizing helping the other teachers during his break with the children instead of completing his paperwork. Amit says his nerves are frazzled and on edge every drive home. When he arrives in his driveway at 6:30 pm he just cries in the driveway before he goes in to see his wife and kids. He sits in the driveway until 7 pm just to pull himself together. Amit knows when he comes home it is safe and he has a wonderful relationship with his wife and two young children who are one and three years old. He walks in the door and his kids jump on him and want all of his attention all night. He just wants to sit and relax. He goes to the kitchen to get a drink of water since he forgot to drink all day. His wife says, "why are you home so late tonight?" He snaps "stop breathing down my back and attacking me." He runs to his room, slams the door, and locks himself in for the remainder of the night.

Inquiry Questions

How does Amit's work impact his home life in this scenario?
Does Amit bring his work stress home with him?
How does this level of stress affect how he interacts with his wife and children?
Why did Amit run to his room and lock himself in the rest of the night when he loves his family so much?

An essential first step on the road to self-care is for teachers to identify and acknowledge the main sources of stress that impact them personally and professionally (Lipsky, 2009). Only after these stressors have become visibly named, can teachers begin to work on ways to manage and reduce the negative impact of this stress on their well-being and daily work with children and families.

When teachers consider their own self-care, they need to think of two distinct types: personal self-care and professional self-care (Sanchez-Reilly et al., 2013).

Personal self-care: Strategies for early childhood teachers that will help them to take better care of themselves including relationships with family and friends, having enough sleep, exercising regularly, opportunities for relaxation and rejuvenation (e.g., vacations, activities), hobbies, engaging in mindfulness activities, and spirituality.

Professional self-care. Professional self-care is helpful in decreasing burnout and compassion fatigue and often includes both individual and team-based self-care (Sanchez-Reilly et al., 2013).

- **Individual professional self-care** activities might include having peers and mentors who provide support, having access to opportunities that support professional learning and growth, strengthening effective communication skills, creating professional boundaries to protect personal time, and opportunities to engage in reflective processes (e.g., reflective supervision, journaling, reflective conversations with colleagues).
- **Team or collaborative self-care** includes opportunities to feel a sense of agency/control in your job, to have meaningful opportunities to contribute to group discussions and decision-making (policies, meeting agendas, etc.), and to collaborate with others.

Self-care strategies are unique to every individual (Gottlieb, Hennessy, & Squires, 2004; Madrid & Schacher, 2006; Sanchez-Reilly et al., 2013). What is considered self-care for one person may not be for another. For example, going for a five-mile walk may be regulating and restorative for one person, going to the beach and sitting and watching the waves for another, while another may find a warm cup of tea and taking some breaths is restorative. All three individuals will define and create a personalized self-care tool-kit.

Examples of Self-Care Strategies

• Eating or sleeping well • Physical activity • Awareness signs of stress in your body • Practicing time management • Spending quality time with family and friends you enjoy being with • Attending self-help activities (e.g. counseling, life coach, spiritual groups, health or healing events) • Practicing deep breathing for relaxation	• Engaging in activities that are meaningful and restorative to you • Taking small relaxing or energizing breaks • Asking for support from others • Participating in a support group • Being involved in activities that are fun or creative to you

Teachers should continually be asking themselves two questions:

- What am I doing to take care of myself?
- What else could I be doing to take better care of myself?
  Adapted from Gottlieb, Hennessy & Squires (2004)

Building a Self-Care Toolbox

People travel to wonder at the height of mountains, at the huge waves of the sea, at the circular motion of the stars, and yet they pass by themselves without ever wondering.

(St. Augustine)

Self-awareness is cultivated with the intentional tuning of your attention to YOU. This includes awareness of your body, mind, and spirit. This can also be phrased as physical (body), intellectual (mind), and emotional (spiritual, psychological) awareness. The world we live in is so busy. In modern times, social media, digital media, and technology have increased our heightened level of distraction from our own self-care and awareness. It is rare to talk to another adult without hearing "I only have five minutes" or you notice them distracted and thinking of other things while they are with you. Look around at a restaurant and notice how many people are not really present with those they are eating with but instead on a form of technology. It becomes even harder with digital life distractions that actually prevent the real time we need to take high-quality care of ourselves and restore our energy. Often it feels like a waste of time and then we continue to put it on hold and prioritize mindless distractions that serve as an escape rather than to restore us. Days go by and then our bodies slowly send signals that we need rest, relaxation, self-care, or positive engaging relationships to restore our positive energy. If we continue to ignore the signs, the outcome can be negative on our health and well-being. There are two key strategies you can use first to develop self-awareness. The first is a temperature check (A). The second is a body scan (B).

- **Temperature Check.** Teachers can use this in many ways. They can check in with themselves each morning before they leave for work, in the middle of the day on a break, after they arrive home, and before bed. Becoming aware of the emotions and emotional intensity they are experiencing in the moment can help teachers develop insight as to whether they need more self-care or self-regulation strategies to restore themselves back to Green (0–3) or optimal state of regulation. Teachers also have the choice in the far-right column to list some things that may be impacting that state of emotion. Emotional self-awareness is an important foundation to not only learn about how you are feeling in the moment and the intensity of your feelings, but it is the precursor to knowing when to use tools for self-regulation support.

Emotional state check in	Scale of emotions check in	Intensity of emotion	What happened? Describe the event/situation/person that impacted this emotional state
Red (hyper-aroused or hypo-aroused)	7–10	Intense	
Orange (early trigger signs)	4–6	Moderate and rising emotion	
Green (optimal state of regulation)	0–3	Calm and regulated	

- **Body Scan.** Pausing and paying attention to how your body feels is important to promote self-care. In our busyness, we forget to pay attention to the clues our body gives us that we are becoming too stressed out. Our body is often the first to send a signal that we have stress. Each person exhibits stress symptoms in different parts of their body. You can check in with yourself throughout the day by putting an X in the silhouette of the body. The X symbolizes where you feel stress—your head, neck, jaws, hands, feet, hips, lower or upper back, neck, eyes, mouth, ears, stomach, or heart? You can place more than one X if there is tension or physical stress being communicated by your body. This pause during the day can help you develop self-awareness about your physical body (Figure 8.1).

Photo A and Photo B are two sample photos of teachers who took a professional development self-care training where they were asked to draw a body scan on a flip chart. They indicated where in their body they experience stress sensations. Notice the images they used to describe their physical stress responses. You can draw your own daily body scan to increase your self-awareness about your level of stress. Body stress can be described with words (stomach pain) or sensations (feels like a volcano erupting in my stomach or a hammer pounding in my head). They can also be described simply by placing in X on the body where you might be feeling discomfort.

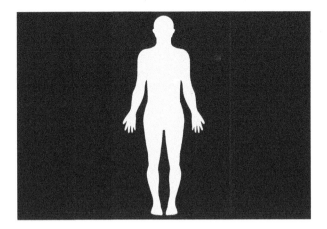

Figure 8.1 Body Scan Outline.

> *The more we take care of ourselves, the more well-being that we have inside and out, the more we can be there for others, more present, more optimistic and more open-hearted.*
>
> Source: Maria LeRose, The Dalai Lama Center for Peace and Education

Sample Photos of Completed Body Scans (Figures 8.2 and 8.3)

Photo A	Photo B

Photo A: Teachers in this break-out group described the following body sensations that were cues to their own stress: hammering in their head, lightning bolts in the head, eye pain, jaw pain, neck tightness, heart racing, a volcano in their heart, hip and lower back soreness.

Photo B: Teachers in this break out group described the following body sensations that were cues to their own stress: Stomach pain and digestive issues, heartburn, shoulder pain, grinding of teeth, hip tightness, head and neck pain.

- **Journaling to Increase Self-Awareness**. Writing your thoughts down on paper can help you slow down and put a temporary pause on the button of life. A car is hurtling down the raceway with one intention and that is to get to a destination first and win. Slowing down feels like you may fall behind or out of the race. However, remember the story of the tortoise and the hare. The hare wanted to get to the finish line the fastest and win. The tortoise took time to smell the flowers and nap along the

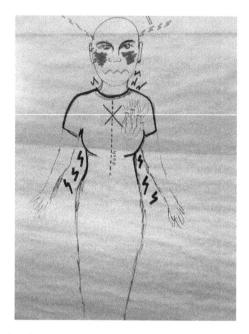

Figure 8.2 Completed Body Scan.

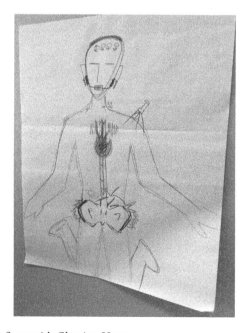

Figure 8.3 Body Scan with Glowing Heart.

way. The tortoise in this fable inched its way ahead of the hare to win the race. Many interpretations of the fable say that the lesson to be learned is that running fast in the race is not the only life objective. Stopping to enjoy life and restoring your energy with a restful nap can aid in winning the race in the long run. Which path do you want to choose? If you fast forward to the end of your life, will you want to be remembered by how fast you went or the quality of life you lived? To achieve a high-quality life, taking time for self-awareness by pausing through journal writing, creates time to reflect on caring for yourself and increases self-awareness such as who you are, what you want and how you want to live each day. We have outlined some key things to think about when you begin the practice of journaling.

- **First make your own journal or purchase one that you feel most reflects your spirit**. Some adults go to the bookstore or online and/or search for journals. Some choose those with recycled plain paper and others with fancy designs and again some prefer one with a lock. In some instances, there are apps that can safely secure your journal entries.
- **Decide what your journaling practice will be in the first three to six months**. Developing a habit takes practice that is consistent. Your new practice can be daily or a few times per week. After three to six months, re-evaluate if you can increase or if you should reduce the number of days in your routine.

Suggestions for Journal Entry Themes and Ideas

Pausing, Breathing, and Checking-in Journal Entry. Close your eyes and take in a deep breath through your nose and release it through your mouth. Repeat three times and then open your eyes. Take this chart and identify how you are feeling in the moment you are writing the journal entry.

Emotional state check in	Scale of emotions check in	Intensity of emotion	Emotional state check in
Red (hyper-aroused or hypo-aroused)	7–10	Intense	Red (hyper-aroused or hypo-aroused)
Orange (early trigger signs)	4–6	Moderate and rising emotion	Orange (early trigger signs)
Green (optimal state of regulation)	0–3	Calm and regulated	Green (optimal state of regulation)

Body Scan Journal Entry. Describe with a body scan a visual symbol or an X how you feel in your body. Examples may include pounding like a hammer, nervous like butterflies in your stomach, rocky like a rocking chair, heavy like a rock, empty like a container, exploding like a volcano, hot like the sun, racing like a roller coaster, buzzing like bumble bees, tight like a rubber band, icy like ice cubes, or angry like a t-rex dinosaur. There are many visuals that can describe how your body feels and you can draw that image or simply an X mark where your body may be feeling stress.

   Physical, Mental, and Emotional Journal Entry Check In. Another journal entry can include a check on how you are doing physically, mentally, and emotionally.

- **Physically**. The physical body is the container for all of emotions. When the physical body suffers due to a lack of self-care and unhealthy managing of emotions, symptoms may arise such as headaches, body aches, facial tension, neck pain, and so on. Checking in with the body throughout the week is important in preventing symptoms physically from getting worse. The body can be giving clues as to how one feels. Also, physical health includes a healthy eating and exercise plan. When self-care is prioritized, the body can operate physically in the most optimal way. Below are some topics you can journal on regarding physical health:
  - Exercise and physical activity routine
  - Eating and nutrition
  - Sleep
  - Physical and well-check exams
  - Medical check-ups for potentially concerning symptoms
  - Body scan to identify cues in your body that indicate stress symptoms

- **Mentally**. What internal dialogue do you say to yourself when you do a journal entry? Is it self-critical? Do you have thoughts ruminating with regret about past events or interactions? (e.g., why did I do that? or I am so stupid?). Do you feel worried about the future? (I will fail and everyone will laugh at me.) Are you happy with how things are right now? (I feel content and am accepting of how things are and I recognize I can learn from this experience.) Most people do not take time to step away and think. They are more reactive and impulsive. How can we get adults to be less reactive and more responsive and thoughtful of how their actions will impact others for the greatest good and outcome? Stepping away and thinking things through is critical to making decisions that are not impulsive and reactive. The mind has the potential to analyze and look at all sides of a situation to weigh options before making a decision. When journaling, you can write and identify the possible outcomes of a choice and determine which choice produces the least harm.

Positive Strength and Asset Journal Entry. Noticing your strengths can promote a more balanced mental mindset. When we are stressed we tend to focus on the things we don't do well or don't like about ourselves. We can get caught in a cycle of negativity and habits of self-talk that are self-deprecating and negative (I hate myself, I am not good at anything, no one likes me, etc.).

Sample journal entry: *"Today I notice one of my strengths. I am very good at helping others, especially the infants in my classroom. I know exactly how to calm each one and I am good at it. Babies love me and they easily stop crying because when I hold them or rock them they calm down easily in my care."*

- **Emotionally**. All feelings are valid. As children we may have grown up with adults that did not know how to help us make sense of our emotions. Some of us as children were not allowed to have emotions and others had to learn to stuff them down for fear of being made fun of or reprimanded for showing emotions. Others were only allowed certain feelings such as happy, content but those such as anger were not allowed. Perhaps the females and males in your family had different standards for expressing certain emotions. If you did not have adults growing up who helped you identify, express, and communicate emotion, then it is likely you grew up with some difficulties identifying how you feel and/or expressing emotions in a healthy way. An example of healthy expression of feelings is to talk to a trusted confidante about how you feel. An unhealthy expression of feelings might be drugs, alcohol, or the use of overeating to numb out the feelings that are uncomfortable. However you were raised, this is an important strategy to develop as the more self-aware you are about your feelings and emotional state, the easier you have the ability to express your internal state in a healthy way.

Use this chart as a guide to describe your physical, mental, and emotional state in the moment.

Physically	Mentally
Great	Great
Good	Good
Average	Average
Poor	Poor
Not good	Not good
Other:	Other:

Emotionally			
Sad	Powerlessness	Content	Disgusted
Angry	Depressed	Anxious	Judgmental
Joyful	Defeated	Afraid	Grumpy
Encouraged	Discouraged	Bored	Angry
Creative	Embarrassed	Distracted	Annoyed
Connected	Rejected	Scattered	Envious
Happy	Sad	Overwhelmed	Frustrated
Proud	Tired	Self-critical	Closed-minded
Satisfied	Remorseful	Other:	
Thankful	Heartbroken		

Sample journal entry: *"This morning I feel great physically and mentally but emotionally I feel frustrated and powerless. I don't want to go to work because I am frustrated with the new teacher that just started. She gets upset with the children and seems uncaring. I am frustrated with the way she is with the children and I don't know how to say something about it."*

Self-Regulation Journal Entry. After you check in with your emotional temperature, do a body scan and determine how you are physically, mentally, and emotionally. What do you do if you find you have intense levels of emotion? What if you are dysregulated and feel reactive and even drained emotionally? If your emotional state is in the red zone, or on the scale of seven to ten, you can use or develop a toolbox of self-regulation strategies. With increased self-awareness you will learn that emotions are only a temporary state and always changing. If we react when our emotions are in the red zone, or on a scale in the seven to ten zone, you may act in ways that hurt others, yourself, or property. It is better to get in the habit of stepping away and taking a tool from your self-regulation toolkit. One question you could explore through journal writing is what are the self-regulation tools available for calming your regulatory system? What tools do you use right now that help you calm down, regulate, or come back to that optimal zone of regulation? One way to start with self-regulation is to reflect in your journal entry with the following inquiry questions:

- What healthy strategies do I already use to bring me calm and self-regulation?
- Make a list of five strategies that bring me calm and regulation that I use at home? Five at work? Five outdoors or in the community? Other?
- Which strategies do I use that are not calming but that cause me more dysregulation?

- Are there any tools I already use daily? Weekly? Occasionally?
- Are my self-regulation strategies healthy (does not harm me, others, or property)?

You can complete this table in your journal. The first is a sample of one already completed and the second is a sample you can use for your journal entry

Sample self-regulation strategy	Is your strategy healthy for yourself, others, or property?	Where do I use this strategy?
Going for a walk	Yes	Park
Talking to a trusted friend	Yes	Phone or out with friends
Breathing	Yes	Anywhere
Listening to music	Yes	Car or on a break at work
Reading a book	Yes	Break at work or home before bed
Having a cup of tea or coffee	Yes	Work or home
Taking a bath	Yes	Home
Walking or petting a loved animal	Yes	Home in the evening
Playing a game	Yes	With family at home
Eating a box of cookies	No	Home
Yelling at my kids	No	Home

Self-regulation strategy	Is your strategy healthy to yourself, others, or property?	Where do I use this strategy?

Problem-Solving or Solution Focused Journal. If you are in an optimal state of regulation (after identifying emotions, emotional intensity, and using self-regulation strategies to bring you to a state of calm) and have a problem you are facing, journaling can help you map out various solutions and outcomes. Thinking through solutions can prevent over reactions or impulsive life moves that can be detrimental to you or harmful to others.

Sample journal entry: "This morning I feel great physically and mentally but emotionally I feel frustrated and powerless. I don't want to go to work because I am frustrated with a new teacher that just started. She gets upset with the children and seems uncaring. I am frustrated with the way she is with the children and I don't know how to say something about it. Some possible *solutions:*

- *Request a job transfer*
- *Talk to my supervisor*
- *Talk to her directly*
- *Wait and observe if things change since she is new*

I think I will wait since this teacher is so new. I just want to watch and see if things change. If they do not I might first consult with my supervisor to think through possible strategies and to gain her support. I am nervous to talk with her directly because I don't want to hurt her feelings."

Gratitude Journal. It seems easier for our brains to scan for danger, what is wrong in life, and to get fixated in a loop that is negative and damaging to our mental health and well-being. In order to cultivate a more balanced mindset, practicing gratitude can help you cast your attention to the things you can be thankful for that you may not otherwise notice. Every day in your journal write one thing you are thankful for. Writing each day one thing of gratitude will help you develop balance mentally and a protective buffering when the negative thoughts come floating to your mind. Negative thoughts can be like Velcro and stick with us, but positive experiences are like Teflon and can more easily slip away from our mind. By keeping a gratitude journal, you help the positive "stick" in a way that builds your mental strength and resiliency. By balancing negative thinking with optimism, it does not mean you are blind to the realities of a situation. It just helps you become balanced in how you look at problems, seeking to look at both the downsides and benefits to a problem.

Gratitude Journal Entry. Writing about things I am thankful for in my life. A gratitude entry helps us focus on the positive and helps us create a mindset that does not just focus on the negative. It is easy to focus only on the negative but through an intentional focus on the positive, we can help our mental health to have more balance.

Sample journal entry: "Today I am thankful for my mother whom I talk to daily and she accepts me and loves me unconditionally. When I talk to her she listens and I feel supportive. I am so thankful she is in my life as she helps me feel grounded and calms me when I feel stressed."

Random Act of Kindness. Doing for others helps us feel we have purpose and meaning. When we do a small act of kindness to help others, it builds our sense of efficacy and well-being. It also allows us to not be so self-focused and absorbed but rather to focus our attention on making a difference for others in the world. You can use your journal to track a weekly or monthly random act of kindness.

Sample journal entry: "I decided that I would do one random act of kindness each month. I started this practice a year ago. This month it was simple. I was at a restaurant with my family and received exceptional service from the waiter. I asked the waiter to speak to his supervisor. I could tell he was nervous and thought he was in trouble. Both the supervisor and the waiter were shocked when I gave specific and descriptive positive feedback about his intentional, responsive, and caring service of our family during our meal. The supervisor said that rarely does anyone ask her over to provide positives. I felt so good being able to point out intentionally something that someone did in the world that was positive instead of complaining when the service is poor."

Note: You will find additional ideas in this chapter to help you think of journal entries!

Mindful Awareness. Mindfulness is the continuous awareness (self-reflection) and nonjudgmental respect for our emotions, thoughts, and bodies (Siegel, 2007). Mindfulness does not control the mind but rather it *transforms the mind to be more present and clear.*

Mindfulness is generally believed to be a learned skill that enhances attention self-regulation because it challenges us to stay in the moment and create a state of active attention on the present (Baer, 2003; Siegel, 2007). In the early education field, mindful practice and concentrated attention are central. When teachers are mindful they are present to what is going on in the classroom and can attend more closely to the children's needs. Mindfulness supports adults to develop executive attention skills that will help to manage their attention toward accomplishing goals by reducing distracting stimuli. Such skills could be negatively impacted if teachers experience secondary traumatic stress as a result of being exposed to the children's trauma.

When teachers make time to relax through mindful practices, they give their bodies and minds time to restore and heal from the day to day stressors they experience. An activity like taking deep breaths in and out is one example of a tool teachers can use to slow down a racing body and mind and bring them back into the present moment. When they can focus their attention on the present moment rather than worrying about the past or future, they can slow down their racing, worried minds. Mindfulness approaches may help build a protective buffer for teachers who face many daily stressors in their jobs taking care of young children.

MINDFULNESS WITH YOUNG CHILDREN

The early learning environment may well be that particular time and place to introduce mindful caregiving practices that promote young children's emotional resiliency to overcome unfavorable conditions and nurturing regulatory and executive functions within them.

Although mindful practice in preschool education is not well researched, it is increasing in popularity (Greenland, 2010; Lillard, 2011). In both education and mindful practice, concentrated attention is central. Attention is a complex system comprised of three primary networks: the alerting network, responsible for achieving and maintaining an alert state; the orienting network that directs attention toward sensory information; and the executive network, which is central to the regulation of emotions, behavior, and cognition, and correlated with executive functions (Posner, 2008).

Mindful teaching practices are aimed at helping focus children on paying attention to their internal experiences, including their emotions and their behavior (Greenland, 2010), and could naturally fit with trauma-informed teaching practices. The game Simon Says is a typical mindful game for teachers to use to activate the attention network system in young children. When the teacher says, "Simon says," jump on one foot, children jump on one foot, but when the teacher does not say "Simon says" and carries out the action, there is a discrepancy between what children hear and see. It is the executive attention network that scans the competing message, enabling young children to execute instructions from one source while inhibiting instructions from another. As the children intentionally direct their attention in a new way, they are creating a fresh experience that changes the activity and ultimately improves the structure of their brains (Siegel, 2007).

Another advantage of introducing mindful practice with young children is the positive impact these practices can have in the development of emotional resiliency and pro-social development.

Children's understanding of self and other emotions, and engaging in positive shared peer play activities that facilitate empathy, relationship skills, and self-reflection, is similar to a mindful practitioner who acts with compassion and empathy in a nonjudgmental way with clarity and insight (Epstein, 1999). According to Siegel (2007), such reflective skills activate the prefrontal cortex and build children's ability to focus and pay attention, in addition to strengthening their prosocial behavior, empathy for others, and self-regulation.

Much of what promotes mindfulness in the developing child has to do with the presence of attuned adults who are aware of their own emotions and align with the child's emotional state (Siegel, 2007). Siegel (2001) explains that alignment, a component of affect attunement, is one way in which the caregiver alters her own emotional state to be "in tune" with the emotional state of the child. It is the attunement of the teacher with the children she is caring for that creates the foundation for children to become mindful.

Mindful Training in School-Age Education

Mindfulness has been taught to over 18,000 school-age children and 750 teachers in 53 American schools; approximately 70% served have been low-income children (Mindful Schools, 2010). The results reported by the Mindful School Program (2010) suggest that it improved attention and social skills, reduced test anxiety, and facilitated a sense of calm. The students demonstrated better focus and concentration; enhanced self-awareness; decreased stress; improved the school-wide culture of calm, focus, and connection; better conflict-resolution skills; healthier ways to respond to difficult emotions; and increased empathy and understanding of others.

Our minds drift to and fro, buffeted by sensation like a boat upon stormy seas. The breath serves as an anchor, something to which we can tether our minds so that we can be present for the real.
                                                                (Gates & Kenison, 2002)

Breathing. Breathing is a tool you can use to calm your regulatory system. Learning how to breath can help you recover and manage small or large stressors. When your body is stressed, hormones are released that propel you into a fight, flight, or freeze mode. When in that state, the ability to think is limited and you become more reactive. In order to manage your stress, taking deep and mindful breaths can benefit you emotionally. It can help you feel calm, develop self-regulation skills, and provide access to your "thinking brain" rather than only the reactive part of your brain. If you practice breathing daily, it can become a part of a routine choice you use from your personal self-care toolkit.

One simple thing you can do to help with stress is to make deep breathing a part of your daily practice and turn it into a habit. It can be done anywhere, does not cost anything, and helps support self-regulation. Follow this simple ritual:

• Sit up or stand up straight
• Take a long, slow deep breath through your nose and then release all the air through your lungs

- Next, take in a deep breath through your mouth and into your lungs and slowly release the air
- Focus on your breathing for at least two minutes, noticing how your body responds
- Try deep breathing at work for a moment, when stuck in traffic, or anywhere you need to refocus.

The Important Role of Supervisors in Teacher's Self-Care

Supervisors and program leaders have a critical role in providing ongoing support to their staff and reducing the negative effects of burnout and compassion fatigue. When teachers feel supported, validated, and valued by supervisors, they find it easier to manage the stress and demands associated with their jobs. Research evidence highlights that when adults perceive their organizations to be supportive, they experience decreased levels of trauma (Lipsky, 2009).

The single most important skill of a supervisor is to provide emotional support to those they supervise. There is no other factor that buffers toxic stress and acts as a co-regulator than a supervisor who shows concern and compassion for the well-being of their employees.

Strategies Supervisors Can Use to Create a Trauma-Informed, Trauma-Sensitive Workplace

- Using reflective conversations that are two-way and include the ideas, voice, and opinions of the teachers
- Promoting workplace self-care initiatives
- Promoting individual self-care for the teacher
- Provide opportunities and pathways for growth
- Have a network of peers to offer support and reflective conversations
- Offer professional development opportunities
- Training opportunities that support growth
- Setting clear limits and expectations
- Offering teachers a voice and input in the construction of policies, procedures, and meeting agendas

---

Next, we introduce the Healthy Brain Map for Quality Self-Care Tool. It is designed to help you explore the balance between stress and restorative activities so that you have enough energy reserves to cope effectively with day to day stressors and to promote high-quality living. Just like there are recommendations for healthy and balanced food eating, we have designed a tool for you to think about healthy and balanced care for your mind, your body, and your spirit.

Healthy Brain Map for Quality Self-Care Tool

Make a list of all the restorative activities and strategies you use (middle column) and new strategies you could begin to add (far right column) in each of the nine categories. If you have at least one strategy listed in each area that you can integrate into your life on a monthly basis, you will increase your likelihood of preventing burnout, compassion fatigue, and secondary traumatic stress.

	List the strategies you use	List new strategies you could add or begin to use
Play and fun	Dancing, playing golf, scrapbooking, cooking.	
Self-reflection	Write in my journal, talking with my best friend, meditation.	
Daydreaming and mind wandering activities		Long hikes alone to think and dream on weekend. Take five minutes in my car before I go into work and before I go into the house to have some thoughtful reflection and a mindful moment.
Sleep		Less phone and TV usage before bed to promote better sleep. Go to bed at a routine time. Less sugar and/or caffeine before bed.
Relationships	Spending time with my mom and brothers regularly. Spending time with my children and partner.	Reducing time with friends that cause me stress.
Environment	Taking a bath, which is my only safe and quiet space to get away in my home! Everyone knows that at bath time don't bother me! Pictures of my loved ones that make me realize how lucky I am. Flowers to give me a connection to nature and beauty.	Go to bed earlier and have my children go to bed more on a predictable routine so that I have a quiet, reflective, and safe space to myself before bed.

Physical activity	Walking during my break or lunch.	Zumba class after work at community center.
Intellectual stimulation		If I get to bed earlier and do the strategy under environment "Go to bed earlier and have my children go to bed more on a predictable routine so that I have a quiet, reflective, and safe space to myself before bed" then I would have time to read.
Work	Asking my supervisor to help me prioritize my tasks since it feels overwhelming at times. Saying no if I am able to or not volunteering to say yes to everything—being more careful.	Use my vacation time more for a well day off to restore and do things I enjoy.

Examples for Each Category in the Healthy Brain Map Framework

The following are examples of the types of activities that fall into each of the categories listed above. These are just examples and do not reflect all of the activities you might list for each of these categories. We list them to help you begin to think about your own Healthy Brain Map … where your strengths are and gaps or areas you need to attend to. You will see that many of these categories overlap and are not mutually exclusive.

Play and fun	Activities that are enjoyable and done for fun rather than as a task to be completed or for practical purposes. Examples: dancing, listening to music, going out with friends, arts and crafts, creative cooking, going on adventures, travel, exploring something new, taking a class.
Self-reflection	This refers to time we tune inward and reflect on our life. So much time is casting the spotlight of our attention outward that focusing inward can keep us in tune with our emotional state and well-being. Examples: counseling, therapy, talking with a friend, journal writing, praying, meditation, yoga, mindful walks.

Daydreaming and mind wandering	The opposite of paying attention is daydreaming. Letting your mind wander while exploring ideas or creative thoughts. This activity allows the brain to live in a creative mode that often allows for new ideas and insights. Examples: lying on a blanket while looking at the stars or clouds, lying in bed and letting your mind wander, walking and thinking of ideas, writing and thinking of ideas, talking out loud with someone who allows you to explore creative ideas.
Sleep	Each person's body needs a different amount of sleep. Only you will know what you need to feel rested and restored.
Relationships	Surrounding our self with those who restore our energy, provide support, and who care about us can help buffer toxic stress. When we choose to be with others who drain us or promote stress then this can add to our already existing stress. Some of these relationships are in our control and out of our control. For this section, think about what you have control over. Examples: being around friends who listen and support you, having relationships that challenge your thinking in a positive way, spending time with those who are fun and restorative, being with people who are healthy or help you grow and become a stronger person.
Environment	We can think about the environments that helps us feel safe and restored. For some it is predictable routines, others it is unpredictable and going with the flow. Some like physical objects of beauty around them and some need things in order. Others may lean toward an environment where there is space to get away and then on the opposite are those who are restored when surrounded by friends or family. It may be if you are introverted, you prefer quiet and more reflective environments and more time alone. If you are more extroverted, you may get energy from being social.
Physical activity	How much physical activity one needs is individual, but it is recommended by the CDC to have an average of 150 minutes of mild to moderate exercise per week. Examples: walking, running, the gym, yoga, crossfit, hiking.
Intellectual stimulation	Activities that help grow the mind and knowledge are things such as reading, taking classes, going to school, searching the internet, watching a documentary.
Work	Well, who needs to explain this one! How much you work and how stressful and restorative it is, sometimes falls in or out of your control. However, what choices do you have to minimize the work stressors you may face. Examples: taking vacation days, saying no to tasks if you are able, prioritizing, not volunteering unless you have the energy.

Referring to the category descriptions above, put an X next to the strategies that you engage in regularly. **These are your Healthy Brain Map strengths.**

Play/fun	X	Self-reflection	X	Daydreaming/mind wandering	
Sleep		Relationships	X	Environment	X
Physical activity	X	Intellectual stimulation		Work	X

Next, we want you to identify your **Healthy Brain Map gaps.** Place an X in the areas below where you need to place greater attention.

Play/Fun		Self-reflection		Daydreaming/mind wandering	X
Sleep	X	Relationships		Environment	
Physical activity		Intellectual stimulation	X	Work	

Now it's time to think of some new strategies you would like to work on adding to your daily and weekly self-care plan to create more balance in your life for healthier outcomes and restored energy.

Based on the Brain Map ratings above, below are some self-care strategies that could be added to a self-care plan. These are self-care strategies I can engage in daily and/or weekly to support my self-care plan. Some examples might include the following:

1. Go to bed earlier so that I have some quiet time, reflection time, and a safe space to myself before bed. Ideally, I would also have a few minutes to read.
2. Less phone and TV usage before bed so I get a better night's sleep. Less sugar and/or caffeine before bed.
3. Zumba class at the community center after work.
4. Spend at least one hour every week doing something that restores me and something I really enjoy.
5. Take five minutes in my car before I go in to work and before I go into the house to have some thoughtful reflection and a mindful moment.

There are benefits to self-care and preventing burnout. When teachers' stressors are buffered with wellness and caring routines, their energy becomes restored and renewed and they have more reserves to pull from for creating safe and predictable environments, building relationships, maintaining a calm and regulated state, seeking to understand the meaning of children's behavior, and using sensitive strategies that heal and protect children rather than worsen their stress and trauma. Working with children with histories of trauma is physically and emotionally draining and complex work. The only way that teachers can sustain attuned responsive care that supports children to heal from trauma and builds their resiliency is by working in environments that acknowledge and value the importance of supporting them to attend on a regular basis to their own self-care.

Teacher Tip for Self-Care

As an adult, you cannot eliminate stress in your life, but you can find ways to take care of yourself so that you have more restored energy to support others. You can only help children when your emotional energy stores are full for that day, enabling you to have the self-awareness and self-regulation necessary to provide quality care. The more life stressors you have, the more self-care and restorative activities will be needed to replenish the strong emotional energy reserves that will be so vital and necessary for you to cope with the challenges you face daily in both your professional and personal life.

If you come to work rested and restored, you will have more energy to help the children, be able to model healthy behaviors, and manage the stress you experience as a result of the challenges you face. If you come to work stressed and depleted, then your brain will be filled with lingering stress that will impact how you connect and react with children. Children are sensitive too! They pick up on your energy even when you think you are not showing it.

Personal Reflection: DaMonica Robinson, Preschool Teacher (Figure 8.4)

About a year ago, I began to prioritize my own self-care. I started to develop certain routines and practices to restore my energy. I began to notice I was feeling increasingly stressed. When I was stressed, I noticed I was more short-tempered with my colleagues and the children, I was quick to speak, uptight, and more reactive. After implementing more of these self-care practices, I started to feel calmer and I could handle more stress including the children with challenging behaviors. Now I am slower to speak, I listen to others more, I am less reactive, and I can remain calm in the middle of chaos. Some of the strategies I use for self-care include:

- Taking time to be alone
- Breathing techniques to stay calm
- I have prayer time before work every morning
- I eliminated negative media such as the news
- I go to concerts with friends for fun
- I have lunch with my good friends for connecting time

Figure 8.4 DaMonica Robinson.

- I eat a healthier diet
- Every evening I do 80 arm circular reps as it is meditative and relaxing for me before bed.

Research examining the effects of mindful practices and their effects on attention is showing positive results. Empirical investigation of mindfulness training in adults showed significantly improved performance in the functioning of attention (Jha, Krompinger, & Baime, 2007). This same benefit could potentially improve the development of young children exposed to traumatic stress in the areas of memory as these children may forget things simply because they are not in an optimal state of arousal and paying attention to their teachers.

Linking to Policy

In contemporary early childhood, there is a push for quality improvement, systems building, and workforce initiatives, which means that many child care providers and early childhood teachers working in public programs are feeling overwhelmed with the stress and increasing demands of their jobs. They not only have more children in their care who require intensive support, they are also managing the demands that these initiatives are introducing into their professional lives including coaching and Quality Rating and Improvement plans. Other teachers and providers, especially private licensed programs and family child care providers, have few if any resources available to support them with children who challenge or puzzle them. TIP should be built into programs to align with other initiatives, instead of being "one more thing" providers and teachers must do.

Unless we develop high-quality initiatives that support teachers in gaining trauma-sensitive tools and skills, our most vulnerable children will continue to struggle in our programs, teachers will continue to burnout, and the cost to society in supporting the children who are not healed in their early years will continue to escalate every year they are in school. Dr. Bruce Perry states the brain is easiest to modify between zero and five and takes high-quality caregiving to do so.

Bruce Perry: www.youtube.com/watch?v=RYj7YYHmbQs

Coaching and TIP in Action

Mary is a teacher in a preschool program in California. Jackie, her coach, was observing her classroom one morning in preparation for a coaching meeting scheduled later in the day with the room's team of teachers. Jackie walked outside where the children were gathered to let Mary and the others know she had arrived and to ask their permission for her to observe. Something felt different about Mary as Jackie approached her. She appeared shut down. Her face was blank, somewhat unresponsive, and her body movements rigid. Coach Jackie asked if she was okay because that day she felt something was different about her in. Mary curtly responded that she had a doctor's appointment and would have to leave early from the coaching meeting. She mentioned little more than that. Later, she did open up when they were meeting alone as part of the coaching session. It was then that Mary let her know she was planning on giving notice that week so that she could move to another position. She went on to explain that she had always been responsible for napping the children and knew which ones needed more individual support to fall asleep. She described with detailed examples some of the strategies she employed. However, her supervisor changed Mary's break time, which meant the other teacher in the classroom had now taken on this responsibility. Mary explained the other teacher refused to nap the kids in an individualized way. The other teacher stated, "I don't want to spoil them by giving them too much attention." As a result, Mary would come back from her break to kids who were awake and dysregulated. This impacted her ability to get necessary paperwork done. Moreover, she shared that she felt bullied by the other teacher.

Mary described examples where the teacher made comments to her such as "you are too soft with the kids," "you coddle them," "you give them too much attention." Mary felt stressed under the constant scrutiny of this teacher belittling her style of caring for the children. Mary went on to explain that a little while after this change, she had been rushed to the hospital for work-related stress in the form of a panic attack, and now she felt it coming once again. She admitted that these things really build up for her and lead to high stress levels. The only avenue of escape she saw was to move on to another location.

After Mary shared her story with her coach, she appeared visibly more relaxed. Her face softened, her body was less rigid in movement. Together, other options were explored besides giving notice. She felt like there was a weight off her heart and became capable in that moment of thinking of alternative solutions such as approaching her supervisor about the break schedule and talking to the other teacher directly about how much her comments and actions impacted her. Together, they practiced talking through these conversations in coaching. Now it was in Mary's hands to make it happen.

When Coach Jackie returned a month later for her next coaching visit, Mary was still in the same classroom and appeared calmer. She was smiling, playing with the children and laughing. It was not difficult to guess her demeanor this time during her outdoor observation, she was clearly much happier. After the observation, they had their individual coaching meeting together. She said that she spoke with her supervisor about her concerns, and her break time had been changed back to her preference. She said it was so much easier to talk to her supervisor then she imagined. Her supervisor was supportive and really listened to her. She had bravely approached the other teacher to talk about why she uses individualized strategies with the children and their successful outcomes. She went on to share how the disparaging comments made her feel. Unfortunately, the other teacher continues to make these same comments, but Mary said she felt that communicating how she felt seemed to create a dynamic where the other teacher allowed her more freedom or as she described it "had more respect" for her way of working with the children. Mary said talking had really helped her calm down and think through alternative solutions to her problem.

Trauma Sensitive Coaching Strategies Used with Teacher Mary

- **Co-regulation**: The use of your own internal sense of calmness to help calm the internal state of intense emotions Mary is having.
- **Listen and attune to the story Mary is experiencing**. Helping someone tell their story regulates their big emotions and calms their sensory system.
- **Helping Mary identify what she was feeling and sensing inside her body** and how that was related to her own experience of what was happening to her in the classroom. Helping her verbalize her

feelings helped calm her down so she could think through solutions next.

- **Coach Jackie did not jump to her own solutions right away.** It was important for her to use strategies of listening, attuning, and supporting the calming of the reptile (fight, flight, or freeze) and mammal brain (which was flooded with intense emotions). Once Teacher Mary appeared calm, Coach Jackie was able to support her in using the Executive part of her brain to think through solutions.
- **Once calm, using reflective inquiry questions to help Mary "think" of her own solutions** instead of Coach Jackie jumping in with what she thinks Mary should do. It is empowering and gives Jackie a sense of feeling in control when Jackie supports the solutions coming from Mary first. Jackie can ask the right reflective questions to help Mary look at all the different options she can choose.

CONCLUSION

Given the significant percentage of young children who experience trauma in their earliest years, early childhood teachers need to create trauma-sensitive, trauma-informed early learning environments that provide consistent, caring, and responsive relationships, predictability, and feelings of physical and emotional safety. We offer several recommendations for teachers and their administrators who are eager to get started in creating trauma-informed programs and want to know how to begin.

Teachers can:

- Commit to learning about trauma and trauma-informed teaching practices. This is the most important first step anyone can take to support young children impacted by trauma.
- Develop self-awareness of your own reactions to stress and practice self-care and self-compassion.
- Practice self-reflection and use inquiry to strengthen your self-awareness, self-regulation, and ability to be attuned and responsive to young children, especially when they are dysregulated.
- Learn about resiliency and how you can help children strengthen it.
- Integrate social-emotional activities into your curriculum.
- Make referrals to appropriate professionals—especially mental health providers—when one of the children in your care requires additional support. Teachers need to work in partnership with other professionals to best support children with histories of complex trauma.
- Take a risk to try and practice one or more of the trauma-sensitive strategies described in this book.

Administrators can:

- Support a school- or program-wide culture for trauma-informed teaching and trauma-sensitive classrooms.
- Understand and respond to teachers' needs and acknowledge the difficulties in teaching young children exposed to trauma.
- Develop a comprehensive professional development plan to support teachers' understanding and implementation of trauma-sensitive strategies.
- Build partnerships with organizations that can provide mental health consultation for staff, children, and families. Specifically ask them to support teachers to learn and practice a wide range of strategies they can use to support children and families impacted by trauma. There are many organizations and systems actively implementing trauma-informed care. Look for opportunities to collaborate and participate in cross-disciplinary partnerships in your community.
- Implement an integrated trauma-informed training for your staff that includes trauma-informed family engagement strategies and an understanding of racial equity and culturally responsive practice.

Although teachers and administrators have powerful roles to support young children's healing and well-being, they cannot do this work alone. This means that researchers, policymakers, and all staff working on behalf of young children and families need to lean in and learn about trauma, so we can collectively strive to shift our programs, organizations, and systems to become trauma-informed, and healing for young children, families, and the workforce that serves them.

Trauma-informed early childhood programs are rooted in empathy and validation of all young children's life experiences. They have compassion for children exposed to trauma and understand that they have developed adaptive behaviors to manage their feelings of terror and feelings of helplessness in the face of adverse experiences. They acknowledge children's strengths, creativity, and persistence instead of focusing solely on their complex and challenging behaviors. They understand the profound responsibility and privilege adults have to support the development of healthy neural pathways in children's brains. And most importantly, they have an unwavering commitment to build consistent, caring, and attuned relationships with every child, every day, so they can communicate to each one that they are deeply loved, full of promise and possibility, and will be safe and protected in their care.

RESOURCES ON TRAUMA AND TRAUMA-INFORMED PRACTICES

Books for Adults

Mathieu, Francoise. (2012). *The compassion fatigue workbook.* New York, NY: Routledge.

A wonderful resource to provide tools for those who are in the helping field. Understanding the cost to an individual of caring, the risk when self-care is not prioritized, and the benefits to everyone when a person in the helping field prioritizes their own self-care and restorative energies.

van der Kolk, B. (2014). *The body keeps the score: Brain, mind, and body in the healing of trauma.* New York, NY: Penguin Books

Dr. van der Kolk uses neuroscience to demonstrate the impact of trauma on the physical brain, body, and behavior. He unveils evidence-based treatments and supports that help bring the body and mind back online so that individuals can have healthier tools for living.

Books for Children

Holmes, Margaret M. (2000). *A terrible thing happened: A story for children who have witnessed violence or trauma.* Washington, DC: Magination Press and republished by Dalmation Press, LLC by permission of the APA.

This book is a wonderful tool that can be used by adults to help young children who have been witness to traumatic events and/or violent crimes. A caring adult can learn how to support children to become in touch with and to communicate the feelings and sensations attached to the event/s they witnessed.

Ippen, Chandra G. (2016). *Once I was very very scared.* San Francisco, CA: Piplo Productions.

With the support of caring adults, a child can be supported to explore their feelings associated with a scary/traumatic experience/s. By reading this book together, the adult can create a safe place for the child to express themselves.

Garcia, Gabi. (2017). *Listening to my body.* Austin, TX: Take Heart Press.

A guide for adult caregivers to use with young children to help them understand the connection between sensations in their body and feelings.

Apps (Mobile Applications)

Stop, breath & think adults

For adults who want to take one to seven minutes a day to practice mindfulness, pausing and reflecting on how they feel in their mind and body. The app allows for a brief guided meditation after the initial prompts.

Videos

Dr. Nadine Burke Harris TEDMED. (2014) talk. *How childhood trauma affects health across a lifetime.*
https://ted.com/talks/nadine_burke_harris_how_childhood_trauma_ affects_health_across_a_lifetime

Pediatrician Nadine Burke Harris describes the science behind Adverse Childhood Experiences (ACEs) explaining the impact of toxic stress (abuse, neglect, and parents struggling with mental health or substance abuse issues, etc.) on the development of the brain. A groundbreaking talk that inspired a national conversation about the need to screen for ACES in early childhood.

Videos Featuring Bruce Perry

Your brain reflects the work you grow up in—"Roots of empathy" (2 min, 50 sec) www.youtube.com/watch?v=q6CXy5g8DDs. This video is short but powerful in that it explains the importance of positive relationships to support children in building empathy.
Trauma, brain and relationship: Helping children heal (5 min) www.youtube.com/watch?v=RYj7YYHmbQs. Several professionals in the field of early childhood trauma including Dr. Bruce Perry and Dr. Peter Levine. Dr. Perry states the brain is easiest to modify between zero and five. The importance of attuned, caring relationships is the most important tool.
Six core strengths for healthy child development: An overview (4 min, 31 sec) www.youtube.com/watch?v=skaYWKC6iD4. Dr. Bruce Perry describes the six core strengths for healthy child development in his model from the Child Trauma Academy:

1. Attachment being the first neurobiological need for a child to develop a strong foundation (relationships are the most important);
2. Self-regulation;
3. Connect socially and emotionally to others around you (friendship skills);
4. Begin to observe differences in others in reactions, looks, personality;
5. Become tolerant of others and unfamiliar situations;
6. Respect diversity and strengths that others have that you don't have.

Websites

ACES Connection
www.acesconnection.com/

ACEs Connection is a social and community action network that brings together people around the world around the topic of trauma, adverse childhood experiences to help heal and develop resilience.

ACES Too High
https://acestoohigh.com/

This website is a news site that reports on updated research related to adverse childhood experiences, the consequences of toxic stress, and the implementation of practices based on the research. The information provided is cross-sector and includes reports from education, juvenile justice, criminal justice, public health, medicine, mental health, and social services. ACEs Connection is the companion social network website.

Center for Disease Control and Prevention: Adverse Childhood Experiences
www.cdc.gov/violenceprevention/acestudy/

This website offers numerous resources around violence prevention for all ages which includes ACEs, research, strategies, and prevention tools.

Harvard University's Center on the Developing Child
https://developingchild.harvard.edu/about/

This website offers articles, videos, and other resources on toxic stress, trauma, and resiliency to support early childhood professional working with children and families.

The National Child Traumatic Stress Network
www.nctsn.org

This website was established to improve access to care, treatment, and services for children and adolescents exposed to trauma.

The National Child Traumatic Stress Network (NCTSN) was established in the year 2000 to improve access to care, treatment, and services for children and youth who have experienced trauma. They have taken a national lead focused on policy, research, treatment, education, and training. The website lists definitions of the different types of trauma, resources, and evidence-based treatments as well as products that can be accessed for free or minimal cost. For providers working with children ages zero to six, they have a link to resources with information on trauma's impact in the early years and strategies for building resiliency for young children and their families (http://www.nctsn.org/what-is-child-trauma/trauma-types/early-childhood-trauma). NCTSN is funded by the Center for Mental Health Services (CMHS), Substance Abuse and Mental Health Services Administration (SAMHSA), US Department of Health and Human Services, and jointly coordinated by UCLA and Duke University

National Institute for the Clinical Application of Behavioral Medicine
www.nicabm.com

This website provides research and clinical knowledge into health and mental health practices. They offer distance learning courses and free resources in areas like brain science, PTSD, mindfulness, and mind/ body medicine.

Sesame Street in Communities: Traumatic Experiences
https://sesamestreetincommunities.org/topics/traumatic-experiences/

Sesame Street recognizes how a child with a history of trauma impacts the family, the community, and our society. Their website features familiar characters from the show and provides activities, videos, printable resources, and articles on key topics to support adults working with children who have experienced trauma. It also includes two apps, "Breathe, Think, Do with Sesame" and "Art Maker" that allows children to express their feelings after a traumatic experience.

Understanding the Effects of Maltreatment on Brain Development
www.childwelfare.gov/pubPDFs/brain_development.pdf

This fact sheet has information on how the brain develops, the effects of maltreatment on brain development, implications for practice and policy, and additional resources and references.

REFERENCES

Acharya, S. & Shukla, S. (2012). Mirror neurons: Enigma of the metaphysical modular brain. *Journal of Natural Science, Biology and Medicine, 3*(2), 118–124. doi: 10.4103/0976-9668.101878

Adams, R., Boscarino, J., & Figley, C. (2006). Compassion fatigue and psychological distress among social workers: A validation study. *American Journal of Orthopsychiatry, 76*(1), 103–108. doi: 10.1037/0002-9432.76.1.103

Almond, D. & Currie, J. (2011). Killing me softly: The fetal origins hypothesis. *The Journal of Economic Perspectives, 25*(3), 153–172. Retrieved from www.ncbi.nlm.nih.gov/pmc/articles/PMC4140221/pdf/nihms443660.pdf

Als, H. (1982). Toward a synactive theory of development: Promise for the assessment and support of infant individuality. *Infant Mental Health Journal, 3*(4), 229–243.

American Psychological Association. (2011). www.apa.org

Applegate, J. S. & Shapiro, J. R. (2005). *Neurobiology for clinical social work: Theory and practice.* New York, NY: Norton.

Azevedo, F. A., Carvalho, L. R., Grinberg, L. T., Farfel, J. M., Ferretti, R. E., Leite, R. E., Filho, W. J., Lent, R., & Herculano-Houzel, S. (2009). Equal number of neuronal and nonneuronal cells make the human brain an isometrically scaled-up primate brain. *Journal of Comparative Neurology, 513*, 532–541. doi: 10.1002/cne.21974

Baer, R. A. (2003). Mindfulness training as a clinical intervention: A conceptual and empirical review. *Clinical Psychology: Science & Practice, 10*(2), 125–143.

Balbernie, R. (2001). Circuits and circumstances: The neurobiological consequences of early relationship experiences and how they shape later behaviour. *Journal of Child Psychotherapy, 27*(3), 237–255.

Blair, C. & Diamond, A. (2008). Biological processes in prevention and intervention: The promotion of self-regulation as a means of preventing school failure. *Developmental Psychopathology, 20*(3), 899–911.

Bowlby, J. (1969/1982). *Attachment and loss, vol. 1: Attachment.* New York, NY: Basic Books.

Bowlby, J. (1980). *Attachment and loss, vol. 3. Loss: Sadness and depression.* New York, NY: Basic Books.

Briggs-Gowan, M. J., Ford, J. D., Fraleigh, L., McCarthy, K., & Carter, A. S. (2010). Prevalence of exposure to potentially traumatic events in a healthy birth cohort of very young children in the northeastern United States. *Journal of Traumatic Stress, 23*(6), 725–733.

Bronson, M. (2000). *Self-regulation in early childhood.* New York, NY: The Guilford Press

Brownn, E. (2014). *Self-care is not selfish.* Retrieved from http://www.eleanorbrownn.com/blog2/self-care-in-not-selfish

Center on the Developing Child (2011). Building the brain's "air traffic" control system: How early experiences shape the development of executive function. *Working Paper No. 11.* Cambridge, MA: Harvard University. www.developingchildharvard.edu

Cochran-Smith, M. & Lytle, S. L. (2009). *Inquiry as stance: Practitioner research for the next generation.* New York, NY: Teachers College Press.

Conkbayier, M. (2017). *Early childhood and neuroscience: Theory, research and implications for practice.* New York, NY: Bloomsbury Academic.

Cozolino, L. (2006). *The neuroscience of human relationships: Attachment and the developing social brain.* New York, NY: Norton.

Cozolino, L. (2012). *The neuroscience of human relationships: Attachment and the developing social brain.* New York, NY: Norton.

Craig, S. (2016). *Trauma-sensitive schools: Learning communities transforming children's lives, K–5.* New York, NY: Teachers College Press.

Cunliffe, V. (2016). The epigenetic impacts of social stress: How does social adversity become biologically embedded. *Epigeomics, 8*(12). Retrieved from https://doi.org/10.2217/epi-2016-0075

Epstein, R. M. (1999). Mindful practice. *Journal American Medical Association, 282*(9), 833–839

Felitti, V.J. & Anda, R. F. (2010). The relationship of adverse childhood experiences to adult health, well-being, social function, and health care. In R. Lanius, E. Vermetten, and C. Pain (Eds.), *The effects of early life trauma on health and disease: The hidden epidemic.* Cambridge, Cambridge University Press.

Felitti, V. J., Anda, R. F., Nordenberg, D., Williamson, D. F., Spitz, A. M., Edwards, V., Koss, M.P., & Marks, J. S. (1998). The relationship of adult health status to childhood abuse and household dysfunction. *American Journal of Preventive Medicine, 14*(4), 245–258.

Figley, C. (2002). Compassion fatigue: Psychotherapists' chronic lack of self-care. *Psychotherapy in Practice, 58*(11), 1433–1441. doi:10.1002/jclp.10090

Gates, R. & Kenison, K. (2002). *Meditations from the mat: Daily reflections on the path of yoga.* New York, NY: Random House.

Ghosh Ippen, C., Harris, W., Van Horn, P., & Lieberman, A. (2011). Traumatic and stressful events in early childhood: Can treatment help those at highest risk? *Child Abuse and Neglect, 35*(7), 504–513.

Ghosh Ippen, C., Noroña, C., & Thomas, K. (2012). From tenet to practice: Putting a diversity-informed services into action. *Zero to Three, 33*(2), 23–28.

Gray, D. (2007). *Nurturing adoptions: Creating resilience after neglect and trauma.* Indianapolis, IN: Perspectives Press.

Greenland, S. K. (2010). *The mindful child: How to help your kid manage stress and become happier, kinder and more compassionate.* New York, NY: Free Press.

Hanson, R. (2009). *Buddha's brain*. Oakland, CA: New Harbinger Publications, Inc.

Heffron, M. C. & Murch, T. (2010). *Reflective supervision and leadership in infant and early childhood programs*. Washington, DC: ZERO TO THREE Press.

Herculano-Houzel, S. (2009). The human brain in numbers: A linearly scaled-up primate brain. *Frontiers in Human Neuroscience, 3*(31). doi: 10.3389/neuro.09.031.2009

Iacoboni, M., Woods, R., Brass, M., Bekkering, H., Mazziotta, J., & Rizzolatti, G. (1999). Cortical mechanisms of human imitation. *Science, 286*(5449), 2526–2528

Jha, A. P., Krompinger, J., & Baime, M. J. (2007). Mindfulness training modifies subsystems of attention. *Cognitive Affective & Behavioral Neuroscience, 7*(2), 109–119. doi:10.3758/CABN.7.2.109

Kaplan, M. & Mead, S. (2017). *The best teachers of our littlest learners? Lessons from Head Start's last decade*. Washington, DC: Bellweather Educational Partners. Retrieved from https://bellwethereducation.org/sites/default/files/Bellwether_HeadStartWorkforce.pdf

Koplan, C. & Chard, A. (2014). Adverse early life experiences as a social determinant of mental health. *Psychiatric Annals, 44*(1), 39–45. doi: 10.3928/00485713-20140108-07

Krasny Brown, L. & Brown, M. (1996). *When dinosaurs die—A guide to understanding death*. New York, NY: Little, Brown and Company.

Ladson-Billings, G. (2009). *The dreamkeepers: Successful teachers of African American children*. San Francisco, CA: Jossey-Bass.

Leiter, M. P. & Maslach, C. (2004). Areas of worklife: A structured approach to organizational predictors of job burnout. In P. L. Perrewe & D. C. Ganster (Eds.), *Research in occupational stress and well-being*, (Vol. 3 pp. 91–134). Oxford, UK: Elsevier.

Levine, P. & Kline, M. (2007). *Trauma through a child's eyes: Awakening the ordinary miracle of healing. Infancy through adolescence*. Berkeley, CA: North Atlantic Books.

Lieberman, A. (2018). *Video: Teacher stress and low compensation undermine early learning*. Washington, DC: New America Foundation. Retrieved from www.newamerica.org/education-policy/edcentral/video-teacher-stress/

Lillard, A. S. (2011). Mindfulness practices in education: Montessori's approach. *Mindfulness, 2*(2) 1–12.

Lipsky, L. (2009). *Trauma stewardship: An everyday guide for caring for self while caring for others*. San Francisco, CA: Berrett-Koehler Publishers

Madrid, P. & Schacher, S. (2006). A critical concern: Pediatrician self-care after disasters. *Pediatrics, 117*(5), 454–457. doi: 10.1542/peds.2006-0099V

Maltzman, S. (2011). An organization self-care model: Practical suggestions for development and implementation. *The Counseling Psychologist, 39*(2), 303–319. doi: 10.1177/0011000010381790

Maslach, C. & Jackson, S.E. (1986). *The Maslach Burnout Inventory* (2nd ed.). Palo Alto, CA: Consulting Psychologists Press.

Massachusetts Advocates for Children (2005). *Helping traumatized children learn. Trauma and learning policy initiative*. Retrieved from www.massadvocates.org

Mathieu, F. (2007, March). *Transforming compassion fatigue into compassion satisfaction: Top 12 self-care tips for helpers*. Workshops for the Helping Professions. Retrieved from compassionfatigue.org

Mesibov, G., Shea, V., & Schopler, E. (Eds.) (2005). *The TEACCH approach to autism spectrum disorders*. New York, NY : Plenum Press.

Mindfulness Exercises Library. *Positive psychology program*. Retrieved from https://positivepsychologyprogram.com/wp-content/uploads/2017/07/Mindfulness-Exercises-Library.pdf

Monk, C., Feng, T., Lee, S., Krupska, I., Champagne, F. A., & Tycko, B. (2016). Distress during pregnancy: Epigenetic regulation of placenta glucocorticoid-related genes and fetal neurobehavior. *American Journal of Psychiatry, 173*(7), 705–713. Retrieved from https://ajp.psychiatryonline.org/doi/abs/10.1176/appi.ajp.2015.15091171

National Traumatic Stress Network (2016). *At intersection of trauma and disabilities: A new toolkit for providers.* Culture Consortium. Retrieved from www.nctsn.org/sites/default/files/resources//spotlight_on_culture_intersection_of_trauma_and_disabilities_new_toolkit_for_providers.pdf

O'Brien, J. L. & Haaga, D. A. F. (2015). Empathic accuracy and compassion fatigue among therapist trainees. *Professional Psychology: Research and Practice, 46*(6), 414–420. Retrieved from http://dx.doi.org/10.1037/pro0000037

Osgood, J. (2012). *Narratives from the nursery: Negotiating professional identities in early childhood.* London, UK: Routledge.

Osofsky, J., Stepka, P., & King, L. (2017). *Treating infants and young children impacted by trauma: Interventions that promote healthy development.* Washington, DC: American Psychological Association.

Pally, R. (2000). *The mind–brain relationship.* New York, NY: Other Press LLC.

Pawl, J. H. (1995). The therapeutic relationship as human connectedness: Being held in another's mind. *Zero to Three, 15*(4), 2–5.

Perez, L. (2009). Intergenerational dynamics of trauma. *Journal of Infant, Child, and Adolescent Psychotherapy, 8*(3–4), 156–168.

Perez, L. (2011).Teaching emotional self-awareness through inquiry-based education. *Early Childhood Research and Practice, 13*(2). Retrieved from https://files.eric.ed.gov/fulltext/EJ956380.pdf

Perry, B. (2001). The neuroarcheology of childhood maltreatment: The neurodevelopmental costs of adverse childhood events. In B. Geffner (Ed.), *The cost of child maltreatment: Who pays? We all do* (pp. 15–37). San Diego, CA: Family Violence and Sexual Assault Institute.

Perry, B. (2002). *Childhood trauma.* (Video modules of the understanding, identifying and responding to childhood trauma.) Lake Zurich, IL: Magna Systems.

Perry, B. (2013). Bonding and attachment in maltreated children: Consequences of emotional neglect in childhood. *Child Trauma Academy.* Retrieved from https://childtrauma.org/wp-content/uploads/2013/11/Bonding_13.pdf

Perry, B. (2014). The cost of caring: Understanding and preventing secondary stress when working with traumatized and maltreated children. *CTA Parent and Caregiver Education Series, 2*(7). Houston, TX: The Child Trauma Academy Press.

Perry, B., Pollard, R. A., Blakely, T. L., Baker, W. L., & Vigilante, D. (1995). Childhood trauma, the neurobiology of adaptation, and "use-dependent" development of the brain: How "states" become "traits." *Infant Mental Health Journal, 16*(4), 271–291. doi: 10.1002/1097-0355(199524)16:4<271::AID-IMHJ2280160404>3.0.CO;2-B

Pines, A. & Aronson, E. (1988). *Career burnout: Causes and cures.* New York, NY: The Free Press.

Posner, M. I. (2008). *Training attention and emotional self-regulation.* Retrieved from https://sharpbrains.com/blog/2008/10/18/training-attention-and-emotional-self-regulation-interview-with-michael-posner/

Posner, M. I. & Rothbart, M. K. (2007). *Educating the human brain.* Washington, DC: American Psychological Association.

Porges, S. (2011). *The polyvagal theory: Neurophysiological foundations of emotions, attachment, communication, and self-regulation.* New York, NY: Norton.

Ray, S., Wong, C., White, D., & Heaslip, K. (2013). Compassion satisfaction, compassion fatigue, work life conditions, and burnout among frontline mental healthcare professionals. *Traumatology, 19*(4), 255–267. doi:10.1177/1534765612471144

Rogers, K. (2011). *The brain and the nervous system.* New York, NY: Britannica Educational Publishing.

Rogoff, B. (2003). *The cultural nature of human development.* New York, NY: Oxford University Press.

Rojas-Flores, L. (2017). *Latino US-citizen children of immigrants: A generation at high risk. Summary of selected young scholars program research.* New York, NY: Foundation for Child Development. Retrieved from www.fcd-us.org/latino-us-citizen-children-immigrants-generation-high-risk/

Rothbart, M. K. & Posner, M. I. (2006). Temperament, attention, and developmental Psychopathology. In D. Cicchetti & D. J. Cohen (Eds.), *Handbook of developmental psychopathology* (pp. 465–500). New York, NY: Wiley.

Rushton, S. (2011). Neuroscience, early childhood education and play: We are doing it right! *Early Childhood Education Journal, 39*(2), 89–94. doi: 10.1007/s10643-011-0447-z

Sanchez-Reilly, S., Morrison, L., Carey, E., Bernacki, R., O'Neil, L., Kapo, J., Periyakoil, V., & Thomas, J. (2013). Caring for oneself to care for others: Physicians and their self-care. *Journal of Community and Supportive Oncology, 11*(2), 75–81.

Schnall, M. (2017). Exclusive interview with Zen master Thich Nhat Hanh. *The Blog. Huffington Post.* Retrieved from www.huffingtonpost.com/marianne-schnall/beliefs-buddhism-exclusiv_b_577541.html

Schön, D. (1983). *The reflective practitioner: How professionals think in action.* London, UK: Temple Smith.

Schore, A. N. (1994). *Affect regulation and the origin of the self.* Mahwah, NJ: Erlbaum.

Schore, A. N. (2003a). Early relational trauma, disorganized attachment, and the development of a predisposition to violence. In M. F. Solomon & D. J. Siegel (Eds.), *Healing trauma: Attachment, mind, body, and brain* (pp. 107–167). New York, NY: Norton.

Schore, A. N. (2003b). The human unconscious: The development of the right brain and its role in early emotional development. In V. Green (Ed.), *Emotional development in psychoanalysis, attachment theory, and neuroscience* (pp. 23–54). New York, NY: Brunner-Routledge.

Schore, A. N. (2005). Attachment, affect regulation, and the developing right brain: Linking developmental neuroscience to pediatrics. *Pediatrics in Review, 26*(6), 204–211.

Schore, A. N. (2010). Relational trauma and the developing right brain: The neurology of broken attachment bonds. In T. Baradon (Ed.), *Relational trauma in infancy: Psychoanalytic, attachment and neuropsychological contributions to parent-infant psychotherapy* (pp. 19–47). New York, NY: Norton.

Schuder, M. R. & Lyons-Ruth, K. (2004). "Hidden trauma" in infancy. Attachment, fearful arousal, and early dysfunction of the stress response system. In J. D. Osofsky (Ed.), *Young children and trauma intervention and treatment* (pp. 69–104). New York, NY: Guilford Press.

Siegel, D. J. (2001). Toward an interpersonal neurobiology of the developing mind: Attachment relationships, "mindsight", and neural integration. *Infant Mental Health Journal, 22*(1–2), 67–94.

Siegel D. J. (2003). An interpersonal neurobiology of psychotherapy: The developing mind and the resolution of trauma. In M. F. Solomon & D. J. Siegel (Eds.), *Healing trauma: Attachment, mind, body, and brain* (pp. 1–56). New York, NY: Norton.

Siegel, D, J. (2007). *The mindful brain. Reflection and attunement in the cultivation of well-being*. New York, NY: Norton.

Siegel, D, J. (2012). *The developing mind: Toward a neurobiology of interpersonal experience*. New York, NY: Guilford Press.

Shahinfar, A., Fox, N., & Leavitt, L. (2000). Preschool children's exposure to violence: Relation of behavior problems to parent and child reports. *American Journal of Orthopsychiatry, 70*(1), 115–125.

St. John, M. S., Thomas, K., Noroña, C., & Irving Harris Foundation Professional Development Network Tenets Working Group (2012). Infant mental health professional development: Together in the struggle for social justice. *Zero to Three, 33*(2), 13–22

Stein, P. T. & Kendall, J. (2004). *Psychological trauma and the developing brain. Neurologically based interventions for troubled children*. New York, NY: The Haworth Maltreatment and Trauma Press.

Stern, D. (1985). *The interpersonal world of the infant*. New York, NY: Basic Books.

Stroud, B. (2010). Honoring diversity through a deeper reflection: Increasing cultural understanding within the reflective supervision process. *Zero to Three, 31*(2), 46–50.

Thomas, P. (2000). *I miss you—A first look at death*. Hauppauge, NY: Barron's Educational Series.

Twardosz, S. (2012). Effects of experience on the brain: The role of neuroscience in early development and education. *Early Education and Development, 23*(1), 96–119.

Twardosz, S. & Lutzker, J. R. (2010). Child maltreatment and the developing brain: A review of neuroscience perspectives. *Aggression and Violent Behavior, 15*(1), 59–68. doi: 10.1016/j.avb.2009.08.003

VandenBerg, K. A. (2007). State systems development in high risk newborns in the neonatal intensive care unit. Identification and management of sleep, alertness, and crying. *Journal of Perinatal and Neonatal Nursing, 21*(2), 130–139.

van der Kolk, B. A. (1994). The body keeps the score: Memory and the evolving psychobiology of posttraumatic stress. *Harvard Review of Psychiatry, 1*(5), 253–265.

van der Kolk, B. A. (2014). *The body keeps the score: Brain, mind and body in the healing of trauma*. New York, NY: Penguin Books

Villegas, A. M. & Lucas, T. (2007). The culturally responsive teacher. *Educational Leadership, 64*(6), 28–33

Whitebook, M., Phillips, D., & Howes, C. (2014). *Worthy work, STILL unlivable wages: The early childhood workforce 25 years after the National Child Care Staffing Study, Executive Summary*. Berkeley, CA. Retrieved from http://cscce.berkeley.edu/files/2014/ ReportFINAL.pdf

Wolfe, P. (2007). *Mind, memory and learning: Translating brain research to classroom practices*. Napa Valley, CA: Association for Supervision and Curriculum Development (ASCD).

Zero to Three (2001). Infant Mental Health Task Force. Definition of infant mental health. Retrieved from https://www.zerotothree.org/espanol/infant-and-early- child hood-mental-health

APPENDICES

Fight, Flight, Freeze Planning Sheets and Observation Tools

Because children mobilize the fight/flight/freeze nervous system when they are triggered, we have designed an observation tool and planning strategy that caregivers can use for each of the three possible responses. To assist in the learning process there is a case scenario, an observation form, and a trauma-sensitive child support plan that can help caregivers identify key elements that contribute to an individual child being triggered and how to provide trauma-sensitive strategies to the child who is in a dysregulated fight, flight, or freeze state.

It is important for caregivers to recognize that trauma-sensitive strategies need to be individualized to the needs of a particular child. It is also critical for them to understand that selecting an incorrect strategy could further dysregulate a child or at best not work at all. Instead, it is better for caregivers to take the time to get to know each child and learn individual strategies that may be effective in helping a child to obtain an optimal state of regulation when triggered by an event or another person in the classroom. To do so, may take several focused observations and reflections on the child's behavior.

When performing a focused observation on a child who is in a dysregulated state, it is critical for caregivers to look for environmental triggers that contribute to the child's behavior and try strategies that re-regulate the child's distress. It is important to consider that situations in the environment or reactions from the caregiver can cause a child to become triggered and/or dysregulated. In responding to the child's behavior, it is helpful if the caregiver begins to learn strategies that will work to prevent a trigger and/or calm and regulate the child.

Finding strategies in the environment or that the caregiver uses in their response and tailored uniquely to that child is key to implementing supports that are trauma-sensitive. The goal is to see the child behind the behavior, recognize the behavior is communicating a need, and that the child can only learn new strategies and responses from a caring, attuned caregiver with whom they have a strong relationship with

FIGHT scenario with Susan (2.5 years)

- **"Fight" stress behaviors**: Susan, age 2.5 years, has frequent and prolonged tantrums when there are unexpected schedule changes that leave her caregivers frustrated and not knowing what to do. If the caregiver raises her voice to get Susan's attention, Susan starts to kick and scream. The caregiver reports that a quiet area and comfort items help Susan calm.
- **History**: Susan was a medically fragile preterm infant who spent the first two months in the intensive care nursery with unpredictable invasive procedures.

Trauma-Sensitive Child Support Planning Sheet

FIGHT Scenario

Child's Name: Susan   Age: 2.5 years   Date: 5/14/18

Child triggers	Child behaviors	Caregiver responses
Adults raising their voice Unexpected schedule changes	Frequent and prolonged tantrums	Frustrated
Environment strategies	**Caregiver attunement strategies**	**Outcomes or reflection on event**
Calming area Quiet space Comfort objects	Using a calm voice, instead of raising voice to get the child's attention to calm and co-regulate her	**What worked?** Using a calm and quiet area to sooth Susan Objects that comfort her and support regulation **What did not work?** Raising voice Adult dysregulated

Trauma-Informed Classroom Observation Form

Name: Susan   Date: 6/1/18   Observer: MH

Describe Triggering Situation
Unexpected schedule changes and when the caregiver raises her voice to get Susan's attention

---

Trigger

☐ Sudden loud noise	☐ Lots of activity	☐ Light level
☐ Drop off/departure	☐ Transitions	**X** Schedule change
☐ Room change	☐ Change in caregiver	☐ Unfamiliar adult
☐ Sudden touch	☐ Approach quickly	**X** Other: Adult raising voice

---

Setting/activity

X Inside classroom	☐ Outdoor play	☐ Inside play
☐ Nap time	☐ Meal time	☐ Circle time
☐ Structured play	☐ Unstructured play	☐ Other_____

Child's response

☐ Yells/screams/cries	**X** Acts out/tantrums	☐ Bites/kicks
☐ Runs away	☐ Withdraws/immobile	☐ Sullen
☐ Hides	☐ Random play	☐ Other_____

Meaning of child's response

☐ Seeks attention	**X** Expresses emotions	☐ Irritated
X Feels Scared	**X** Over-aroused	☐ Seeks or avoids sensory input
☐ Wants space	☐ Under-aroused	☐ Other_____

Teacher's response

X Raises voice	☐ Corrective	☐ Blaming
☐ Punishing	☐ Stern face	☐ Shows disapproval
☐ Controlling	☐ Approaches quickly	☐ Other_____

Meaning of teacher's response

X Frustrated	☐ Anxious	☐ Feels out of control
☐ Concerned	**X** Doesn't know what to do	☐ Other_____

Teacher attunement strategies

X Remains calm	☐ Eye level proximity	☐ Soothing tone of voice
☐ Eye contact	☐ Approaches slowly	☐ Acknowledges feelings
☐ Emotionally connected	☐ Close proximity	☐ Other_____

Environment strategies		
Quiet area	X Comfort items	Regulating/calming activities
Feeling posters	Supportive transitions	Consistent/predictable schedule
Visual prompts	Available teacher	Other_____

FLIGHT scenario with Michael (4.0 years)

- **"Flight" stress behaviors**: Michael's (age 4.0 years) caregiver has observed him stopping an activity and running toward a quiet area when he hears loud noises and/or when adults enter the classroom. When the caregiver approaches Michael quickly and insists that he return to the activity, he hides his face and starts crying. When the caregiver approaches Michael slowly and uses a calming voice, he gradually comes back to the activity.
- **History**: Michael recently observed his grandmother being taken in an ambulance with a loud siren to the hospital.

Trauma-Sensitive Child Support Planning Sheet
FLIGHT Scenario

Child's Name: Michael   Age: 4 years   Date: 11.1.18

Child triggers	Child behaviors	Caregiver responses
Loud noises Adult enters class and approaches child too quickly Unpredictable events Quick transitions Child unprepared for transitions	Running away Hides face Cries	Approaching too quickly Insists on returning to activity
Environment strategies	**Caregiver attunement strategies**	**Outcomes or reflection on event**
Quiet areas Safe space or calming corner	Approach child slowly Use calm voice	**What worked?** Slow or gradual transition Calm voice Quiet area **What did not work?** Approaching child quickly Unexpected adults or transitions Loud noises Insisting on doing something Using a voice that is not calm

Trauma-Informed Classroom Observation Form

Name: Michael   Date: 10/15/18   Observer: NM

Describe Triggering Situations:

Loud noises, when an adult enters the classroom, when the teacher approaches him too quickly

Trigger		
X Sudden loud noise	☐ Lots of activity	☐ Light level
☐ Drop off/departure	X Transitions	☐ Schedule change
☐ Room change	☐ Change in caregiver	X Unfamiliar adult
☐ Sudden touch	X Approach quickly	X Other: Unpredictable events

Setting/Activity		
X Inside classroom	☐ Outdoor play	☐ Inside play
☐ Nap time	☐ Meal time	☐ Circle time
☐ Structured play	☐ Unstructured play	☐ Other_____

Child's response		
X Yells/screams/cries	☐ Acts out/tantrums	☐ Bites/kicks
X Runs away	☐ Withdraws/immobile	☐ Sullen
X Hides	☐ Random play	☐ Other_____

Meaning of child's response		
☐ Seeks attention	☐ Expresses emotions	☐ Irritated
X Feels scared	X Over-aroused	X Seeks or avoids sensory input
☐ Wants space	☐ Under-aroused	☐ Other_____

Teacher's response		
☐ Raises voice	☐ Corrective	☐ Blaming
☐ Punishing	☐ Stern face	☐ Shows disapproval
☐ Controlling	X Approaches quickly	☐ Other_____

Meaning of teacher's response		
☐ Frustrated	☐ Anxious	☐ Feels out of control
X Concerned	X Doesn't know what to do	☐ Other_____

Teacher attunement strategies		
X Remains calm	☐ Eye level proximity	X Soothing tone of voice
☐ Eye contact	X Approaches slowly	☐ Acknowledges feelings
☐ Emotionally connected	☐ Close proximity	☐ Other_____

Environment strategies		
☐ Quiet area	☐ Comfort items	☐ Regulating/calming activities
☐ Feeling posters	☐ Supportive transitions	☐ Consistent/predictable schedule
☐ Visual prompts	**X** Available teacher	☐ Other_____

FREEZE scenario with Laura (6.0 years)

- **"Freeze" stress behaviors:** During transition from home to child care, Laura, age 6.0 years, is often subdued and expressionless. During the day, Laura seems withdrawn and has problems paying attention in class. The teacher is concerned that it takes a lot of effort to get Laura's attention to participate in class. If she raises her voice, Laura seems to withdraw even further. The teacher aid has been developing a relationship with Laura and notices that during music class Laura likes singing and dancing.
- **History:** Laura's parents recently separated and she has had little contact with her father with whom she has a close relationship.

Trauma-Sensitive Child Support Planning Sheet
FREEZE Scenario

Child's Name: Laura Age: 6 years Date: 1.14.18

Child triggers	Child behaviors	Caregiver responses

Transition from home
Adult raising voice
	Subdued
	Expressionless
	Withdrawn
	Difficulty
	  paying attention
	Lack of participation in
	  class
		Raising voice

Environment strategies	**Caregiver attunement strategies**	**Outcomes or reflection on event**

Music class
Singing and dancing
	Building a relationship
	  with Laura
	Noticing what calms
	  and dysregulates
	  Laura
		What worked?
		Discovering that a raised
		  voice did not help her
		Relationship with
		  Teacher's assistant
		Using music or singing as a
		  regulation strategy
		What did not work?
		Raising voice

Trauma-Informed Classroom Observation Form

Name: Laura   Date: 1/14/18   Observer: D.M.

Describe Triggering Situation
Drop off from home to school, teacher's raised voice

Trigger

☐ Sudden loud noise	☐ Lots of activity	☐ Light level
X Drop off/departure	**X** Transitions	☐ Schedule change
☐ Room change	☐ Change in caregiver	☐ Unfamiliar adult
☐ Sudden touch	☐ Approach quickly	**X** Other: Raised voice

Setting/Activity

☐ Inside classroom/	☐ Outdoor play	☐ Inside play
☐ Nap time	☐ Meal time	☐ Circle time
☐ Structured play	☐ Unstructured play	**X** Other: All day at school

Child's response

☐ Yells/screams/cries	☐ Acts out/tantrums	☐ Bites/kicks
☐ Runs away	**X** Withdraws/immobile	**X** Sullen
☐ Hides	☐ Random play	**X** Other: Difficulty paying attention

Meaning of child's response

☐ Seeks attention	**X** Expresses emotions	☐ Irritated
☐ Feels Scared	☐ Over-aroused	☐ Seeks or avoids sensory input
☐ Wants space	☐ Under-aroused	☐ Other: Difficulty paying attention

Teacher's response

X Raises voice	☐ Corrective	☐ Blaming
☐ Punishing	☐ Stern face	☐ Shows disapproval
☐ Controlling	☐ Approaches quickly	☐ Other_____

Meaning of teacher's response

☐ Frustrated	☐ Anxious	☐ Feels out of control
X Concerned	☐ Doesn't know what to do	☐ Other_____

Teacher attunement strategies

X Remains calm	☐ Eye level proximity	☐ Soothing tone of voice
☐ Eye contact	☐ Approaches slowly	☐ Acknowledges feelings
☐ Emotionally connected	☐ Close proximity	**X** Other: *see below

---

Environment strategies

☐ Quiet area   ☐ Comfort items   X Regulating/calming activities

☐ Feeling posters   ☐ Supportive transitions   ☐ Consistent/ predictable schedule

☐ Visual prompts   X Available teacher   X Other: Music and singing

---

* Identified when she engages and is calm.

REPTILE BRAIN, EMOTIONAL MAMMAL BRAIN, OR ZONE OF OPTIMAL REGULATION

Signs a child is in the Brainstem or Reptile Brain (Survival = Fight, Flight, Freeze):

- Hurting others
- Hurting themselves
- Destroying property
- Yelling and screaming
- Swearing
- Crying or tantrums
- Threatening
- Bullying
- Shut down or dissociative (out of it or in another world)
- The child appears frozen or without words
- The child is running away
- The child is hiding, avoiding, or escaping a situation
- Can't listen to instructions, guidance or words
- Is not responsive to redirection

Some things to do or say when in Reptile Brain:

- Help the child identify the sensations in their body by pointing to images or where in their body they are experiencing the sensations
- Be still with the child using minimal words and just be present, letting them "borrow" your calm state
- Send a gentle message, "you are safe, you are here with me now"
- Walk or sit with the child
- Match the level (if they are sitting see if they can tolerate you sitting with them, if they are needing to walk see if you can walk with them,

if they are shutdown, tell them you see them and will be nearby when they are ready). It depends on how the child will tolerate you in their space—will it be comforting or dysregulating? Make sure not to send a message of abandonment (example would be just walking away and leaving them there with no words)

- Ask if they want to walk with you over to the safe space in the room
- Use a calm, neutral voice
- Use few words of direction and correction
- Don't problem solve as their cortex is not accessible at this time
- Let the child know you are here when they are ready
- Get down to their level to appear less threatening or intimidating
- Don't ignore the child
- Don't say the child is "just trying to get attention"
- Don't use stern tones and quick abrasive movements
- Find a safe space they can go that is more regulating in the environment

Signs a child is in the Emotional/Mammal Brain:

- Emotions are escalated (anger, sadness, frustration)
- The child is telling you what happened to them with intensity and their own perspective
- The child is telling you what happened through nonverbal means such as drawing, writing, art
- The child can still be in both reptile and emotional brain at the same time so you may see some of both areas
- The child's stories do not include empathy to others, perspective taking, or solutions
- The child has a story filled with how they were wronged and the other is wrong
- Stories can have elements of exaggeration "I will die or I will hurt them"
- If they share solutions they are often exaggerated and may not be logical
- The child is crying or yelling or shutting down while talking
- The child may or may not be able to express their emotions with words depending on the level of emotional intensity
- Both the mammal and reptile brain are often called the "downstairs brain" and dance together with the intensity of Fight, Flight, and Freeze

Things to do or say when in Mammal Brain:

- Use a calm and neutral voice.
- Use body language that conveys safety (allow children to borrow your calm energy until they regulate)

- Help them feel safe
- Help them feel that you care for them and what they experienced
- Help the child name what they are sensing in their bodies
- Help the child name what they are feeling with words
- Help the child tell their story without agreeing or disagreeing and without correction or direction
- Don't guide to solution when emotions are intense
- Use sensory objects in the classroom to manage energy (sand, water, music, pinwheels, safe space, bubbles, coloring, play dough, walking, etc.)
- Use words that de-escalate or are neutral such as "that happened to you," "how did that feel," "you must have felt X," "I wonder if." These words help them tell their story
- Attune to the internal experience and story of the child to calm their dysregulation
- Use calming areas or activities that will support optimal regulation (healthy ways to calm energy (listening to music, sensory objects such as art, stress balls, fidgets), or expel energy (walking, running, movement)
- Acknowledge their feelings, don't try to make them go away or minimize what they are feeling (that is silly, you are so dramatic, that did not happen)
- Don't call the child out. Create a sense of privacy for their story
- Offer a break (water, walk, calming area)

Signs a child is back in Optimal Regulation:

- The child is not hurting self, others, or property
- The child is responsive to your words
- The child's body appears calm and back in the present moment
- The child is more logical and open to thinking of solutions
- The child is open to ideas or suggestions
- The child can think of choices
- The child has the capacity to see or hear the other sides of a problem
- The child is open to talking things through with adult or peers
- The child tells their story with words

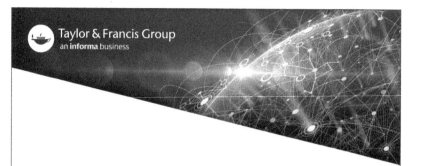